Market and Sales Forecasting
A Total Approach

THIRD EDITION

GORDON BOLT

KOGAN
PAGE

First published in 1971
Second edition 1981
Second edition, paperback, 1983
Second revised edition, paperback, 1987
Reprinted 1988
Third edition 1994

Kogan Page Limited
120 Pentonville Road
London N1 9JN

British Library Cataloguing in Publication Data
A CIP record for this book is available from the British Library.

ISBN (Paperback) 0 7494 0913 4   ISBN (Hardback) 0 7494 1364 6

Typeset by BookEns Ltd, Baldock, Herts.
Printed and bound in Great Britain by Biddles Ltd, Guildford and Kings Lynn.

Contents

12 Monitoring and Controlling Forecasting and the Forecast 332

Index 356

Preface
to the First Edition

'If you can look into the seeds of time, and say which grain will grow and which will not, speak then to me.'
          Banquo to the three weird sisters in *Macbeth*

On occasions, when visiting a company either as a consultant or as an educationalist, I am astounded to find quite sizeable organizations that claim either that they do no forecasting or merely 'add 10 per cent to last year's sales figures' without reference to the market. I usually ask these executives, 'When are you leaving?' for the odds that they can go on obtaining effective forecasts using this 'head in the sand' approach with impunity are very much against them. If the market declines by 10 per cent the company will have heavily overproduced, and tied-up capital in the shape of stocks will fill the 20 per cent gap. Alternatively, if the market increases by 25 per cent, the company will have missed a marketing opportunity and lost part of its share of the market that may be hard to regain in a highly competitive field. In many cases very elementary prediction techniques will take a lot of the guesswork out of forecasting.

In other companies I find that naive extrapolation of historic sales data is used as a forecast without reference to the changing market or the environments in which the companies operate.

In the vast majority of companies I visit I find a range of forecasting methods being used that produce predictions varying in their effectiveness.

Most books on forecasting treat the subject from a narrow, specialized or partial-subject point of view. Some briefly examine forecasting as a part of overall marketing activity, others are collections of statistical tecniques that ignore subjective, non-statistical methods and the overall forecasting/marketing process. Some books ignore the environments in which companies operate and sales performance takes place, others examine the problems of forecasting the economy and certain markets but avoid the problems of company sales forecasting. Approaches are many: statistical, non-statistical, behavioural, subjective, objective, etc. This book seeks to bring together all of these approaches, examining the market environment and marketing influences, and suggests an effective plan of forecasting that can be used as a framework of operations.

The material in this book has emerged over a long period, with systems, methods and techniques obtained from many sources including simple experience. Their development and application comes from the sheer necessity of evolving tailor-made forecasting systems to operate in ever-changing market and company situations.

Whilst this book presents a total approach to marketing and sales forecasting in the sense that it suggests a complete philosophy and an effective overall framework, it would not be possible to list every forecasting technique. But it does suggest a range of methods that show the principles of most forecasting categories and examines a number in detail that have practical applications or implications for all engaged in market and sales prediction.

The book is intended for marketing and other company executives in small/medium sized companies, but also for marketing researchers, forecasters, and management trainees in large organizations. Academically it is aimed at management and business studies students at universities, business schools, polytechnics, and other colleges of further education. It is particularly applicable to CNAA and university degree courses in Business Studies, Advanced Marketing Diplomas, the Diploma in Management Studies, the Diploma in Marketing, and Higher National Diploma and Certificate courses in Business Studies.

Just as forecasts are affected by the environment in which a company operates, so the author has been influenced by the environment in which the book has been written. I would therefore like to thank the wide range of people who have helped me, some personally and some through their writings. Their names would be too many to list, ranging as they do from executives of client companies, other business acquaintances, fellow members of the Institute of Marketing, to colleagues.

However, I would particularly like to thank Richard Carless who reviewed the manuscript at the later stages of its development, making valuable suggestions with regard to sequence and layout. I would also like to thank Gordon Brand who reviewed Chapter 4 and made a number of useful observations as to content; also Arthur Mugridge who reviewed Chapter 5 and who made a number of suggestions including the multiple correlation example.

Preface
to the Second Edition

In this revised edition some earlier techniques have been further developed and 'new' ones have been added. The problem is what to leave out rather than what to put in. I have tried to continue the earlier practical approach to the subject and I would like to thank everyone who has helped me, especially colleagues at Bristol Polytechnic and numerous friends in industry and commerce. I would also like to thank my wife for her continued support and patience and for indulging me in one of my hobbies, this fascinating subject of forecasting.

In researching and/or applying these methods in company situations it is noticeable that many organizations rely on 'part-time' forecasters. It is significant that the approach in this book (and therefore appropriate techniques) is particularly of use to the 'part-time' forecaster.

Some companies appoint specialist forecasters or market analysts to make market and sales forecasts, but in many organizations the forecasting (particularly short term) task is treated as an adjunct to the main role of such personnel as salesmen, sales managers, management accountants, brand or product group managers, depot managers, etc. Some companies use these 'operations personnel' to develop a short term forecast (eg a six to 12 months ahead operations forecast) but use centralized marketing specialists or others to develop a forecast as the basis of a three to five years ahead corporate plan. Many of the former group of operations personnel have little experience of formal forecasting techniques or know how to develop a forecast objectively. Consequently in some cases highly suspect 'guesstimates' are added into the cumulative forecast.

Sometimes the forecasting function conflicts with the main role of a job/position, perhaps because of time constraints, the nature of the job, the nature of the person, etc.

Although all budgets in an organization are ultimately dependent upon forecasts of how many products and/or services an organization should or could sell or provide, in various companies the forecasting activity is given different degrees of priority depending on how its importance is perceived by an individual, his or her manager, and management generally.

The result is often an effort by the 'operations personnel' to 'make the forecast happen' rather than to take advantage of changing market conditions and do what is best for an organization 'in the market place'. For example, if during the forecasting period sales are down, pressure is put on the sales force to increase sales. The sales force tends to sell what is easiest to sell, which may not be what is in stock, or which causes problems of an unanticipated 'stock out' situation on some lines. In industries with relatively fast changing technology some not-so-easy-to-sell lines may be left in stock and they may have to be heavily price discounted or risk becoming obsolete. This in turn may affect the profit forecast. In some cases, to ensure that forecasts happen, over-ordering takes place, resulting in a disproportionate amount of capital being tied up in stock at the year end, cash flow problems and, possibly, price discounting.

It would appear that if organizations are to depend particularly in the short term on 'part-time' forecasters, some training in elementary forecasting is necessary to obtain more meaningful forecasts in the first place.

Very rarely does one see sessions on forecasting in a training programme for salesmen, sales managers or brand or product group managers. Sometimes this is because it is not the prime part of the job (eg a salesman must be able to sell or he will not have anything to forecast) or because it is considered that one has to have an advanced qualification in mathematics to do 'formal' forecasting. It is possible, however, by using appropriate examples, to develop so called non-numerate operations personnel into more credible forecasters. Also it is possible to show methods which develop a rolling forecast that is easily updated so that the forecast for the next period is not such a formidable task to obtain.

The fact that these 'operations personnel' are closer to the customer/market place than others within an organization means that they already have, to some degree, one of the essential forecasting abilities, ie 'understanding the forces at work in the market place'. Giving them guidance in forecasting methods may mean that they can produce more viable forecasts.

Conclusion
Somewhere, sometime, the author read:

> Market and sales forecasting is too crucial to an organization to be reduced to simple guesswork, prayer, or the toss of a coin. The

'inspired amateur' is still with us and the question is how much longer can organizations afford him; on the other hand his activities should not be confused with real subjective forecasting, or the application of human experience and judgment to 'mechanical' forecasting methods.

Forecasting has many skeletons in organizational cupboards and these need to be brought out into the open because forecasting accuracy has a direct effect on an organization's strategy, tactics and performance. A poor forecast today can haunt a company tomorrow in the form of insufficient or excessive capacity and/or inventory, the cost of which will eventually be reflected on the profit line of the balance sheet.

This must be more true today than the day it was written.

Preface
to the third edition

For many years the major problem in making considered market and sales forecasts was the 'number-crunching', ie the handling and processing of large amounts of data, the comprehension and application of statistical and mathematical methods and formulae. But with the wider availability, the declining price, and the increased power of personal computers, forecasters are able to carry out a broader range of complex forecasting tasks, formerly too complicated and/or too time consuming to be done routinely.

While still continuing to cover basic statistical and elementary mathematical methods and formulae, this new, revised edition, examines the various aspects of computers and computing that are of direct relevance to market and sales forecasting and the work of the forecaster. It examines computer types and their role in forecasting, relevant peripheral equipment, the various categories of software (giving examples of forecasting-specific packages), and provides information sources for all other software packages that are currently available. Such software packages cover the mathematical/statistical methods shown in the book and many others.

Associated with this increased application of information technology to forecasting, sources of information have been updated and increased in Chapter 3, 'Collection of data for forecasting', and a specific section covering on-line Databases has been added.

While the 'number-crunching' aspect (especially of historic sales data) may have declined as a forecaster's problem, the identification, weighting and prediction of key market-related factors that affect the level of sales, has become more problematic as, in many cases, markets have become more erratic.

The ability to identify direct and indirect market-related factors that affect an organization's sales performance in a particular market segment, measure, interpret and predict their future direction, intensity and velocity, and integrate their combined effects with the right amount of weighting, is crucial to effective forecasting. A new chapter (Chapter 4) has been introduced to cover this specific area.

Since the last edition of this book, the need for effective forecasting has increased, not diminished, as international and national markets have become more competitive for a variety of reasons.

The controversy continues as to which is more effective, objective/ quantitative forecasting techniques or subjective/judgemental forecasting techniques, and this edition continues to cover basic techniques of both types. A multi-technique approach of the two types appears to be the most effective compromise, with the emphasis changing according to the economic/market/company situation, and the final forecast is validated by a mixture of relevant experience, intelligence and informed judgement.

Forecasts should rely more heavily on the predictions provided by objective/quantitative methods, as long as there are no fundamental changes in the various environments in which the organization operates. However, when and if such changes do take place, subjective/judgemental techniques should be given more weight. But leaning solely on either polarized position may lead either to 'paralysis by analysis' or 'extinction by instinct'.

1

The Forecasting Environment

'A good database and detailed market surveillance are crucial to good forecasting'

A Wilson

There is an old saying in business. 'If you don't know where you are going, any road will take you there . . .'. In a changing, challenging and competitive business environment, however, the continued success, or even survival, of an organization without some element of business planning is unlikely.

The business person is therefore encouraged to lessen the business risk by engaging in 'strategic planning'. This involves making decisions about co-ordinating viable alternative business strategies that balance an organization's mission statement, objectives, capabilities and capacity, with the current and expected future business environment, and of taking advantage of imaginative market opportunities to achieve success.

Marketing research can determine the present business environment and market opportunities, but various types of forecasting methods are needed to predict their future shape and direction. Those methods of forecasting that are directly relevant to the effective management of an organization include:

- economic forecasting (either international, national or regional);
- technological forecasting;
- market and/or industry forecasting;
- product/service/process forecasting;
- sales forecasting; and
- profit forecasting.

Although this book is mainly about market, product/service and sales forecasting, it is important to acknowledge the impact the other areas mentioned above have on them.

Forecasting relevant international economic factors and their potential effects, for example, implies acknowledging the economic concept of the law of comparative costs, ie that countries/regions will tend to specialize in those business activities in which they

17

have the greatest possible advantage or the least possible disadvantage. Government subsidies and activities in various forms can distort the 'natural' advantages of countries/regions, but will nevertheless affect relative competitiveness and therefore sales.

The forecaster needs to identify those aspects of international activity that could have an effect on an organization, and its 'freedom' to market its products/services/processes and endeavour to forecast (or at least be aware of) their trends regarding future size and speed of change. These factors could include such aspects as the degree of free or artificially restricted trade, the impact of international trade blocs (eg the European Community), terms of trade, changes in country boundaries, the effects of weak or strong currencies and exchange rates, and many others.

Likewise, the forecasting of (or at least being aware of) relevant aspects of the direction of national and regional economies that could affect an organization's business activities is crucial to commercial success. Relevant aspects could include, for example, the state of the economy (boom or recession, decline, stagnation or growth), the degree of inflation, strength of currency, government policy towards and support of business and business organizations (privatization v public ownership), levels of taxation, subsidies and grants, interest rates, strength of scientific and technological research, and many others relevant to a particular organization.

Sources of information for making such international, national and regional economic forecasts are shown later in Chapter 3, 'The collection of data for forecasting'; additionally a number of actual forecasts are produced by 'experts' and are mentioned in that chapter.

The area of technological forecasting is examined in Chapter 6.

Profit forecasting is the realm of the individual entrepreneur or board of directors and, in the context of the organization's mission statement and objectives, sets the predicted cost imputs against the predicted future sales, in terms of volume/value to produce expected profit levels. Whether these are acceptable or not is a business judgment.

Value satisfactions and buying motives

While the aim of an organization is normally its profitable operation, to achieve this, its immediate objective must be the discovery, creation, attraction and satisfaction of customers. Psychologists have listed what they consider to be primary and secondary human needs which, if converted into everyday living, become satisfactions that consumers/users value and because of their needs, become buying motives. If these needs and motives are recognized and the marketing approach and promotional appeal based upon them, consumers/users are more likely to react in the way desired by the marketer.

Customers do not buy what a company has put into a product, process, or service, but what they can get out of it. No one has ever sold a product or service; what customers buy and consequently what companies must sell (and forecast) are groups or combinations of consumer/user value satisfactions. These satisfactions include logical benefits (actual product/service differences or performances, thrift, saving, economy, profit, safety, convenience, etc); psychological benefits (prestige, approval of others, status, freedom from fear, love, affection, curiosity, fashion, appeal of aesthetic design, etc); added subjective values, price/value relationships, and even the satisfaction of dealing with a particular company (the attraction of corporate image) or buying from a particular salesperson.

Further, value satisfactions/buying motives can also be identified as consumer orientated (eg most of those listed above are in this category), industrial (eg improved efficiency, lower maintenance costs, faster working speeds, reduced/cheaper labour required, lower price, safer operations, better working conditions, etc), and service based (eg risk reducing, applications advice, life-prolonging, performance enhancing, expert/counselling advice, capital reducing, profit-making, sales-increasing, effort-reducing, maintenance and repair needs, efficiency-increasing, profit-producing, etc). As the purchase of many products includes or requires some element of service (eg the spare parts availability and/or the after-sales servicing of a car), the value satisfactions of the latter must be integrated with those of the product.

To complicate matters, different consumer/user types will be motivated by different priorities and combinations of benefits and satisfactions at different stages during the life cycle of a product/service. It is possible, with a minimum of marketing research, to compile a list of buying motives appropriate to a particular life cycle stage and develop a 'typical' consumer/user profile in any marketing situation.

However, in framing the buying motive appeal, it must be remembered that the purchaser is not necessarily the consumer/user, and the value satisfactions/buying motives of both groups should be reflected in the marketing appeal; this applies to both consumer and industrial markets. Particularly when marketing industrial products and services, it is important that the buying motives of everyone who can influence a purchasing decision (eg works directors, personnel managers, supervisors, etc — and even the titular buyer) should be assessed, and marketing appeal weighted accordingly.

Effective marketing, therefore, can be defined as providing consumer/user satisfactions (at a profit), and any perceived changes in them or in the marketing appeal strategy will affect sales and therefore sales forecasts.

Company resources and competitive elements

Optimization of profit can be achieved only by making the fullest use of company resources and competitive advantage, and by seizing marketing opportunities that are perceived for the short-, medium- and long-term. It follows that, to put the market and sales forecast into context, what is known as a SWOT (an organization's Strengths, Weaknesses, Opportunities and Threats) analysis needs to be carried out. This is a critical assessment of an organization's strengths, weaknesses and limitations, both perceived and apparent to potential customers and competitors, and those that are known to the company, but are passively hidden or deliberately concealed from the market-place. It also involves the realistic assessment and appraisal of the market opportunities and market threats for the short-, medium- and long-term.

In some cases where necessary and/or appropriate, SWOT analysis should be carried out, not only on the organization, but also on its competitors, distributors, customers and end-users, etc, according to the company situation. This is shown in Figure 1.1.

An effective way of conducting SWOT analysis is through a

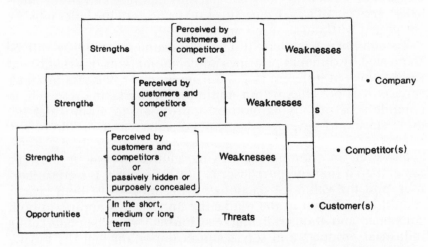

Figure 1.1 *SWOT analysis*

brainstorming session by 10 or 12 appropriate persons, as normally an individual manager's assessment is either too optimistic or too pessimistic, reflecting the person's own perception of the organization. Nevertheless, by this method, it should be possible for a company to build on and emphasize its strengths and/or avoid or do something about its weaknesses, and make realistic plans for the future.

Controllable and non-controllable factors

The profitable success of a business unit will depend upon its ability to identify and appreciate the interaction of external (and largely non-controllable) factors, and of internal (largely controllable factors) that bear upon it, its particular market(s) and the industry situation. An example is given in Figure 1.2, where certain external factors (market and environmental forces) are seen to directly affect a particular business, and where certain activities within the company (and therefore controllable), namely the marketing mix, are arranged in the most effective way to meet the challenges of the external factors. The importance to the success of a business (and especially of effective forecasting), of identifying controllable and non-controllable factors, is seen in great depth in Chapter 4. However, it is important to examine them briefly in the context of other marketing concepts and practices.

External influences

External non-controllable factors lay down the broad environmental limits within which an organization will operate. They include such forces as the general economic and political environment, the state of science and technology, climatic factors, cultural, ethnic and social forces, demographic factors, standard and cost of living factors, and appropriate international considerations, both as they exist and as they may develop in the future.

The total environment also includes government controls, influence and intervention over the product/process/service, over competitive and restrictive practices, over pricing, over advertising and sales promotion, intellectual property, over other company activities and business generally; all normally enforced by legal instrument or government pressure. A further part of the external business environment will be moulded by the general legal system of the country, such as accepted customs, common and statute law (especially the law relating to contract, agency, sale of goods, etc), and the attitude of the courts.

The attitudes and habits of consumers and potential customers,

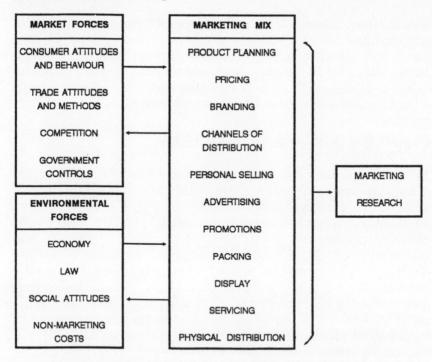

Figure 1.2 *Controllable and uncontrollable factors in marketing*

and those of trade channels of distribution, particularly those reflected in trade structures, practices and procedures, will form an important part of the broad business environment. Competition (national and international), in its many forms (eg price, non-price, choice, service, direct and indirect, etc), is a further aspect of the business environment, within which a business must operate and which will have an impact on forecasts.

Internal factors

Among the many internal controllable factors are a number that do not come within a company's marketing programme, but which can affect forecasts and forecasting, and which decisions made regarding them need to be made in terms of what is good for the company 'in the market-place'. These would include such factors as the company's financial strength, particularly with regard to the money available or obtainable for expenditure upon product/service research and development, and for financing the marketing programme. Especially important are those parts of the marketing programme that require investment. These are sometimes without an immediate or apparent return in the short-term (eg marketing research or public relations), or are cumulative in effect over a period of time (eg advertising). The company's financial strength is also a vital factor, where new or improved products/services or new ventures introduce the possibility of operating losses in the early stages of the life of a project.

Other internal business factors that will have an impact on a company's marketing effectiveness are its specialized experience or know-how (in manufacturing, marketing, scientific research and development, and management techniques), its plant capacity, its material resources and skilled personnel available, its image and reputation, and its position in the market. Also important are its location with regard to markets, raw materials sources and transport links, labour and basic utilities. Lastly, the ownership or control of technical monopoly through intellectual property (patents, registered designs, trade and service marks, and copyright) is a powerful internally controlled factor.

The marketing mix

From the marketing point of view, the most important group of internally controlled factors that can affect forecasting are known as the 'marketing mix'. This refers to the way in which the various component parts and techniques of the marketing effort are combined and emphasized.

Market-orientated organizations are constantly striving to discover the optimum marketing mix under existing and potential marketing situations, ie the marketing mix that will achieve company objectives and/or produce maximum profits in the short-, medium- or long-term.

Furthermore, the pattern of the progressive life of a product and/ or service and its implications has caused the concept of the *product/service life cycle* to evolve (examined later). It is necessary to recognize at this point that the composition of the marketing mix needs to be different, because its task is different, during each stage of the life cycle of a product and/or service.

The marketing mix analyzed

An example of the component parts of a particular marketing mix is shown as part of Figure 1.2, although this does not show the size, scope, operation or emphasis of the individual parts. Because each organization's marketing mix will (of necessity) be different, writers, academics, consultants and some practitioners have tended in recent years to use the 'umbrella' formula of 'the 4 P's', ie Product,

Price, Place and Promotion, to describe the component parts of the marketing mix.

However, marketing thinking does tend to change to accommodate emerging market conditions, and some 'authorities' have amended their thinking in recent times. For example, Philip Kotler in his many writings over the years (and in particular his book with Armstrong, *Principles of Marketing*[1]) has advocated the use of the four P's.

However, in the journal, *Marketing Business,*[2] Philip Kotler is quoted as saying, '. . . the four "Ps" of product, price, place and promotion — should become the four "Cs". . . .' Kotler wants to see the four 'Ps', which he describes as 'a seller's mix', transformed into 'a buyer's mix.' Product, for example, from the buyer's point of view, is customer value. Price is the cost to the customer, which is more than the physical price charged; it also includes the energy cost and time cost. Place for the buyer equals convenience; the seller offers place but the customer will be attracted by convenience. And finally, promotion, which is what the seller uses to inform and promote, should be communication — the buyer wants dialogue. So for product, price, place and promotion, substitute customer value, low cost, convenience and communication — that should be the modern marketing mix.

In some cases companies have added extra 'Ps' to the original four where it is appropriate to their type of business and market. For example, one 'fast moving consumers goods' have added 'P' for packaging which is a crucial part of their market mix in retail 'self service' situations. Yet others in the marketing of services have added 'people' (because of their direct/immediate contact with customers) and 'physical evidence' (because the direct service company, eg a hotel, provides the environment and premises).

Sales (and therefore forecasting) will be affected by the impact on the customer of a wider marketing mix than the four 'Ps' and the following twelve 'Ps' would seem more appropriate for marketers to choose from and for forecasters to use:

Product This category to also include services and processes, as well as quality, features, sizes, before and after-sales service, guarantees and warranties, patents, registered designs and trade or service marks, product development and strategy.

---

[1] *Principles of Marketing,* Philip Kotler and Gary Armstrong, Prentice-Hall Inc., page 45.
[2] 'Silent Satisfaction', Laura Mazor, in *Marketing Business,* December–January, 1991–92, page 24, Chartered Institute of Marketing, Moor Hall, Cookham, Berkshire.

Price This part of the marketing mix should include competitive pricing policies (cost plus pricing, 'what the market will bear' pricing, average pricing, marginal pricing, premium pricing, skimming market segment pricing, penetrating the market pricing, 'sliding down the demand curve' pricing, fraction below competition pricing, expansion pricing, price differentiation, price discrimination, etc), customer's perceived price/quality/value relationships, recommended prices, functional, promotional and performance discounts, credit periods and terms.

Place This should include methods and channels of distribution, warehouse and facility locations, inventory or strategic stocks and transport alternatives.

Promotion This should include advertising, branding, sales promotion, merchandising, selling and (where appropriate), after-sales service.

Public relations This is separated from promotion because, although it includes marketing to the public (consumers, retailers, wholesalers, etc), it also includes other 'publics', such as shareholders and the financial community, employees, local communities, opinion formers in local and central government, etc.

Position The deliberate decision to position the product and/or service in a market segment in relation to competitors.

Packaging The protection in transit and storage, to persuade and project a strong identity, to give customer satisfaction (possible re-use) and trade appeal.

Physical environment This is mainly relevant in the provision of services on the company's premises, eg hotels, restaurants, leisure centres, health care, etc.

Probe This involves being seen to be conducting research into customer needs, the environment, etc; applying the research to the company's 'offerings'; and using it for promotional purposes.

Personnel This is particularly relevant to the direct marketing of services, as company personnel are in direct customer contact, and includes attitudes, commitment, behaviour, selection and training, amount of discretion allowed, and skill in handling interpersonal situations.

Plan This would include such inputs as the company 'mission', corporate aims and objectives, key corporate skills and strengths, internal and external analysis and major inputs from other departments. Also, the identification of major market alternatives outside present products and markets, strategy for present products and/or services, optimization of present operations, methods of market entry, actions to be taken, and the control of operations.

Perform The manner, approach (proactive or reactive), style, commitment, enthusiasm, etc, with which the above plan is implemented.

Profit The policy, acceptable profit/loss levels, long-, medium- and short-term profits, what the market will bear, excess and/or monopoly profits, return on capital invested, pay-back periods and discounted cash flow policies.

An organization's marketing mix describes the way in which the various component parts and techniques of its marketing effort are combined and emphasized. Using the extended marketing mix described above will ensure that every aspect of a company's port-folio of products and/or services will have the desired impact in the market. A dynamic, proactive marketing mix, appropriately amended to meet changing market and marketing situations, will ensure that marketing and sales objectives (including forecasts) are achieved.

The product/service life cycle

All products and services have life cycles; the implications of the shape of sales curves have been generally understood for a long time, and have often been used as the basis for marketing strategy. There is a life cycle for the individual company's product/service, ie a *brand life cycle* and there is a life cycle for a *whole product category*. The latter is the sum total of all individual company brand life cycles for a grouping of products/services that are very similar or that offer similar customer satisfactions. It will be appreciated that an individual company can influence the shape, speed and size of its own brand life cycle in relation to its market situation and resources. But the extent to which it can affect the whole product life cycle will be limited, and more difficult (though still possible) to achieve, except under conditions of monopoly and duopoly.

The product/service life cycle permits the identification of the out-of-phase relationship between the sales curve and the profit curve, normally experienced by companies in competitive markets. Recognition of this factor is vital, for although the forecasting of sales is necessary for the effective operation of a company, it is more meaningful to relate them to the anticipated level of *profits* in view of the basic company objective.

Furthermore, the concept of the product life cycle is a useful device as a planning and forecasting time unit. Even when the exact timing of a product life cycle cannot be determined, it is often more realistic than arbitrarily imposed accountancy time units, when considering the future of a product and/or service.

Each market situation produces its own pattern for a particular product category life cycle. The various stages of both the whole product/service category and the brand life cycle category tend to have their own particular characteristics in all cases, although the duration of each stage may differ considerably. A typical product/ service life cycle in a hypothetical case could be as shown in Figure 1.3.

From a forecasting viewpoint the product/service life cycle can be considered in two ways:

1. As a potential curve. In this case a prediction of size, shape and speed must be determined by an analysis of the underlying internal and external factors that will mould it. A company can adjust the type and emphasis of its marketing activities to suit the current and future stages of its product/ service life cycle. Or, thinking in terms of a product/service life cycle stage, it will help a company to pick out the right combination of marketing mix factors, and determine the right timing so that a market will be 'created' for its product/service.
2. As a realized curve. In this case it is the result of marketing policies and strategies operating within the constraints of the underlying internal and external factors. By using retrospective analysis, the determining factors that caused the life cycle's shape, size and speed can be identified, and the results can be used to produce more effective forecasts.

The product/service life cycle analyzed

An appreciation of the various stages of a fully exploited product/ service life cycle, as shown in Figure 1.3, is vital to forecasters if they are to allow for the dynamics of marketing in a forecast. The actual stages of a life cycle can be identified by a combination of various characteristics, some examples of which are shown immediately below the graph in Figure 1.3.

Just as there are characteristics that identify life cycle stages, so there are ideal strategies and responses appropriate to each stage, if a company is to take maximum advantage of the market situation in which it finds itself.

The situation during each stage is briefly described as follows.

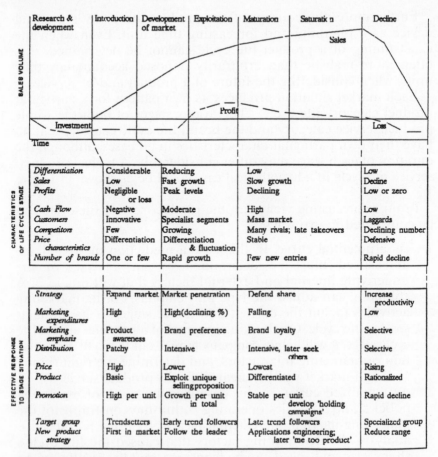

	Research & development	Introduction	Development of market	Exploitation	Maturation	Saturation	Decline
CHARACTERISTICS OF LIFE CYCLE STAGE							
Differentiation		Considerable	Reducing	Low			Low
Sales		Low	Fast growth	Slow growth			Decline
Profits		Negligible or loss	Peak levels	Declining			Low or zero
Cash Flow		Negative	Moderate	High			Low
Customers		Innovative	Specialist segments	Mass market			Laggards
Competitors		Few	Growing	Many rivals; late takeovers			Declining number
Price characteristics		Differentiation	Differentiation & fluctuation	Stable			Defensive
Number of brands		One or few	Rapid growth	Few new entries			Rapid decline

	Introduction	Development of market	Exploitation / Maturation / Saturation	Decline
EFFECTIVE RESPONSE TO STAGE SITUATION				
Strategy	Expand market	Market penetration	Defend share	Increase productivity
Marketing expenditures	High	High (declining %)	Falling	Low
Marketing emphasis	Product awareness	Brand preference	Brand loyalty	Selective
Distribution	Patchy	Intensive	Intensive, later seek others	Selective
Price	High	Lower	Lowest	Rising
Product	Basic	Exploit unique selling proposition	Differentiated	Rationalized
Promotion	High per unit	Growth per unit in total	Stable per unit develop 'holding campaigns'	Rapid decline
Target group	Trendsetters	Early trend followers	Late trend followers	Specialized group
New product strategy	First in market	Follow the leader	Applications engineering; later 'me too product'	Reduce range

Figure 1.3 *A hypothetical product/service life cycle applicable to an individual brand or a whole product category; the characteristics of the life cycle stage and suggested effective responses to each stage situation are shown beneath each stage of the life cycle.*

1. The research and development stage

The opening stage of the product/service life cycle commences when the market-orientated company identifies market opportunities, growth markets, and when product/service concepts or ideas are explored, researched, screened, evaluated and developed. It is a period of 'tailoring' a product/service process to satisfy the particular needs of an identified group or groups of potential customers in relation to actual or potential company resources, and of assessing the short-, medium- and long-term profit potential. It is a period of expenditure outwards without revenue inwards, but it is one that should be viewed as a period of investment in a project rather than a loss. It is also a period when price must be determined and related to volume at different levels so that a viable forecast can be made.

2. The introduction stage

During this stage, if the product/service and market have been carefully and extensively researched; if the product has been tested and prepared for the target market segment and is acceptable to potential customers; and if the correct mix of marketing activities has been properly assessed and the product launch correctly timed, sales will commence and will normally increase throughout this period. However, as Figure 1.3 indicates, it is unlikely that overall profits will be made until a later stage.

3. The market development stage

In this stage, if the new product/service is successful, the rate of sales growth gains momentum as there is a significant increase in consumer/user demand. This increase occurs as information regarding the product/service is spread by advertising, sales promotion, and 'word of mouth advertising', and more consumers/users purchase.

Two factors are responsible for the expansion of demand for the new product/service: one is the effectiveness of the marketing mix and the other is the market reaction. Market reaction should develop according to the pattern anticipated in the market and sales forecasts.

The fundamental factor is the whole 'bundle of consumer/user value satisfactions' (not just the product/service) that is being offered. Often it is relatively easy to create initial demand for a new product/service, particularly when the uniqueness, novelty or curiosity factor is high. But a fundamentally good bundle of of consumer/user satisfactions is necessary to foster repeat or recommended sales.

The market development stage tends to be a period in which demand is 'created' rather than waiting for it to occur by accident or through the incidence of time. By 'creating' demand, companies can operate at the optimum level output and, in many cases, achieve economies of scale.

4. The exploitation stage

The full development of a particular segment of the market by a company marketing a particular product/service does not lead to the 'maturity' of the market as a whole. The product/service life cycle cannot proceed to its maturation stage until a variety of different product/service alternatives and marketing options are available to the main market segments that comprise the total potential consumer/user group. There is, therefore, an intermediate phase, that of the *exploitation stage*. The company exploits its marketing situation, emphasizing the unique features of the product/service and other marketing advantages (price, quality, performance, utility satisfaction, status, convenience, etc).

In the introduction and market development stages, a single generic product/service type tends to be offered to a main segment of the market. In the exploitation stage, sales propositions are evolved by market-orientated companies that appeal not only to some parts of the existing market, but also to completely new segments, thus extending the market further.

5. The maturation stage

Some exponents of the product life cycle use the terms 'maturation' (or 'maturity') and 'saturation' synonymously, to describe the stage before the decline of the cycle. However, in the majority of cases, two rather different sets of circumstances, one following the other, normally exist during both the company and the overall industry life cycles, between the exploitation stage and that of decline. It is appropriate to describe the first as maturation and the second, saturation; both have distinct effects on forecasting.

The life cycle moves into its maturation stage when a variety of different product alternatives have been made available to each of the main market segments that comprise the total potential consumer group.

Maturation is a gradual process. Product improvements and differentiation continue during the early part of the stage, but later there tends to be a decline in the rate of new or improved product development. In the early part of the stage also, consumers are faced with an increasing range of brands and need 'educating' as to what each brand offers. Later, the market settles down as consumers become skilled in the evaluation of brands.

Furthermore, over the period there tends to be a gradual decrease in the number of new entrant companies. However, the degree of competition between existing companies will tend to increase during the maturation stage as there will be an increased supply of the various versions of the product/service into a market that is growing only very slowly. Another characteristic of this stage is that price levels tend to decline in real terms, mainly because of the increase-in-competition factor. They also decline because of the increased scale of production operations and mass production techniques that permit a reduction in fixed cost per unit as overheads are spread over a greater sales volume.

It is a dynamic, transitional period; the early part characterized by many improved and differentiated products/services, shifting brand loyalties, fluctuating market shares and prices, but later culminating in the maturation of products/services, markets, competition and prices.

The maturation stage is one where supply is catching up with general demand, and specially 'tailored' versions of products/services are freely available to many specialized market segments. This situation has arisen because companies that contemplated entry into the particular market during the development stage made individual company production equipment investment and marketing policy decisions. Such decisions, made in isolation, and in ignorance of other companies' plans, are based upon early life cycle data and the predicted steepness of the curve in the two previous periods. This often leads to excess production capacity in the industry in the maturation stage.

By the time the maturation stage is reached, three distinct types of demand have emerged. Each requires a different approach if a company's marketing effort is to be effective. Marketing personnel (and therefore forecasters) need to distinguish between expansion demand, replacement demand and repeat demand. *Expansion demand* relates to completely new consumers or users entering the market for this type of product/service. *Replacement demand* is associated with consumer durables and industrial capital goods and is caused by users replacing existing products/equipment. *Repeat demand* is concerned with frequently purchased consumable products/services. The forecaster needs not only to identify the type of demand that exists but also to allow for the impact of internal factors (eg advertising) and movements in external factors (eg economic recession) that will excite or retard them.

6. The saturation stage

This stage is characterized by intense competition with a high level of sales promotion activity, as the main suppliers in the market tend to increase production and seek to take from competitors some of their brand share of the market.

Overall expansion demand for the product/service will have almost ceased, as consumers that make up the existing market are satisfied with the existing design or composition of the product/service. New consumers are offset to a great extent by some existing consumers changing to a 'new' substitute product/service, ie leaving this life cycle. Within the overall category market, individual company market shares, and consequently their sales volume, can and do change, depending on how competitive the industry is, and the degree to which consumers of one brand can be persuaded to switch their loyalty to a competitor's product/service. The saturation stage may be indicated in its early phases by a weakening of brand preference, itself indicated by a higher cross-elasticity of demand among leading brands.

In the early part of this stage, price competition is typical and, in many cases, forcing down prices towards costs, makes economies of scale crucial to survival; hence the need to increase production. In the latter part of the saturation stage, this highly competitive situation causes the structure of the industry to change, ie the number of product/service companies to be reduced but not necessarily the number of product alternatives. The over-production resulting from planning decisions in earlier life cycle stages, leads to the rationalization of products and processes. But, as designs and/or composition becomes standardized and the most efficient production methods become established, there will be a tendency for products to look the same or similar within each market segment (eg cars, detergents, petrol, etc).

During the saturation period, most companies in the market realize that they must change to a new type of marketing mix, appropriate to the latter end of the product/service life cycle. Because all brands of a particular product type are beginning to look the same, the emphasis will tend to be upon psychological and emotional appeals rather than on basic product/service differences. Furthermore, it may be possible to extend the saturation stage. For example, a new or differentiated product or market fragmentation is often possible, creating a new market situation; alternatively, the product/service will move eventually into the last stage, that of decline.

7. The decline stage

The decline stage cannot be avoided in the long-term, as sales will fall eventually as the product/service concept is superseded. Decline can often be anticipated with fair accuracy by effective market and sales forecasting techniques. A product/service can then be withdrawn at an appropriate time during this stage, or another product/service introduced to replace the sales volume of the existing product/service when it is phased out. Anticipation is important to large-scale producers because the replacement product/service must be of a potential level of sales (when the declining product/service is phased out), to ensure continued economies of scale of large-scale operation in a volume market.

The decline stage can be caused by a variety of factors, the most important of which are changes in consumer/user tastes, needs or habits, a changed rate of market acceptance, impressive improvements in competitors' or substitute products/services, and normal product/service degeneration.

Often, because of intense competition during the saturation stage, companies become less consumer-orientated and more competitor-orientated. The obsession with beating competition at all costs often results in activities that effectively challenge competitors, but are not necessarily ideal for providing the best combination of consumer value satisfaction. Consumers often become dissatisfied and search for substitute products/services and methods of satisfying their needs.

The decline stage is characterized by a pronounced downward trend in sales volume. This indicates, in the case of a company life cycle, that consumers are buying other brands, or in the case of an overall product/service category life cycle, that the generic product/service concept has been superseded by one that has more consumer appeal or provides additional satisfaction. By this stage in the overall product/service life cycle, there appears to be enough familiarity, sophistication and acceptance of the product/service concept to permit consumers to compare not only brands, but also to compare the price/value alternatives of existing and substitute products/services.

The decreasing demand in the decline stage tends to be of the repeat purchase type, with decreasing levels of brand loyalty. Brand loyalty uncertainty is fostered by the disappearance of well-known brands of volume producers who no longer find the contracting market attractive, or by the introduction of improved or replacement products/services, accompanied by different claims in the area of product/service performance or satisfaction.

The extension of a product/service life cycle will depend in the short-term upon the marketing strategies of companies supplying the market. This emphasizes a basic difference in the approach of the economist, compared with the marketing person. The economist looks upon demand as something that exists and believes that income and price are determinants of demand, changes in either having a direct effect upon demand. The marketer believes that income and price are determinants of marketing potential and opportunity, and for these to be realized as actual consumer demand, marketing effort must be expended in the form of an appropriate and effective marketing mix.

The marketing mix, or the way in which the various component parts and techniques of the marketing effort are combined and emphasized, will need to be changed in each phase of the life cycle. The marketing task is different in each stage, and companies that do not recognize the phase change and continue to use the marketing mix from an earlier era, will not optimize their results, and at worst, meet with fairly serious difficulties.

Life cycles in multi-product/service companies

The multi-product/service company has to contend with a number of brand life cycles and an overall product/service category life cycle. Not only will different products be in various stages of their life cycles, but all will be of varying degrees of profitability at a given time. It is obvious that there will be an optimum combination of sales of the various products if maximum profits are to be achieved. Thus, with a range of four products, A, B, C, and D, in a hypothetical company situation, the highest profit level may be reached if three of A are sold to seven of B, three of C and one of D; this relationship is referred to as the *product mix*. Marketing effort must be expended to achieve this pattern of sales and has a direct effect on sales forecasting. As each brand life cycle will have a different life span and the stages of each will be of varying duration, it will be necessary to review profitability of the product and/or service mix at frequent intervals.

An appreciation of the product/service life cycle concept will also ensure that a company will have continuity of profit balance, ie not having all its products/services in the introduction stage or all in the decline stage at one time. Products and services can be scheduled into the product/service range to ensure that as one market becomes saturated and eventually begins to decline, another product/service is ready to enter the exploitation stage. This is particularly important to large-scale producers, who must ensure volume follow-on products/services to replace former volume products/services in declining markets.

Selection of data for the product life cycle

When using the product life cycle as a planning or forecasting technique, or as a method of control where actual sales performance is compared with it, care must be taken in the selection of data. It is possible to measure sales volume by ex-factory delivery movements and/or by ultimate consumer sales (over-the-counter sales). In some industries, where products are produced in a range of colours, sizes, styles, qualities, etc, these two sets of data could produce two brand life cycles with very different shapes, having considerable implications for forecasting.

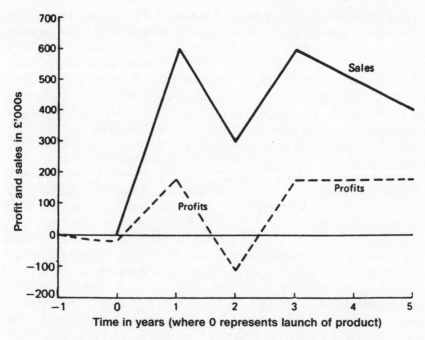

Figure 1.4 *The ex-factory sales and resulting profits/loss (brand life cycle) for a brand of paint*

Take, for example, a brand of paint; the ex-factory sales (brand life cycle) could be as shown in Figure 1.4. This brand life cycle bi-modal pattern is due to the heterogeneous nature of brands of paint. Differences are caused not only because of the need for a range of colours and different sizes of cans, but also because of the need for a range of different finishes, ie undercoat, gloss, matt, 'silk' finish, emulsion, etc, to be available in retail outlets. The number of combinations with such a range of alternatives is considerable. Thus, the high level of sales in the first year of a new or replacement product could be partly attributed to the need for wholesalers, builders merchants and retailers to put into stock a complete range, so as to be able to offer adequate customer service and choice.

In the second year, sales would tend to reflect the normal market growth rate of true consumer sales (from a point on the normal life cycle in Figure. 1.3), ie of 300,000. In Figure 1.4, the move to the 600,000 sales peak in year three, could come from the normal development of the ultimate consumer life cycle (Figure 1.3), ie from the increased consumer brand acceptance/demand and from the extension of distribution through new wholesale and retail outlets.

35

It is particularly noticeable in the market development stage that as the rate of consumer/user acceptance increases, so trade (wholesale and retail) attitudes tend to soften, and acceptance by parts of the trade, which initially were not persuaded to stock the new product, gradually takes place. In some cases the consequent filling of wholesale and/or retail warehouses causes the ex-factory deliveries to far exceed the 'over-the-counter' sales, subsequently causing a sharp decrease in factory sales in the ensuing periods as the trade 'lives off its stocks'. Replacement stock ordering will take place but will be less than stock-building unless the product gains further acceptance by consumers/users in the market generally.

This situation tends to result in the overall product category life cycle, the twin peak (bi-modal) pattern as shown in Figure 1.4. In the market development stage, the innovating company may still dominate the market, but once it has shown that a definite market exists for the new unique product, it is joined late in this period by a number of competitors, who, observing a potential profit and/or marketing opportunity, enter the market with a slightly different and more improved product and/or sales proposition. The apparent profit opportunity is magnified to potential new entrants, by the relatively large ex-factory sales of the innovating company, while the trade channels are stocking up with the complete range of colours, sizes, styles, qualities, etc. Thus, new investment in production and marketing facilities takes place, often based on ex-factory sales movements, whereas in fact consumer/user purchases are moving at a much slower rate and in a different pattern (ie as in Figure 1.3). Gradually, excess supply over the true market growth rate causes some new entrants to offer abnormal discounts to wholesalers and/or retailers to secure channels of distribution, to obtain market share, and, in some cases, to suggest lower prices derived from production economies or lower gross margins.

It should be noted, however, that differences in the timing of ex-factory life cycles and ultimate consumer life cycles will often occur when middlemen are used, although this will not alter the pattern or stages. These timing differences are important as they can affect sales and therefore forecasting. For example, in the scheduling of advertising and marketing effort, a Christmas product requiring heavy promotional effort to appeal to consumers in October, November and December, will require trade press and trade mail promotion, together with personal selling pressure, in August, September, October or even earlier.

Segmentation, target marketing, and positioning

It is crucial to the marketing effort of a company (and to successful forecasting) that these concepts/practices are are applied.

'Target marketing' is the process of formulating market and marketing coverage policies for a company or organization. A carefully considered decision has to be made as to which of the following market coverage strategies will produce the optimum results:

1. *Undifferentiated marketing* This ignores segments of the market and seeks to attack the whole market, aiming to satisfy the common needs of potential customers.
2. *Differentiated marketing* This operates in several market segments and designs separate product/service combinations for each.
3. *Concentrated marketing* This aims for a large share in one or a few segments.
4. *Niche marketing* This aims to identify a specialized sub-set market in a particular market segment on which to concentrate. This approach is particularly useful to small and medium firms, not wishing direct confrontation with larger competitors who are not interested in 'the niche' as a special market because it does not have the volume over which to spread its large overheads. Niche marketing can be defined in terms of market type, customers, product/service combinations and variations in marketing mix.

The decision as to what strategy to adopt will be influenced by the following factors:

1. Company strengths and weaknesses which will determine the extent of coverage that is not only desirable but also viable.
2. Heterogeneity and homegeneity of products/services and market; the more heterogeneous they are, the greater the pressure for points 2, 3, and 4 above. The more homogeneous they are, the greater the pressure for number 1 above — undifferentiated marketing.
3. The current stage of the product/service life cycle. Generally it is appropriate to go for wide, undifferentiated coverage in the early stages of a product/service life cycle and target for specific segment(s) or a particular niche in the later stages, especially where high levels of competition are met and a niche would be more profitable to dominate.
4. Competitors' and especially the market leader's past, present, and potential segmentation strategies. A company may wish to target market segments ignored or neglected by competitors or

potential competitors in which it has the best possible advantage or the least possible disadvantage.

'Segmentation' is the process by which a company partitions its prospective customers (the market) into sub-groups or market segments. Companies have found that if they can identify a viable sub-market, they can cater for the special needs of that segment exclusively, and gain a degree of dominance that probably would not be possible with the total market.

Segmentation strategies allow a company to relate its strengths and weaknesses to a marketing opportunity by arranging its marketing approach in such a way that will ensure a concentration of resources in those areas where the company has the best possible advantage or the least possible disadvantage. There is a tendency for companies to enter a market initially in one segment only and when successful to add other segments. There are two main strategies to define appropriate segmentation:

(a) To start with an existing product/service/market and study customers and potential customers of the generic product/ service to determine if there are differences in needs between different buyers, to determine differences between what suppliers are offering and what customers want, and to identify groups of buyers that respond to similar marketing stimuli.

(b) To start with preconceived notions (hopefully backed by past experience and/or good business judgement), of what the critical segment variables are.

Segmentation bases in consumer product/services may be by consumer characteristics such as:

1. Socio-economic factors, ie
   (a) Social class — identified through income, education, occupation, etc.
   (b) Ethnic race — nationality, religion, etc.
   (c) Demographic — age, sex, family size, life cycle, population movements, etc.

2. Life-style dimensions — activities, peer and affinity groups, interests, status, opinions and demography, type of housing, pattern and standard of living, etc.

3. Attitude style — successful idealists, affluent materialists, comfortable belongers, optimistic strivers, disaffected survivors, etc.

4. Geographic factors — inner-city, urban or rural, advanced economies and developing areas/regions, etc.

5. Psychological factors — these may be based on personality,

needs v wants, aspirations, status, motives, values, perceptions, preferences, buying behaviour, brand loyalty, etc.
6. Buyer behaviour factors — preferences, brand loyalty, awareness, conviction, rating, where people buy, readiness to buy, amount they buy, logical, illogical and psychological purchasing motives.

Segmentation bases in industrial product/service combinations may be customer size, geographic location, industrial classification (the Standard Industrial Classification as a framework for this), usage rate, type of organization (eg importer, manufacturer, processor, wholesaler), product type, etc.

Both consumer and industrial segmentation is possible on the basis of customer response to products/services, quality, brand, performance, price, advertising and sales promotion, distribution, etc.

Effective segmentation and sub-segmentation (niche marketing) in which a company intends to operate should produce a better forecasting focus and improved accuracy in forecasts.

Market positioning

The market position adopted by a company for one of its products/ services is created by its policy on quality, performance, design, prices and discounts, image (both company and product/service), brands, and combinations of these, as well as the marketing mix required in any targeted segments of the market. This is its market position relative to competitors and can be both real and/or apparent.

It is real because in retrospect it will be possible to see by sales, market share and segment analysis the market position of a product/service relative to competitors in a past period. It is apparent because, although the company may think that its product/service is in one position in the market, customers may perceive it to be in another. Thus a company which markets what it perceives to be a high quality/performance product/service will have problems if customers perceive it as a medium quality or unjustified high price product/service.

Furthermore, forecasters must recognize that the market position as perceived by customers in one market segment will be different to that perceived by customers in another; therefore, market position is linked with the concept of market segmentation. The relationship can be viewed through the use of a matrix format as in Figure 1.5. In each market segment, the objectives and strategies will be different, particularly in view of existing and potential competition.

The importance of the concept of market position to forecasters

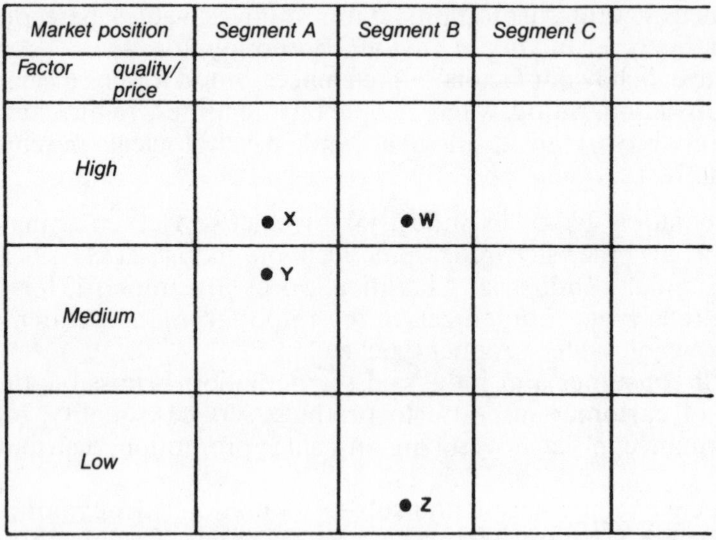

Market position	Segment A	Segment B	Segment C	
Factor quality/ price				
High	• X	• W		
Medium	• Y			
Low		• Z		

Figure 1.5 *A matrix format indicating market position in the context of quality and price*

can be seen from Figure 1.5, segment A, where the marketing function of a company believes it has placed a particular product/ brand in position X, ie the lowest price in the high quality market category. However, stockists and the ultimate customer perceive it to be the highest-priced product in the medium-quality category, ie position Y.

In the circumstances, it will be difficult to persuade stockists to stock and/or the ultimate customer to buy, at the high-quality price and there will be further dissonance if the advertising 'promises' for the product/service are perceived to be different to what customers consider feasible.

Also in Figure 1.5, there will be similar marketing/forecasting problems in segment B if a company positions a product range at point W (ie relatively low in the high-priced, high-quality market) when the need/gap/opportunity is for a very low-priced, low-quality product/service, ie at point Z.

Market positions are also linked with other aspects of marketing/ sales planning, ie product/service/packaging description, market/ brand share, customer/user target groups, basic customer buying motives and benefits, desired image, promotional and profits policy, etc.

Forecasting's special relationship with marketing research

Marketing research is about the past and the present; forecasting is about the present and the future; in fact, in some organizations, forecasting is considered part of the marketing research function. Whatever the organizational implications, the effectiveness of marketing research can have a direct impact on forecasting, and the techniques of marketing research can be useful to the forecaster in obtaining the information on which to base a forecast.

Marketing research has been defined as '. . . the systematic and objective search for, and analysis of, information relevant to the identification and solution of any problem in the field of marketing . . .'[1] This can form the basis or at least the initial stages of the forecasting process.

It can also be defined by reference to a multi-dimensional model relating marketing research information types to research types and to the overall marketing research process as shown in Figure 1.6.[2]

The marketing management information obtained from the ten marketing research types shown in Figure 1.6 are obtained through a variety of methods indicated in the diagram as the 'Marketing Research Process' and this can be easily emulated or adapted to meet the needs of forecasting and the forecaster.

Marketing research serves as professional and/or technical expertise in collecting, classifying and storing relevant information. It should also recommend, execute, interpret, and present marketing research studies to marketing management. It is a management tool for reducing managerial risk-taking by providing facts that enable judgements and decisions made by management to be more soundly based. As such it should be a systematic, continuing study and evaluation of all factors bearing on any business operation which involves management decisions to be made in terms of what is good for the company in the market.

Good forecasting decisions must be based on good information; through the interface with the marketing research function of the company, there can be a beneficial two-way communication process.

Forecasting and marketing management

The effectiveness of an organization's marketing activities (including its ability to forecast) will depend not only on their quality and per-

[1] Green, PE and Tull, DS (1974) *Research for Marketing Decisions*, Prentice Hall, New Jersey.
[2] Bolt, Gordon J (1973) *Marketing in the EEC*, Kogan Page, London, p 23.

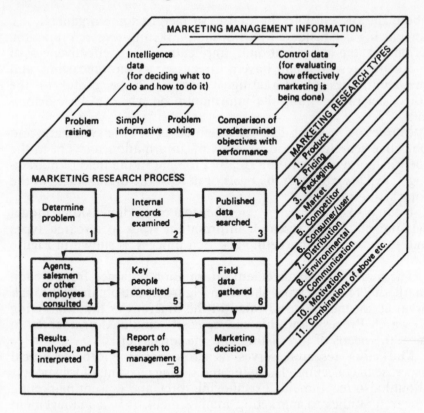

Figure 1.6 *Marketing research as a multi-dimensional model relating information types to research types and the overall process*

formance but also on how well they are managed, ie planned and controlled.

Planning and control can be divided into five main activities:

1. Identifying with the organization's mission, setting aims and objectives, identifying key tasks, setting acceptable performance levels, standards, goals, etc.
2. Developing a programme to achieve these objectives.
3. Measuring performance against predetermined goals.
4. Interpreting trends and results.
5. Knowing where, when and how to take corrective action.

A further aspect of control is recording performance information for use as a guide in planning and forecasting future operations; this also highlights marketing opportunities. Special marketing decision areas in this management function relate to acceptable profit levels, optimum marketing mix, appropriate pricing strategies,

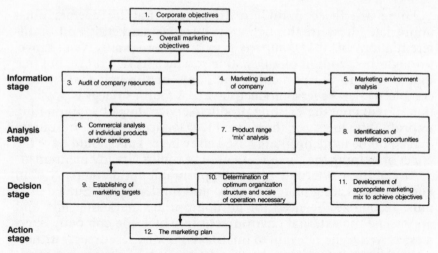

Figure 1.7 *Stages in the development of an operational marketing plan*

attractive trade discount structures, viable credit policies, imaginative branding policies, etc.

A particular planning role is the development of an operational marketing plan with stages suggested in Figure 1.7.

Just as the effectiveness of marketing planning depends to a great extent on viable market and sales forecasting, it must be appreciated that market and sales forecasts will be affected by policy decisions made in marketing planning.

The best methods of measurement and control are through the use of a variety of communication devices. These include marketing audits, budgets, performance appraisals, field inspections, ratio analysis, reports, job descriptions, critical path and network scheduling, conferences, the application of the profit centre concept, sales and cost analysis, etc.

In practice, effective marketing management control is not used simply to determine how good or bad marketing has been in the past, but also to set effective goals to determine what action to take to obtain optimum results in the future.

Conclusion

Marketing is a dynamic process. As the market situation changes, reflected by the various stages of the life cycle of a product and/or service, so the composition and emphasis of the marketing mix must change to keep the company ahead of competitors in any new market situation. Companies move forward or slip back; they must grow, not necessarily in size, but in effectiveness of operation.

There are three main growth routes that forecasters must appreciate; these are through more effective marketing and/or differentiation of the company's existing product/service range, through the addition of an existing product/service range, but one that is new to the particular company, or through marketing a completely new generic product/service. A fourth strategy is possible, that of reducing the existing product/service range by eliminating unprofitable 'lines', or those products/services that use resources that could be more profitably used elsewhere. This should have the effect of helping the three main growth routes already mentioned.

Any of these alternatives can be profitable for a company if an effective marketing plan is evolved and implemented. Such a plan must recognize the need for an appropriate marketing mix and appreciate the external environment in which the company operates, as well as be relevant to internal company resources. Furthermore, the marketing plan should take account of changing market/marketing needs as the life of a product/service develops, and should be one that is based on an effective forecasting system to predict the market in general and company sales in particular.

2
Market and Sales Forecasting

'It is bad enough to know the past; it would be intolerable to know the future'.

W Somerset Maugham

The forecast's planning role

Market and sales forecasts are important tools of company management and decision-making as they assist in the appraisal of investment projects, in the analysis, measurement and improvement of current marketing strategy, and in the identification and/or development of new products and new markets. Further, they promote and facilitate the proper functioning of the many aspects of company activity, ie production, marketing, finance, research and development, purchasing, etc.

The scale of operation of a company will depend upon the sales and potential sales available in a particular market and/or its ability to find and enter new markets. The sales forecast will therefore have a vital role to play in company planning in general and marketing planning in particular. An effective market and sales forecast enables management to plan fundamental marketing strategies and tactics, and compile an overall marketing plan to achieve realistic as well as desirable predetermined profit targets or other objectives in the short, medium and long term. In this marketing planning role, it enables management to integrate a company's general objectives and its operating plans and schedules, with marketing opportunities in existing and/or potential markets or market segments.

The forecast as a target

The ideals of various company functions can be crystallized at the optimum profit level through an effective sales forecast in its role as a target. The production function's ideal is simplification, standardization, long planning periods and absence of time pressures, no under-utilization of plant, and long, even production runs.

The marketing function's desire is for innovation, diversification, a wide variety of products and high levels of stock. The demand by the finance function is for low stocks, low costs, high turnover, high return on capital invested, predictive cash flow, and low credit risk. These ideals often conflict, but the best possible combination of them can be built into the company plan based upon effective market and sales forecast information. In fact the sales forecast should form the basis of all budgets throughout a company. This is because, in the last analysis, all budgets depend upon, or are limited by, how many units a company can sell and/or the level of sales revenue. The sales forecast therefore plays the role of regulator of company resources as there is little point in using technical, financial, marketing or managerial resources unless the resulting goods and/or services can be sold.

Forecasting targets are set in some companies at an artificially higher level than 'realistic' forecasts. This is rationalized on the basis that sometimes the forecast becomes a maximum rather than a minimum aim.

The need for continuity and system

The overall process of forecasting should be continuous and systematic. It should be continuous to enable the assembly of adequate information and possibly the updating of forecasts to allow for changing environmental patterns or freshly revealed information. It should be systematic to be effective; the assumptions made, the logical processes and the methods used, must be explicit and well-defined. Systematic forecasting provides the managers of a company with an effective method of control and measurement of performance, and indicates the various limitations within markets. It will be possible to compare forecasts with actual sales both within time periods and between time periods, thereby permitting the analysis of the difference between the two and enabling the overall forecasting process to be improved. Furthermore, it keeps management informed of sales progress and trends, and results can be interpreted indicating where and when to take remedial action.

The cost of having a continuous detailed forecasting system for a large number of product variations or markets can be high in terms of money and time. Bearing in mind the widely quoted 80/20 rule, ie 80 per cent of profits comes from 20 per cent of products, one approach is to forecast individually and in detail those products/services that make the greatest profit contribution. The growth factors or other indicators that are discovered can then be applied to the remainder in several appropriate groupings. It may be necessary to supplement this 'secondary' type of forecasting with ad hoc, periodic forecasts.

Pre-forecasting considerations

Before forecasting can be considered, however, an overall assessment of company activities must be made; for example:

1. What business is the company in? This must be defined broadly in terms of consumer or user requirements rather than in terms of products or immediate services: the home laundry business rather than detergents; the public transportation business rather than railways; the food preservation business rather than refrigerators; home-heating rather than oil-fired boilers.
2. What products will the company be making in the future to meet the anticipated needs of customers and potential customers, and how will these products be related to the current product range?
3. In which markets is the company operating and how are they defined, eg in terms of size, region, age groups, location, socio-economic groups of consumers or industrial grouping? Is the total size of each of these markets likely to grow or decline?
4. What are the factors that affect demand in the various market segments that make up the total markets? Are there any gaps in these markets that could be filled by other products?
5. What is the company's present and desired future market share? Without market share knowledge it is not possible to measure true progress in relation to market opportunity. In a growth market it is possible to have rising company sales volume but a declining market share.
6. What are competitors doing and how effective are they in particular markets? As far as possible, a profile of competitors should be prepared showing their production capacity, resources, investment, level of sales, level of advertising, degree of competition in specific product or market areas, etc.
7. What is the price/value relationship between the existing and planned product ranges? What is the value of company products to customers in terms of logical and psychological function and performance?
8. What profit levels are desirable in the short, medium and long term? It was shown in Chapter 1 that in various phases of the company brand and/or product category life cycles the company aims and consequently profit objectives will vary. However, for effective forecasting it will be necessary to recognize

and anticipate the results of these future profit aims by profit gap analysis. One way of looking at future profit goals is by using a profit gap analysis diagram.

All these and other factors will help the forecaster to understand what he or she is trying to forecast.

Profit gap analysis

This is shown in Figure 2.1 where the company's past profit performance is plotted, a straight line trend is fitted (see, later, least squares method) and is projected to some appropriate medium- or long-term point in time (perhaps four to 10 years ahead). This assumes that the present trend will continue, and if for any reason (perhaps the anticipated decline of a product) it can be seen that this will not be the case, an adjustment to the trend will be necessary. If the level of anticipated profits at the future point is acceptable then no further action is necessary. But if the desired level of profits (A in Figure 2.1) and the projected level (B) do not coincide, an analysis of this gap is necessary. Management must then plan strategies and tactics to ensure that profits are lifted to the desired level over the period, and these will affect the volume of sales and must therefore be allowed for in sales forecasting calculations. In some cases three levels of profits are considered, the level that *must*

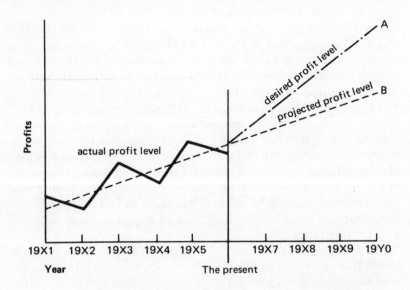

Figure 2.1 *A hypothetical profit gap analysis diagram indicating actual profits, trend, projection and profit objective*

be reached if the company is to continue, the level that *should* be reached, and the level that *could* be reached in certain defined circumstances.

In fact it is necessary to make an appraisal of markets, potential markets and marketing activities.

A comprehensive forecasting approach

The modern approach to market and sales forecasting is to remove as much of the guesswork and as many of the hunches as possible, and to substitute scientifically processed facts to enable predictions to be made. The wide range of variable factors involved in predicting market or company sales makes exact forecasting impossible; a forecast merely provides a means of assessing future probabilities so as to reduce the uncertainty that is always associated with the future. In fact, analysis of the differences between actual sales and forecasts will often indicate the beginning of new trends and cause management to take appropriate action. Any forecast is made with a number of qualifications, eg that the prediction will be within certain limits (for example ± 5 per cent), or that basic economic factors such as demand, real income, relative price, habits and attitudes, etc do not change radically or else change on a predetermined or anticipated course. As far as possible market and sales forecasts should be expressed in terms of probabilities, with the forecaster putting forward the market or sales prediction with the highest probability, but at the same time showing other less probable but nevertheless important possibilities.

Furthermore, the use of statistical information and forecasting methods does not rule out the need for intelligent human judgement and discretion in anticipating future market and sales activity. In fact, the forecaster must avoid attaching too much importance to naive and mechanical extrapolation. There must be a combination of statistical analysis and human judgement to determine and define the variables at work in any forecasting situation. After any purely statistical analysis and prediction, it is necessary to apply intelligent human judgement to validate such a forecast.

Forecasting does imply the ability to determine the primary and secondary underlying forces at work in the international and national economies and the market, and also implies the ability to predict the future importance, growth and trend of these forces. A fundamental premise in predicting the future course of economies, markets and sales is that factors that operated in the past, producing certain situations and sales volume, will continue to be associated to a greater or lesser extent with these situations and sales in the future.

Environmental considerations

All companies operate in, and therefore are affected by, four interdependent environments: those of the international economy, the
national economy, the broadly defined consumer satisfactions
market and the immediate market. Their relationship is indicated
in Figure 2.2. They are basically non-controllable and their effects
must be determined and reflected in the forecasting operation.

The extent of the effect on company operations of the international
environment will depend upon whether or not the company considers the entire world (or parts of it) as its potential market, or the
extent to which it is open to foreign competition in its home markets.
The international marketing concept is that trading should be
carried out not simply by exporting products but also product
parts, exporting research know-how, arranging for products to be
made under licences abroad, setting up companies and/or invest-
ing in other countries and also importing products or parts that are
cheaper or better to incorporate in home products. The nature of
the product and the number and location of potential customers
will also indicate the importance of the international environment;
for example, it will affect a large-scale aircraft or space vehicle
components manufacturer to a greater extent than an ice-cream
manufacturer.

The second interdependent environment is the national economy
and one way of looking at the economy of a country is as the sum
total of all industries within it, the gross national product being an
economic indicator that measures the economy. External and
internal pressures upon the economy will cause pressures upon
industries and consequently upon companies as shown in Figure
2.2. For example, external balance of payments problems may
cause a government to restrict credit and place restrictions on hire
purchase thereby directly affecting sales in a number of consumer
durable industries (television receivers, washing machines, etc).

Consumers can often obtain similar groups of satisfactions from
alternative products in different industries. For example, they can
obtain home heating from coal, oil, gas, electricity and from different applications within these groups. These substitute products
form the third environment in which the company, and consequently the forecaster, must operate. Companies in any of these
very different industries are in fact in competition and are in the
broadly defined consumer satisfaction market of home heating.

The fourth interdependent environment is that of the immediate
market where companies are in direct product competition with
each other, eg one type of oil-fired boiler against another. But even
so, pressures can come from companies in other industries infil-

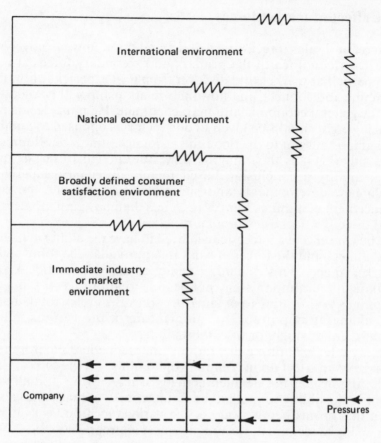

International environment

National economy environment

Broadly defined consumer satisfaction environment

Immediate industry or market environment

Company

Pressures

Figure 2.2 *Environments within which companies operate*

trating a particular market, eg in recent years companies making metal components have lost ground to manufacturers of plastic components. When the marketing researcher or forecaster discovers the beginning of such a trend, the company has the alternatives of maintaining sales by buying new plant and manufacturing plastic components, or of doing nothing and suffering declining sales, or of withdrawing from the particular components market and extending its production of other metal products. Pressures may also come from industries in no way, or only remotely, connected with an industry, eg companies in the tobacco industry under social and medical pressure in their own markets have diversified into many other product fields. In such circumstances the sales forecaster will have to consider how attractive his industry is to outside companies wishing to diversify.

The effect of market forces

Market and sales forecasting will depend upon how effectively the forecaster can unearth the primary and secondary forces at work in a particular market, and discover from past experience how they combine and connect, and how their relationship will be modified by the general economic and market climate. He must decide how much weight should be given to one factor as opposed to another. It is important not to overlook the influence of new developments and situations, as they may be powerful enough to negate or at least modify a conclusion based merely upon past experience. Such new developments and situations may indicate the commencement of minute changes in trends that may gain momentum and directly affect sales in a later period.

Thus the effective forecaster will need to have the ability to identify and understand the forces at work in a particular economy and/or market place. This includes being aware of the ideal data (although the company may not be able to afford its cost in terms of money and/or time to obtain), the sources of relevant data, and the changing importance or momentum of the various market factors, either singly or in combination.

Only after examining the various interdependent environments that have an effect upon company operations will the forecaster be able to consider the detailed activity of forecasting. Initially this implies the ability to predict the future course of market forces. In turn this means being aware of the various techniques available, the ability to identify the techniques most appropriate to the existing and anticipated situation, understanding the strengths and weaknesses of the various techniques and the need to weigh and/or change the combination of techniques in a dynamic market situation.

Short-, medium- and long-term forecasts

The need for, and the distinction between, short-, medium- and long-term forecasts must be recognized. Obviously to different companies in different industries, these terms mean very different things. For example, the short term in an industry such as shipbuilding would obviously be much longer than the short term in the manufacture of a consumer product such as a packaged cake mix, not only because it is takes longer to design and produce the article, but also because consumer demand, habits and fashions change more rapidly in the consumer goods industries than in the capital goods industries.

Short-term forecasts

However, despite the differences in various industries, it is often possible to link the seasonal pattern of demand within an industry with its short-term period. In economics, the short term is a period which is long enough to allow the variable factors of production (direct labour, direct materials, existing machinery and buildings, etc) to be used in different combinations and amounts, to ensure that the maximum profits are obtained. Further, it is a characteristic of such a period that it is too short for new fixed capital (new plant, new equipment production lines, factories, etc) to be planned, purchased and brought into operation. These are important considerations, as any short-term operational sales forecast for a company should not exceed the total product capacity of its present equipment unless it is prepared to sub-contract or purchase outside the company. If an inflated sales forecast figure is achieved in book orders but the production function is unable to meet these orders, the ensuing customer frustration and ill-will caused by delivery delays will only serve as an obstacle to future sales by the company. In certain capital goods industries during a period of boom, this situation does occur and is characterized by 'longer order books'. But these industries remain in this fortunate position only as long as demand remains high, as long as new suppliers do not enter the industry, and as long as competitors (home or overseas) do not introduce other products that can be substituted for the original and which can be delivered more quickly. Further, in such circumstances a mistaken picture of true demand, reflected in forecasts, can be built up by buyers placing orders with several suppliers merely to ensure delivery of part of these orders.

The fact that demand in the short term is influenced by seasonal factors is emphasized more in some industries than in others. The fact that it can be linked with certain periods, such as any of the four seasons, Christmas or the summer holiday seasons, tends to make this factor regular. Consequently, in many industries it is possible to allow for peak sales periods, by manufacturing and stocking in off-peak periods. If seasonal factors are important, it is necessary to make a forecast with a seasonally adjusted estimate of sales rather than a straight line trend. Because of the regularity of seasonal factors and the relatively short time element involved, it is usually easier to obtain a more accurate forecast for the short term than for the medium and long term. Short-term forecasting is necessary for immediate planning and the scheduling of existing resources.

As soon as the time period under review moves beyond the short term, the forecasting time periods (medium- and long-term), in addition to marketing considerations, tend to be dependent upon the time it takes to plan, purchase and bring into operation new fixed capital and assets (new plant, equipment, production lines, factories, etc) and upon the potential operating life of such assets.

Medium-term forecasts

In most industries there is a recognized business cycle in which, although the actual volume of business is either higher or lower than in the past, the pattern of business is characterized by a fairly even cyclical movement. In various industries (particularly capital and industrial goods) this 'business' cycle ranges from two to five years and tends to be more difficult to forecast than the seasonal pattern because of the longer time span involved.

Also, although on such a cycle it is possible to anticipate an increase or decrease in sales in any one period, the magnitude of fluctuations experienced tends to be much greater. However, because of a medium-term recurring business cycle, it is possible in many industries to anticipate future movements of demand in a number of markets. Some companies in the machine tool industries, for example, use such business cycles as one of their techniques to forecast sales, making the necessary adjustments to allow for the disappearance or lessening of some factors that operated in the past and the presence of new influences in the current situation. Medium-term forecasts are required to enable realistic detailed budgeting to carried out, and to ensure the best possible use of company resources. This type of forecast affects marketing planning and policy; it has the effect of either adapting company resources to match the market situation and/or of adjusting the marketing mix to match company resources in the medium term.

Long-term forecasts

The long-term forecast is the most difficult type of forecast to make with any degree of accuracy. This is mainly because of the time factor; obviously the longer the time period the greater the opportunity for new situations to arise and new variable factors to emerge. It is also due to the long-term influences of much wider economic factors such as world trade, international competition, population trends, the general trade cycle, the product life cycle, income trends, changes in standards of living, productivity changes, technological developments, a country's ability to attract and foster growth industries, and many others. But even though such difficulties prevail, a long-range forecast is an essential tool of business activity. It is necessary for the future planning of resources such as finance, buildings, plant and equipment, labour, research and development, raw materials and marketing facilities, etc. It is necessary for long-term consideration of entry into new markets, or for deciding on matters of product diversification as well as for determining the overall direction of a company's policy. Long-term forecasts of between five and 20 years are best approached by considering them as trends rather than highly detailed forecasts. As such predictions are influenced by long-term patterns in the national and international economies, they should be based upon national and international economic and political indicators rather than recent sales experience by a company in a particular market or industry. Long-term forecasts will also be influenced by the progress of the overall product category life cycle. The application of all these factors can be seen in current world energy markets.

Long-term forecasts are made to ensure the availability of resources. In fact, the importance of this type of forecast is in direct proportion to the specialization of the resources to be made available or acquired. Buildings, equipment, materials, skills, etc to be used in company operations that are so specialized that they cannot be used for other than their originally intended purpose need a more accurate sales forecast. For any group of products, the different resources required have different lead times, ie for a factory the necessary lead time could be two to four years, for plant and equipment one to three years, components and materials a month to 18 months. Even specially trained labour may require a lead time of one to 12 months. These points indicate that the term (ie the time unit) of the forecast should be related to the purpose for which it is to be used. Long-term forecasts need updating from time to time, sometimes revealing a substantial change to be made in the allocation of resources. This is particularly true when a need is indicated to convert fixed resources to some other use, eg buildings, plant and equipment, etc, that have been planned, or partially completed.

It will be appreciated that in long-term forecasting precise timing matters much less than with short- or medium-term predictions. This is because the aim of long-term forecasting is to get a picture of the probable level of demand in five to 20 years' time, assuming, of course, that situations have developed according to the anticipated pattern. Generally, it is important to realize that in long-range forecasting it is the general sweep of the economy and the market that is important, not actual and detailed prediction of sales in the twentieth year.

The impact of medium- and long-term factors on short-term forecasting

Because of the differing time horizons of short-, medium- and long-term forecasts and their different uses by various functional areas within an organization, it is often the case that they are each calculated by different people with different roles within that organization. Thus product/brand managers, sales managers and salesmen may be directly involved in making short-term forecasts and the corporate planning group in making a five to seven year corporate plan.

There is a tendency for the short-term forecaster to leave the medium- and long-term considerations to other people. However, Figure 2.3 shows, in a hypothetical situation, the cumulative effect that medium- and long-term business cycles have on the short-term sales patterns.

The seasonal pattern will continue at a higher or lower level depending on the influences of the medium- and long-term cycles. The diagram illustrates why a seasonal recession can be sometimes very minor and sometimes more severe. This is also one of the commonest faults in forecasting: the forecaster gets the pattern right but the level wrong. If the data appears in tabular form this may never be realized and a fundamentally effective method of forecasting may be rejected. By always showing forecasts and sales performances on graphs, patterns that are vertically wrong can be identified, as well as sales patterns and forecasts that have a lead/lag relationship, ie where the pattern of sales leads or lags horizontally. In both cases, the cause may well be the pressure of medium- and long-term cycles and influences upon short-term forecasts or sales performance.

The main problem in either very short-, short-, medium- or long-range forecasting is to determine when a change is about to take place and when a new situation is about to present itself. As minor influences can start new trends, the forecaster must use all the forecasting tools appropriate to his particular company and industry, and get as many opinions as possible about the full meaning of the current data and trends. The magnitude of the problem then lessens because it becomes one of discerning an average trend from a variety of trends and reliable opinions. The multi-technique approach to forecasting is essential.

Sales forecasting definitions

Sales forecasting concerns the potential and prospective sales volume

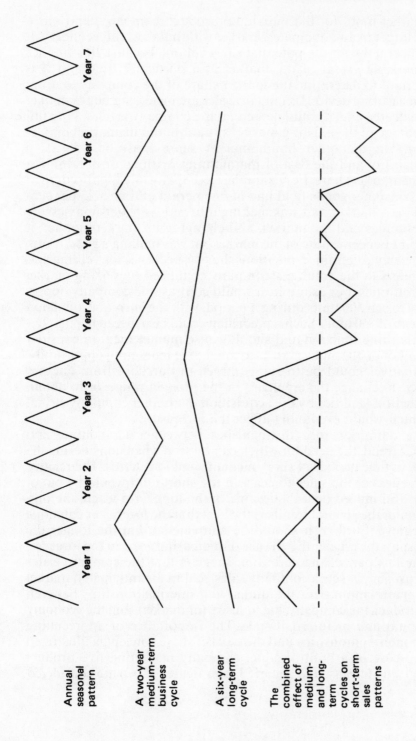

Figure 2.3 *A hypothetical sales situation showing the cumulative effect that medium- and long-term business cycles have on short-term sales patterns*

or market trend for the individual product (company) and sets a sales target in an anticipated market within the overall economy. It is concerned with the potential sales volume because this implies the possible extent of the market at a particular time and it is important to determine the market share of the company to use it as a measuring device. If company sales are increasing but its market share decreasing, it could mean that the company is not taking full advantage of the existing market situation and its market opportunity. On the other hand, market share must be related to profitability and the cost of maintaining existing, or obtaining a higher, market share. For example, a company in a highly competitive consumer goods field had at one period of time a 23 per cent share of a market and was making a huge loss. After re-assessing its resources and the market, and changing its marketing plan, it had a 12 per cent share of the market but was making a good profit.

The above definition mentions the prospective sales volume and this refers to the volume a company could sell by seizing market opportunities. For example, it would contrast the company opportunity to sell 500 units during a period, with the current production capacity of 350 units. Such a prediction could be of use to the marketing planning function and should cause management to consider a number of alternatives so as to maximize marketing opportunity. Alternatives could be to sub-contract, to purchase from another source, to change the emphasis in the product range, or to obtain production facilities by the acquisition of another company etc, all of which would eventually affect the forecast.

The definition also distinguishes between sales volume and market trend, the need for which can be seen when considering the different time periods of short, medium, and long terms. The relative preciseness of the sales forecast in the short term would be out of place and indeed be unbelievable in the long term where the prediction of the general trends is the best that the forecaster can hope to achieve. Further, it should be appreciated that the longer the time span the greater the chance of increasing error in the forecast.

The last part of the definition suggests that the company sales forecast simply sets a company sales goal in an anticipated market and again emphasizes the underlying interrelationships between the product, the company, the industry (or market), and the economy (national and/or international). The importance of appreciating these interrelationships and the market share concept is illustrated in the case of a multi-product company marketing five product groups; the forecast and achieved sales figures of two are considered here:

Product group	Company sales forecast	Actual sales achieved
A	£800,000	£900,000
B	£600,000	£560,000

From the data shown it would appear that a better marketing job has been carried out on group A by increasing sales by £100,000, than on group B where sales were £40,000 down on forecast. But if the size of the market involved and the company's share of the individual market or industry are considered, a totally different picture is revealed.

Forecast:

Product group	Industry or market forecast	Company sales forecast	Forecast share of market
A	£10,000,000	£800,000	8%
B	£12,000,000	£600,000	5%

Achieved:

Product group	Industry or market sales	Company's actual sales	Actual market share
A	£15,000,000	£900,000	6%
B	£8,000,000	£560,000	7%

If the above data is considered, the former assessment of the marketing performance with these two product groups will be reversed. In the case of A the fullest advantage has not been taken of a tremendously expanding market, and the company's market share has dropped from 8 per cent to 6 per cent. On the other hand, the initial assessment of a bad marketing performance for group B must be reconsidered because this market has in fact contracted, and although the product group is down on forecast, the market share has increased from 5 per cent to 7 per cent. It is therefore very important when comparing forecast sales with actual sales to consider (a) whether the market upon which the forecast was based has expanded or contracted, and (b) what was the size of the market share.

The above example also emphasizes the need for effective market forecasts as well as company sales forecasts. It also raises some questions as to the effectiveness and adequacy of the company's market forecasting techniques; these need an urgent, critical reappraisal. Further, if the sales forecasts were the basis of budgets throughout the company, the circumstances in which the purchasing department could make available extra raw materials, and the production function could make available extra capacity for an additional £100,000 of A to be manufactured, would be worthy of investigation.

Another approach to defining a sales forecast could be: 'an estimate of future product/service sales in volume/value over a given period of time regarding current and prospective customers'.

It could be argued in management terms that the forecast is merely the first step and that the sales forecast becomes a budget once it has been costed and accepted. When this happens the budget could be defined as: 'a financial statement of forecast revenue and expenditure over a given period of time'.

It could be further argued that once the original forecast becomes a budget and resources have been committed, then the predicted targets must be achieved. However, the implications of forcibly achieving a forecast/budget must be understood. By various means it is nearly always possible to achieve a sales forecast, eg prices may be cut, trade discounts increased, more money can be spent on advertising and sales promotion, more salesmen can be employed, etc. But all these methods incur increased costs and therefore although the sales forecast/budget may be achieved the profit target may not.

A widely accepted practice is that of updating the forecast or reforecasting at appropriate intervals during the year in the light of the market situation then prevailing.

Setting forecasting objectives

In any form of planned activity it is necessary initially to lay down the objectives, the purpose and the desired achievement. Market and sales forecasting is no exception, and it is essential to lay down individual company objectives because each organization represents a different combination of policies, resources, products and market aims.

One objective could relate to the degree of accuracy; it could indicate what is desirable and what is considered realistic. A company forecasting objective could be to forecast within ± 3 per cent of the monthly sales figure and within ± 5 per cent of the total sales for the year. In complex market situations it may not be possible to obtain a high degree of accuracy because of the influence of a great number of independent variable factors, and the level of accuracy attainable in one industry may not be acceptable in another. In some cases a trend rather than a highly detailed forecast may be adequate in a particular range or market. In other situations 'flexible' forecasting may be appropriate. In a complex market situation or where fundamental changes are likely to take place, a range of forecasts may be made in an effort to cover all eventualities. This could lead to a 'worst' situation forecast, a static situation forecast, an improved situation forecast, and a best situation forecast. Such a sales forecasting exercise provides a fringe benefit for the company as it forces executives to examine possible alternatives and plan accordingly. The accuracy factor, within the feasible levels accepted by a company, can be improved by using a multi-technique approach to forecasting. This is especially so where variations between the forecasts of various techniques can be investigated or where a forecast is built up empirically as in the case of forecasts by salesmen, area managers and regional managers, in addition to statistical techniques.

Forecasting objectives need to be set in relation to costs; a forecast must be obtained around a budgeted cost figure. The cost of obtaining a forecast and the expected profit contribution as a result of using it need to be balanced. But the cost of making a wrong forecast and causing an expansion of company resources or causing them not to be available when needed should be considered; it often follows that a more effective forecasting system is set up.

Other objectives will concern time; a weekly, monthly, quarterly, yearly, five yearly forecast may be needed, but forecasts are required in time to take effective action. If the degree of sophistication of the forecasting system is such that by the time the forecast is ready it is too late to be used, then something less sophisticated must be accepted; the ideal forecasting system must be modified to circumstances.

Because companies have different policies, different sets of resources and operate in different markets they need to emphasize certain aspects of the various company functions (production, finance, marketing, etc) in order to optimize their profits. The objectives of any forecast should reflect the relative importance of various aspects of company activity. But even within the various company functional areas a variety of objectives can be suggested.

1. Forecasting objectives and research and development

Market and sales forecasting objectives in the field of research and development are numerous but in the main are concerned with obtaining longer design and development lead times, assessing how functional features of products will affect sales, providing forecasts in segments rather than total markets and forecasts for product sizes, colours, models, etc.

Such forecasts centre around the questions: is there a market for a product? How big is it? Is it intensive or extensive? How many products can be sold and at what prices? Where is the market located? What are the shares of the market held by competitors? What are the short-, medium- and long-term prospects? What are the implications of the results of product tests and test markets when interpreted into sales in regional, national or international markets? In this area potential profit levels can be anticipated, for there is an obvious link between the range of unit volumes that can be sold at a range of various prices, which in turn is linked to costs.

2. Purchasing

The objectives of a forecast related to the purchasing function is concerned with future material requirements in types, materials, sizes, colours, quantities, qualities and the timing of their purchase. Effective forecasting enables the purchasing function to (a) deal in standard parts or materials, bulk quantities or grouping of orders related to special discounts, (b) purchase at times geared to seasonal price changes, (c) reduce the number of buying occasions, and (d) lower raw material stock levels. It also permits the planning of financial requirements for purchasing and the procurement of special or non-standard material. Depending on individual company needs, objectives should be set giving due consideration to the needs of the purchasing function.

3. Production

The main objectives of forecasting as an aid to the production function concern the scale of operation and the degree of use of existing and future production resources. In industries where economies of scale are possible, volume predictions as the life cycle progresses, are of extreme importance in planning for future production resources. But with any scale of operation, sales forecasts indicate the degree of potential use of existing plant and equipment. This gives management the opportunity to consider new product development projects and to ensure more economical working of production resources in the future. Effective production and product line scheduling, long order lead times, long runs of one product, size or colour, are factors that affect production economy and the forecasting objectives should reflect them. Sales forecasts in this area are therefore likely to take the form of an analysis by brand or product groups, sizes, models, etc.

Stocks have to be financed and, in most cases, inventory costs are high and the aim of a forecast could be to enable a company to carry economic levels of finished and partly finished stock.

4. Personnel

Manpower budgets as well as materials budgets must be planned, and the sales forecast forms the basis of planning for future increased, decreased or static personnel requirements. The objective of forecasts in this company activity area is to give the personnel department the greatest possible lead time, not only to obtain suitable personnel but also, ideally, to permit proper training to take place. Effective market and sales forecasting can also foster good employer/employee/trade union relationships as it gives advanced warning of future changes in the numbers and types of staff the company will be requiring in the future.

5. Finance

The objectives of the sales forecast with regard to the financial function of the company will be to provide appropriate data upon which to forecast stock turn, cash flow, return on capital invested, desired profit margins, profits, and dividends. In many companies the balance between the inflow of cash and the outflow of expenditure is very fine and month by month predictions of volume by product type, price, and market segment will assist financial management. In different markets, and sometimes in different segments of the same markets, accepted credit limits will be different, and the identification of these different credit areas can be carried out by analysis of a forecast by consumer group, type of outlet, or industrial classification.

Further, as the sales forecast should form the basis of all budgets in a company, it therefore assists financial management to determine the company master budget, and also to plan that money will be available at the correct times during the short, medium and long term for working and fixed capital and capital projects.

6. Marketing

Although it forms one of the sub-functional activities of marketing, market and sales forecasting will have a number of uses for other parts of marketing, and in consequence will have a variety of objectives in each marketing area.

The sales forecast will be either the input or the output of various marketing research activities. Its role in the function of the

Time horizon	Marketing	Production	Inventory	Finance	Purchasing	R & D	Top management
	Sales of each product type Sales by geographical area Sales by customer Competition prices	Demand of each product Plant loading	Demand of each product Demand for material Demand for semi-finished products Weather conditions	Sales revenue Production costs Inventory costs Leading indicators Cash in-flows Cash out-flow	Production Cash availability Purchasing of supplies and material		Competition evaluation
Short-term (up to 3 months)	Sales force targets Total sales Product categories Major products Product groups Stock levels	Total demand Demand of product categories and product groups Scheduling employment levels Costs	Demand for material	Total demand Inventory levels Cash-flows Short-term borrowing Prices	Demand for products Demand for material Lead time for purchasing		Total sales Sales breakdowns Pricing

Medium-term (3 months to less than 2 years)	Total sales Product categories Prices General economic conditions Promotional emphasis	Costs Budget allocations Buying or ordering equipment and machinery Employment level		Budget allocations Cash-flow	Demand for products Demand for raw and other materials	New product introduction	Demand for sales other expenses Cash-position General economic conditions Controls Objectives
Long-term (2 years or more)	Total sales Major product categories New product introduction Saturation points Market research emphasis	Costs Investments selection Expansion of plant and equipment Ordering of heavy equipment	Total sales Expansion of warehouses	Total sales Investment selections Capital expenditure Allocations Cash-flows	Contracts for buying of raw material	Total sales Technological, social and economic conditions of future New product development	Total sales Costs and other expenses Social and economic trends Goals and objectives and strategies establishment New products

Figure 2.4 *Uses of forecasting in organization function areas*

marketing effort has already been examined under the heading of general research and development. In advertising and sales promotion the prediction objective might be to indicate the volume markets which in turn will help to determine the appropriate levels of advertising expenditure. Forecasts of the size, location, type of market and consumer, with forecasts of product models, help to determine which media and advertising theme is appropriate to reach such a market.

In the area of packaging the aim of the forecast will be to provide information regarding volume, size and type of pack etc, to enable the economic purchase of unit packs, display outers, and shipment cases.

The sales forecast objective in relation to the sales force is to provide a basis for area, branch, and salesmen's sales target. However, it is essential to ensure that the target does not become an implied maximum to the salesman so that opportunities are missed because the target has been reached. It is better to have a quota that *must* be achieved, together with a target that *could* be reached with considerable extra effort, both being part of the overall potential of the territory. The forecast could form the basis for a remuneration plan for the sales force.

Sales forecasting objectives in the area of physical distribution relate to information for transport, warehousing, location of strategic stocks, and channels of distribution (wholesalers, retailers, etc). In the case of transport, the number of items that will be sold, size of order and geographic spread in various areas will help to determine such factors as whether to use the company's own or external transport services, size of fleet and size of individual vehicle, frequency of delivery, etc. Volume, seasonal factors and a breakdown of size and type of product are important factors when considering warehousing and the placing of strategic stocks. Forecasts help to determine the channels of distribution to be used by a company. When volume is small and/or the geographic spread is wide, manufacturers' agents or wholesalers may be more economic to use than when volume is relatively large, in which case the increased overheads of dealing direct with the retailer or consumer can be spread over a greater sales volume. The forecast may have to allow for longer production lead time if wholesalers are used. For example, it may be that products purchased by consumers in November and December have to be sold into retailers in September and October, but sold into wholesalers in July and August. Further, in forecasting the initial sales of a new product range, the forecaster will need to differentiate between ex-factory deliveries to wholesalers and retailers and the actual over-the-counter purchases by consumers. Initial ex-factory sales may be high as middle-men purchase a variety of the whole range to give consumers a choice and possibly an adequate service; a new range of household paint with a variety of different sizes, finishes and colours is an example of this.

Company-wide uses of forecasts

Because all budgets in a company ultimately come back to the question of how many units the organization will sell, all functional parts of a company will be interested in a forecast. In some cases a functional department will make its own individual forecast for use in a particular way.

Figure 2.4 indicates the various forecasts needed by functional areas of a company, and it will be seen that needs differ in the short, medium and long term. The purpose of Figure 2.4 is to highlight forecasting needs and to indicate where forecasting may be in operation. Any forecaster needs to research his organization to determine whether other personnel have made or are making a similar forecast to the one that is needed. Such research can avoid duplication of effort and save valuable time.

If the marketing department is not responsible for all forecasts, the management implications are that all forecasting activity should be integrated and ideally a composite forecast should be made.

Why, what, how, who, where and when

Setting objectives is in effect giving the answers to a series of questions commencing with the words Why, What, How, Who, Where and When.

Why do we need a forecast? Is it for short-term production scheduling, for financial planning, or to buy advantageously in a seasonal market? The most important primary and secondary reasons should be determined and the forecasting system built around them.

What are we trying to achieve, in terms of accuracy, scope, and effectiveness; do we need a trend or a detailed forecast? What are the particular problems involved in obtaining short-, medium- and long-term forecasts? What are the costs involved in terms of time and money, and what is the forecasting system's contribution to company profits? What sources of information are we going to tap?

How are the forecasts to be compiled and how many techniques are to be used? Is it to be calculated as a total forecast and broken down into product forecasts or started as product forecasts and built up to a total company forecast, or both? How can the forecasting system's adequacy be determined and what checks can be built in to ensure that it is working properly?

Who is going to do the forecasting? Is it to be done at executive level, or by specialist forecasters, or are the routine parts to be delegated to others; or a combination of these? Who will be involved in forecasting: company executives, specialist sales forecasters, marketing researchers, customers, potential customers, key people, salesmen, consultants, etc?

Where will the forecasting be done: in the marketing research section, in the marketing statistics or budgetary control section, in a specialized forecasting section, or in a combination of these?

When will forecasting be done? Will it be done on a weekly, monthly, quarterly, or yearly basis? When and how often will the forecast be reviewed? When and under what circumstances will the forecast be amended, if it is wrong by 5 per cent, 10 per cent, 25 per cent etc of actual sales? When and for what reasons will certain forecasting techniques be dropped and others introduced?

For effective control, objectives must be set so that the success of each forecasting technique is measured by comparing each component forecast with actual sales and any variances analyzed. It is the analysis of these variances, however small, that indicates the beginning of a new up-turn or down-turn in sales.

3

The Collection of Data for Forecasting

'Knowledge is of two kinds. We know a subject ourselves or we know where we can find information upon it.'

Dr Johnson

Scope

The next stage in market and sales forecasting is the collection of relevant and market-related information. This information is usually one of four types: *historic and factual* data referring to the past or present, assumptive information that makes rational assumptions for the future, data based upon the *statistical probability of an event taking place* and information regarding *future plans* and policies.

There are three main classifications of sources of information for marketing research in general and for market and sales forecasting in particular:

1. Desk research into internal records, which is the analysis of available, or potentially available company statistics and historic information. It also involves the collection of information regarding activities planned for the future (viz the marketing plan, etc), and details of company policy and an analysis of their possible effects on the sales forecast.
2. Desk research into secondary sources of information in published or existing material such as government statistics, economic data, trade information, published surveys, etc.
3. Original external field research ranging from informal approaches to key people and customers, regional or national surveys and experiments (ie controlled test marketing, pilot launches, etc).

Within these three areas, data can be obtained covering the external (and largely uncontrollable) factors and the internal (and largely controllable) factors examined in Chapter 1. Unless an adequate picture of the relevant market environment is obtained, even the most sophisticated predictive methods will fail to produce an effective forecast.

Desk research into internal records

This is the most useful, economic and logical starting point for market and sales forecasting. The continuous analysis of sales should be a normal everyday activity of any efficient marketing organization. Facts discovered by such an analysis often provide the solutions to many research and forecasting problems and are found within the company files. It is merely a matter of extracting and processing them into a usable form. The methods and types of internal records analyses are numerous, and their pattern and range will depend upon the problems facing the company, or indeed what information it requires.

However, there are a number of basic groups of data that can be used, improved upon, or rejected, and an analysis of their recent, past and current performance can make market and sales forecasting more effective.

Sales volume

One of the most important is sales volume. Total sales volume, and sales volume by product or product group, or service, is necessary. Such information would indicate the relative importance of each product or service in the company's product mix and in terms of income added to total company revenue or number of units sold. This data and the other groups that follow are extremely useful for statistical extrapolation.

Area sales volume

Area sales volume statistics involve a breakdown of past sales into geographical areas, salesmen's territories, television area coverage, or evening newspaper area coverage. Such data is necessary to relate the actual sales of an area to its potential.

Time sales volume

The analysis of sales over a period of time allows the progress of a company to be assessed, but it should cover not only sales in terms of money, but also sales in terms of units sold. Otherwise, fluctuations in price or (in the long term) the fall in the value of money may seriously restrict the usefulness of this data for forecasting purposes. Analysis of sales over a period of time allows seasonal fluctuations to be isolated and allowed for, as these are often hidden in yearly total figures.

Price/sales volume

Price/sales volume analysis indicating the effect on past sales of changes in price and discount levels is another key area of internal desk research.

Channels sales volume

The sales performance of the various channels of distribution being used by a company makes possible assessment of the contribution that each group, or type of outlet, makes to total revenue and is an indicator in establishing outlet profitability. It highlights current trends in channels of distribution and acts as a guide to a really effective advertising policy which in turn will affect sales.

When the policy of a company is to sell through retail outlets, analysis of the size and number of such outlets, as well as the distribution coverage (ie the number dealt with in relation to all outlets), produces essential forecasting information. Further, analysis of the type of outlets being used and a comparison made with the current trend in the pattern of distribution will enable a company to forecast and adjust to changes. Examples might be the growth of 'giant' retailing, of self-service and self-selection, of composite trading (widening of product ranges available in formerly specialist outlets) and of voluntary chains and groups.

Recognition of these changes will make possible more realistic forecasting of sales by allowing for the current distribution trend and by placing less reliance upon historic data obtained from an 'old' distribution pattern. Such analysis will enable a company to determine the minimum size of dealer or user with whom it is economical to deal direct, and will act as a guide as to whether an increased or decreased use of wholesale channels is indicated. Likewise, when a company is selling through agents, wholesalers, factors or distributors, or selling direct to industrial users, analysis of this kind will allow the forecaster to predict potential and permit marketing management to choose the most profitable method. Often this type of analysis will reveal a pattern of purchasing that can be used in forecasting. Also it may indicate the greater profitability of one type of outlet in one part of the country compared with the same type in another part.

When marketing industrial products, sales by SIC (Standard Industrial Classification) group will reveal the equivalent information regarding sales by types of industry. The Standard Industrial Classification list published by the Central Statistical Office shows industries by broad category (eg Electrical Engineering). It further sub-divides them into more specific groups to which it gives a classification number (eg Electrical Machinery 361, Insulated Wires and Cables 362, etc). The Standard Industrial Classification approach not only allows an industrial marketing company to analyze its sales by user industry type, but also permits a comparison with official statistics and data from other sources using the SIC. As a consequence it may be possible to derive the company's percentage share of the industry market. Internal company data based on the SIC can be linked also with input/output analysis described in Chapter 6.

Order size statistics

The minimum and average size of order statistics are important forecasting indicators, as the size and value of an order must be related to the cost of preparation, handling, administration, and delivery. Such overhead costs have an obvious and direct influence upon sales and profit, and there is a minimum size of order below which it is unprofitable to do business. If the company is in a strong position it can dictate what business it will handle direct and what it will pass through wholesalers. The minimum and average size of order decision will obviously affect sales and therefore forecasting.

Cost data

The actual cost of marketing is a further group of data that can be obtained from company records, and the sales and marketing cost per £ of sales obtained is a useful indicator for period-to-period comparison. It is particularly important in the case of the field sales force, and the sales cost per £ of sales obtained should be broken down into cost per salesman's territory. Marketing cost analysis will indicate particular problem spots in total marketing expenses. Such expenses should be broken down and attributed to all the sub-functions of marketing, from marketing research, product planning, publicity and promotional costs, to direct selling, physical distribution and administration, etc. By comparisons *within* sub-functions, for example, it may be found to be more profitable to have more door-to-door couponing and less television advertising. From comparisons between sub-functions (ie more spent upon advertising and less upon the sales force), it will be possible for marketing management to determine which is the best mix of the various marketing factors and enable predictions to be made that are more realistic. This type of analysis often leads to decisions by marketing management to change the use of company resources. Therefore, forecasters must follow through the consequences of their earlier analysis.

Sales potential

Sometimes potentials have been calculated for the sales force, ie total market potential by area, the number of customers and/or potential customers per area, etc. If they have been calculated carefully, the comparison of increases or decreases in actual sales with potential at regular time intervals is a useful indicator to the forecaster.

Sales force statistics

Data regarding the sales force, ie length of journey cycle and frequency of call, differing time allocation to various classes of customers, changes in the numbers of calls and the effect in different time periods, the number of calls in relation to the orders obtained, and even the effect on turnover of sales training etc, can all be obtained from internal records and in some cases are fundamental to the making of a realistic forecast.

Stock control data

The analysis of stock and the calculation of maximum and minimum stocks that it is economic to carry, both within the firm and in wholesalers and retailers, will bring to light stock control data. However, an economically low inventory must be reconciled with the level of stocks necessary to give adequate customer service or to meet competition and this in turn will have an effect on sales. Closely linked with stock control is the discovery and calculation of stock turn data during various periods of the year. Increasing stock turn will make a product more attractive for wholesalers and retailers to stock and sell actively.

Further, the availability of stock, where it is located and in what variety, will be a further influence upon sales and consequently upon sales forecasting. If stocks are not available, then the demand created by company advertising may be satisfied by competitors.

Accounting ratios

Statistics and facts regarding any aspect of company activity, especially those concerning marketing that are relevant to forecasting, should be extracted from internal records. In fact, the effectiveness of both marketing and general management can be calculated by using appropriate management accounting ratios comparing one period with another, or, if the facility exists, one company with another (eg inter-firm comparisons operated by private firms or trade associations). A statistical picture of company progress can be obtained when such ratios are calculated on a continuous basis.

Historic information

All types of historic marketing data must also be taken into account in forecasting: past marketing research information, the progress of both new and existing products (including product/process/service life cycle data), the expenditure, pattern and emphasis of advertising and sales promotion, and the relationship of sales volume and market share to these expenditures. Also pertinent would be information regarding size and type of sales force, the channels of distribution, methods of physical distribution and information regarding past pricing, branding, and credit policies. Between various time periods, comparison of changes in any of these factors would indicate their effect upon sales and therefore upon future predictions.

Predictable future data

Just as historic information regarding the eight sub-functions of marketing is important, so too are the planned future levels of these factors, particularly if they are to be different from the recent past. Therefore part of internal research will be concerned with the potential repercussions of future plans. For example, what effect will a proposed increase in the advertising budget have upon sales and why is it contemplated? In a growth market a particular increase in advertising expenditure may cause a disproportionate increase in sales. Alternatively, in highly competitive markets such an increase may merely be intended to hold sales at the level attained in the previous period. But where a new company enters a relatively static market, its sales can only come from customers of existing companies, therefore these companies may have to increase advertising expenditure as sales fall rapidly, merely to try to retain a reduced share of a market (a holding campaign). Company plans for the future in all activities (marketing, production, finance, etc) must be considered if forecasting is to be effective. Even a plan to commence, improve, or increase training for salespeople must be taken into account, as this will have an obvious effect upon sales performance.

These examples do not exhaust the range of possible headings under which past and proposed future data can be obtained from within a company, and therefore the individual forecaster must tailor the company's own internal research to suit its particular resources and market situation.

Desk research into secondary sources of information in published or existing material

Effective market and sales forecasting also uses basic economic and industrial data, government or official statistics, data from institutions and trade associations, national and trade press information, data from international bodies, previous surveys covering similar or analogous subjects and markets, and published information regarding competitors' strategy and tactics. To obtain optimum results from this type of desk research, existing information should be regularly updated.

Government sources

Government sources publish a wide range of information that is of great use to the market and sales forecaster. In particular, the Central Statistical Office produces a number of publications that give a comprehensive statistical picture of social and economic aspects of Britain. These publications include:

Social Trends 23
From employment to leisure, education to health and transport to housing, *Social Trends 23* gives a comprehensive insight into how Britain lives. All aspects of British life are revealed through statistics, charts and text in this social brief published annually.

Regional Trends 27
This is the most important source of official statistics about the standard regions of the UK, documenting the life of the nation in intricate detail. A multitude of graphs, tables and maps are presented on population trends, education, law and crime, earnings and industry, etc.

Family Spending — A Report on the annual Family Expenditure Survey
This multi-purpose survey provides a unique fund of social and economic data. It shows how households spend their money; how much is spent on food, travel, housing, etc. It shows how spending

patterns depend upon the income of households, their composition, and where they live, and how this has changed in the last 35 years.

Key Data — UK social and business statistics
This presents a selection of official UK statistics on key social and economic subjects including finance, trade and industry, prices and incomes, employment, defence, law and order, leisure, education, health and social security, environment, energy, etc. The data is illustrated with maps, tables and charts.

Annual abstract of statistics
This provides the latest economic, financial and social figures, drawn together from the Central Statistical Office's monthly and annual statistical publications.

Guide to Official Statistics
An invaluable reference book for tracing primary sources of statistics for the past five years on a range of subjects as diverse as weather and wages, finance and forestry, production and police. Included are all official (and a few non-official) sources of information on the UK, the Isle of Man and the Channel Islands.

Retail prices 1914–1990
From the price of a loaf of bread to the cost of a pint of beer, from electricity bills to petrol prices, the Retail Prices Index is the primary measure of price inflation as it affects consumers in the UK. Monthly figures have been compiled on a similar basis since 1947 and an earlier series — *The Cost of Living Index* — goes back as far as 1914. Besides the overall ('all items') index, there are component indices covering particular goods and services. This volume contains the longest possible time series for each of the indices currently compiled, providing a comprehensive series of information of use for both reference and analytical purposes.

United Kingdom National Accounts
This shows how the nation makes and spends its money. This annual Blue Book looks at all aspects of the UK economy — production, income, expenditure. It covers industry; current, capital and financial accounts for the personal sector, companies, public corporations and central and local government; and the wealth of the nation, investment and capital consumption.

United Kingdom Balance of Payments
This annual Pink Book gives detailed balance of payments data for a range of areas, from the City's contribution to the UK's overseas earning to the total transactions with the rest of the European Community and the UK's overseas assets and liabilities. It contains

information on visible trade, invisible and capital transactions, as well as specific aspects of the balance of payments.

United Kingdom National Accounts — Sources and methods
An essential reference book for users of official estimates of GDP, consumers' expenditure, capital formation and all the other estimates within the national accounting system published annually in the Central Statistical Office's Blue Book.

Standard Industrial Classification of economic activities 1992
As a result of the Single European Market, extensive changes have been made to the *Standard Industrial Classification*. This important revision brings the UK system of classification and indexing in line with that of the European Community. It gives categories for a multitude of items, activities and services.

Indexes to the Standard Industrial Classification
This is the vital companion to the *SIC Revised 1992* and provides two indexes. The numerical index lists each heading of the SIC followed by a list of characteristic activities included within the heading. In the second index, the activities have been arranged alphabetically. Alongside each is the numerical heading to which the activity is classified.

Input-Output Tables for the United Kingdom 1984
Input-output tables present a snapshot of the economy for one time period, illustrating the connection between primary inputs and final demand at industry level. The tables are the first to be compiled since 1984, consistent with the national accounts estimates for that year as given in the 1987 Blue Book. For ease of use a floppy disk containing the tables is included with this publication.

Business Monitors
These are designed for businesses and others undertaking forecasting and market research of all kinds. They provide statistics on manufacturing, energy, mining, service and distributive industries. The Central Statistical Office regularly questions thousands of UK businesses on their output and performance. Some 800,000 inquiry forms are sent out each year, and the statistics are collated and presented by expert government statisticians, using accepted statistical techniques.

Variously published at monthly, quarterly or yearly intervals, 'Business Monitors' are the primary and often the only source of the information they contain. 'Business Monitors' can help you to:

* *Monitor business trends* not only in your own industry but also in your suppliers' and customers' industries.

- *Identify successful products* by following the performance of different products to determine where sales are increasing.
- *Assess your efficiency* by comparing your performance with that of your industry as a whole.
- *Identify new markets* by determining which product sales are on the increase and what new retail outlets are opening.
- *Pinpoint seasonal factors in your business* by studying the trends of different surveys.
- *Market your products* by reference to a list of manufacturer's names and addresses.
- *Compare* the price of your products with those of your industry or sector.

What information do 'Business Monitors' contain?

1. Production Monthly, Quarterly and Annual Sales Series
The PM, PQ and PAS series are the major source of information on sales of UK manufactured products by UK companies. Generally they include import and export data, which enables the forecaster/ researcher to calculate the total market for products in the UK and some include producer price indices and employment figures.

2. Production Annual Series
The Production Annual series covers the Annual Census of Production — the major source of information on the structure and overall performance of the UK manufacturing, energy, mining and construction industries. The series includes tables on output and costs, capital expenditure, stock, analysis of businesses by number of employees, labour costs and operating ratios.

3. Service and Distributive Series
The Service and Distributive series includes statistics on retailing, motor trades and wholesaling. The Monitor SDA 25 Retailing provides detailed results of a regular inquiry into the structure of retail trade. It is supplemented by SDM 28 Retail Sales which contains monthly indices of retailing turnover. Four other monitors are SDA Wholesaling, SDA Motor Trades, SDA Catering and allied trades and SDA 29 Service trades.

4. Miscellaneous Series
The Miscellaneous series contains information on a variety of topics, including Producer Price Indices, travel and tourism, insurance and current cost accounting incides.

Periodicals

Economic Trends This monthly publication brings together all the main economic indicators. The largest section provides time series and graphs over the last five years, preceded by several pages of the latest information and followed by an analysis of indicators in relation to the business cycle over the last 20 years. Other articles comment on and analyse economic statistics. *Economic Trends* is the primary publication for the quarterly national accounts and balance of payment articles.

Economic Trends Annual Supplement This fills two known gaps in the range of official statistical publications. It provides a notes and definitions supplement to *Economic Trends* and contains long runs of up to thirty years' data for some of the main economic indicators.

Monthly Digest of Statistics This provides basic information on 20 subjects including population, employment and prices, social services, production and output, energy, engineering, construction, transport, catering, and national and overseas finance. The Digest contains mostly runs of monthly and quarterly estimates for at least two years and annual figures for several more.

Monthly Digest of Statistics (incorporating the Annual Supplement) This supplement gives definitions of terms and units employed in the *Monthly Digest of Statistics* in more detail than is possible in the headings and footnotes of the tables in the publication itself.

Financial Statistics This monthly publication provides data on a wide variety of financial topics including financial accounts for sectors of the economy, government income and expenditure, public sector borrowing, banking statistics, monetary aggregates, institutional investments, company finance and liquidity, security prices and exchange and interest rates. It is prepared by the Central Statistical Office, in collaboration with the Statistics Divisions of the Government Departments and the Bank of England.

Financial Statistics Explanatory Handbook This handbook provides background notes to the many tables in *Financial Statistics*. It explains their purpose and how they are compiled, shows the relationship between tables and provides further references. Together the two publications are major reference documents for people and organizations concerned with the flow of investment funds, saving media, government income and expenditure, institutional investment, company finance and finance generally.

Statistical News This quarterly periodical provides a comprehensive account of current developments in British official statistics to help all those who use or would like to use statistics. Every issue contains two or more articles dealing with a subject in depth. Shorter notes give news of the latest developments in many fields including, international statistics. Some reference is made to other work which, though not carried out by government organizations, is closely related to the official statistics. Appointments and other changes in the Government Statistical Service are also given. A cumulative index in the winter edition provides a permanent and comprehensive guide to developments in all areas of official statistics.

General

The above publications can be obtained from HMSO Publications Centre, PO Box 276, London, SW8 5DT or its HMSO bookshops and agents. Further information can be obtained from the Central Statistics Office (Press and Information Office), Room 65C/3, CSO, Great George Street, London SW1P 3AQ or at the Business Statistics Library at Newport, Gwent.

Non-government sources

There are many non-government sources of information for appropriate economic, business and market data. The reader is recommended to consult *Sources of Unofficial UK Statistics*, compiled by David Mort for the University of Warwick Business Information Service, published by Gower Publishing Ltd.

This book gives details of more than 1000 publications and services produced by trade associations, professional bodies, consultants, local authorities, employers' federations and others, together with statistics appearing in trade journals and periodicals. Titles and services are listed alphabetically by publisher and each entry contains information, where available, on subjects, content, sources of statistics, address of publisher, frequency, cost, availability, and contacts for further information.

Press sources

The world, national and local press and specialized trade magazines provide valuable current data for the forecaster in general and specific fields. The usefulness of the highly specialized trade press varies from industry to industry with overlapping of information in some areas (much of it calculated on different information bases) and a great number of information gaps in others. A tendency exists for such trade press to emphasize technical and production information although marketing and forecasting data is emerging in some.

Directories

A wide range of directories form an invaluable group of information sources giving details of companies, type of product, company structure, number of employees, addresses of parent companies and subsidiaries, etc. These include:

(a) *The Confederation of British Industry Directory.*
(b) *Rylands.*
(c) Kemps.
(d) Kelly's Directories of Manufacturers and Merchants.
(e) Dun and Bradstreet *Guide to Key British Enterprises.*
(f) Dun and Bradstreet *British Middle Market Directory.*
(g) Roskill's *Who owns Whom.*
(h) GPO Telephone Directories (especially the *Yellow Pages*).
(i) *The Kompass Register.*
(j) Industrial directories published by some trade journals.
(k) Directories of mailing lists offered by some direct mail agencies.
(l) *Stubbs Directory.*

Published surveys

Published surveys also represent another category of information source for the forecaster.

Competitors

Competitors' catalogues, obtained either direct or through customers or from trade fair and exhibitions, are possible sources of data, as well as competitors' advertisements, public relations announcements and financial reports.

Subscription and consultancy services

A range of such services exist and the reader is recommended to refer to *UK Statistics: A Guide for Business Users* by David Mort, published by Ashgate Publishing Ltd. This is a guide to key sources of information in selected subject areas of particular relevance to business users. The coverage, content, methods of collection and limitations of major titles and services in each subject area are described. Of particular use to the forecaster is the chapter on Market Research Data, Advertising and Media Information.

International sources

In the international field, a wide range of information regarding other countries and their potential markets can be obtained from a variety of sources. For example, the United Nations produces a catalogue of specialized publications by its Departments. Of particular use is the *United Nations Statistical Year Book* that includes a world and region summary; population and social statistics; international economic relations; national accounts; government finance; wages and prices; and economic activity covering agriculture, forestry and fishing, mining and quarrying, manufacturing (food, beverages, tobacco, textiles and leather, non-metallic mineral products and fabricated metal products, machinery and equipment), transport and communications, energy, land use, science, technology and intellectual property. Another useful source is *World Resources*, a regular Report by the World Resources Institute in collaboration with the United Nations Environment Programme and the United Nations Development Programme.

A number of useful statistical/descriptive/advisory publications can be obtained from governments worldwide. In the UK, this would include those from the Department of Trade Export Section (in London and at regional centres) which provides a wide range of information on international countries/markets but particularly on the European Community's 'Single Market'. With regards to the latter, its 'Exports to Europe Branch' (EEB), have special 'country desks' so that information can be accessed quickly by telephone. The Central Statistics Office *Business Monitor* (MA20), 'Overseas Trade Statistics of the UK' also contains useful information for the forecaster.

Other international agencies are useful sources of information. The Organisation for Economic Co-operation and Development (OECD) produce specific country and worldwide reports/surveys; their 'Food consumption statistics' publication is particularly helpful regarding information in its specialized area.

The International Monetary Fund publish a variety of statistical reports; of particular use in its specialized area is the *Government Finance Statistics Yearbook* that gives world tables and tables for individual countries.

The World Bank has its own set of useful publications but also *World Tables* are published by the Johns Hopkins University Press for the World Bank.

A further source of information is the International Labour Office but in this specific area *International Labour Statistics: a handbook, guide and recent trends*, edited by R Bean, published by Routledge, London, is particularly useful.

There are numerous regular and *ad hoc* reports and surveys of regions/countries/markets by British and foreign banks and other agencies, as well as a variety of special publications (eg *The World in Figures*, compiled by *The Economist*, published by Hodder and Stoughton), that are available.

Availability of information

The examples of published information sources mentioned above are merely a few from each potential group. The sources chosen by any forecaster will depend upon the objectives of the search/survey, the type of product/service, the market, the industry, and the company concerned.

For local, regional, national or international information, forecasters can find many sources to suit their specific needs that can be combined/compared/cross-referenced to produce more effective forecasts from the variety of libraries available. These include the commercial and/or reference department of local authorities public libraries, specialist libraries (eg Business Statistics Library at Newport, Gwent, the Patents Office, and some embassies or trade missions), libraries of professional bodies (eg Chartered Institute of Marketing, Cookham, Maidenhead), and the libraries of Universities and Colleges many of which are 'open libraries', ie they can be used by individuals and businesses for reference purposes or can be used on a subscription basis. The Association of Special Libraries and Information Bureaux (ASLIB) can also supply information on special sources.

On-line sources of information

In addition to the above sources of appropriate information, a number of specialized computer on-line databases have been developed to contain industry reports, market reviews, marketing research data, and statistics and media data. These often include information on the economic environment, historical market estimates, forecasts of market size, market share details, analyses of market trends, information on competitors and potential customers, and industry comment; some are general and some are industry specific. This information can be accessed immediately by the forecaster via a computer (and modem), saving money and many hours of tedious 'research' work.

Two useful sources of information about on-line databases are the *Directory of Online Databases*, published by Quadra/Elsevier, New York, USA, and the *DIALOG Database Catalogue*, published by Dialog Information Services Inc, Dialog Europe, Oxford,

England. These sources give information such as the database name, details of subject/content, type, producer, geographic coverage, the time span, the online service used, language, update details, conditions/costs, etc.

The marketing research/intelligence applications of on-line databases can be divided into five distinct areas, ie market information and research reports, company information, advertising and public relations, business news, and economic and demographic statistics; some databases cover combinations of these areas.

Some examples of databases that are of use to market and sales forecasters are:

BIS INFOMAT NEWSFILE (Producer: BIS Infomat; Online service Data-Star Dialog Inc). Contents include summaries of business news reports from hundreds of publications world-wide. Covers marketing, advertising and retail sales information on a wide range of diverse industries internationally.

HARVEST (Producer and online service: Harvest Information Services Ltd). Contents include a marketing, advertising and public relations news file, a market overview file containing statistics, analyses forecasts about specific product/service areas, an advertising factfile, a new product news file, a factfinder file involving national and regional economics and household penetration by product, a demographics file (national and regional), and a consumer research file (attitudes and behaviour).

MAGIC (Marketing and Advertising General Information Centre) (producers: Datasolve Ltd and others; Online service: Datasolve Ltd). Contents include a number of specialized files of information on business and industry news, marketing, market research surveys, forecasting, advertising and the advertising industry and public relations. Actual files include:

BRAD (British Rate and Data) provides advertising rates, comparative circulation statistics, etc, on all British media; corresponds to BRAD Directory.

Henley Centre for Forecasting contains full text of leisure futures, analyses and forecasts of social, industrial and economic trends in consumer spending, including a survey of leisure time usage. Also contains full text of *Planning Consumer Market* giving 5 year forecasts on the market of consumer goods and services, published by the Henley Centre for Forecasting.

Marketing Surveys Index contains citations and abstracts of a wide range of business and economic research reports published worldwide. Corresponds to the *Marketing Surveys Index*, published by Marketing Strategies for Industry (UK) Ltd, updated monthly.

MEAL (Media Expenditure Analysis Ltd); see details below under *MEALINK*.

MINTEL covers a range of MINTEL reports on a number of files including Daily Digest, Leisure Intelligence Reports, Market Intelligence Europe Reports, Consumer Goods and Services Intelligence Reports, Personal Finance Intelligence Reports, and Retail Intelligence Reports. Produced by Mintel Publications Ltd.

Campaign contains the full text of 'Campaign', covering the UK advertising industry; and also includes regular detailed surveys on special topics. Published by Haymarket Publications.

Marketing contains full text of 'Marketing'; includes analyses of new marketing techniques with case histories and reviews of newly published statistical data. Published by Marketing Publications.

Media Week contains full text of 'Media Week', providing coverage of the UK public relations industry. Published by Mediaweek Ltd.

PR Week contains full text of 'PR Week', covering all aspects of the media with emphasis on the UK and Europe. Published by Range Nine.

MAID (Market Analysis and Information Database) (producer: MAID Systems Ltd; Online Service: Pergamon InfoLine). Contains news and information on the advertising and marketing research industries. Includes full-text market research reports on various industries. Reports cover manufacturers, retailers, wholesalers, and sales, market shares, sizes, structures, trends, and segmentation, ownership, socio-economic groups and population, seasonal and regional variations and trends, packaging and production. Also includes business news reports, media audit data and advertising expenditure. Users can search by industry, brand or company name, publication name or date and publisher name.

MEALINK (Producer: Media Expenditure Analysis Ltd (MEAL)); On line service Datasolve Ltd (MAGIC see above). Contains data on advertising expenditure in the UK. Data are available by advertising media (eg newspapers, magazines, and television), by brand names, and by product categories.

PIMSsm Database (Profit Impact of Market Strategy) (producer: Strategic Planning Institute: Online service: SPI Strategic Planning Institute). Contains current and historical marketing data on 2,300+ strategic business units in several hundred companies worldwide. Aggregate data on SBU's are provided for income statements, balance sheets, market shares, market growth rates, customer characteristics, and such strategic indicators as degree of innovation and product differentiation/quality.

PTS PROMT (Predicasts Overview of Markets and Technology) (producer: Predicasts, Cleveland, OH, USA). This is a multi-industry database that provides broad, international coverage of companies, products, markets, and applied technologies for all industries. PTS PROMT is comprised of abstracts and full text records from more than 1000 of the world's important business publications, including trade journals, local newspapers and regional business publications, national and international business newspapers, trade and business newsletters, research studies, investment analysts' reports, corporate newsletters and corporate annual reports. PROMT gives information on many industries/markets, including biotechnology, chemicals, computers, electronics and telecommunications, food, finance, health, recreation, transport.

Furthermore, it provides information on competitive activities, market size and share, new products/services and technologies, financial trends, mergers and acquisitions, contracts. joint ventures, new facilities, trade, regulation and many others aspects of international business.

PTS International Forecasts (producer: Predicasts, Cleveland, OH, USA). Contains abstracts of published projections for all countries of the world excluding the USA. The file includes forecasts on general economics, industries, specific products, and end use data.

PTS MARS (Marketing & Advertising Reference Service) (producer: Predicasts, Cleveland, OH, USA). This is a multi-industry marketing and advertising database with abstracts and full text records on a wide range of consumer products and services. Contains market size/share information, product or service introductions, evaluations of markets for existing products and services, researches marketing and advertising strategies, monitors advertising campaigns, budgets and target markets, provides information on products and services, tracks agency changes, new accounts, launch dates, contracts, and appointments.

World Reporter (producer: Datasolve Ltd and others; Online service: Datasolve Ltd). Contains 475,000+ news items, articles and broadcast transcripts from press, radio, and news agencies.

There are a number of other specialized on-line databases available to meet the particular needs of market and sales forecasters; details can be found in the two on-line database directories mentioned earlier in this section.

Gathering forecasting information by original field research

This means direct contact with past, present and potential customers and with any other person able to give relevant market and sales forecasting information.

Whether original field research needs to be used by a company in forecasting the market and sales will depend upon the availability information from internal or published sources. For example, if the subject of a forecast is a completely new product concept or a unique improved product, original field research may be the only source of forecasting information. If competitive factors in a market have changed greatly in recent periods, historic data from desk research may no longer be a reliable source upon which to base a forecast. Further, depending upon cost, time, and accuracy factors, original field research may be the only method of obtaining realistic demand and supply forecasts. Statistically based forecasts often omit vital factors in human behaviour which drastically affect market (demand and supply) patterns. Direct field research provides the opportunity to assess the possible effects of such behaviour on forecasts. It can also fill in gaps in published data.

Types of field research

The types of market and sales forecasting research that can be carried out 'in the field' are numerous, and a company has the choice of doing the work within its own organization, obtaining the services of specialist market research agencies or of using the market research facilities often offered by advertising agencies.

Some of the main areas in which original field research can be useful in market and sales forecasting are classified as follows:

1. Product/Service

It is possible to investigate product/service acceptance by the market of new, improved, or existing products/services, as well as examining the reception of a basic product/services concept. It is also possible to discover the market segmentation pattern and the corporate image associated with a product. The reactions of a representative sample of consumers/users can be studied and it becomes possible to forecast the size of the various parts of the market in advance, subject to other forecasting factors.

2. Market

The geographical location of a market and its size in terms of market segments can be found by field research if they are not available through published data. This also applies to market share analysis. Potential trends, user characteristics (and consequently ideal profile) and user/purchaser attitude research are also possibilities in this area.

3. Packaging

Unit sales volume can be affected by reaction to the packaging of a product and research into product acceptance through the pack, its protection performance in transit and in storage, its marketing performance, its convenience and after-use function. All these factors can help when considering the effect a pack will have on sales volume in the future.

4. Pricing

Price is a function of demand and therefore should be a prime consideration of the forecaster. Price confrontation studies, in which a sample of consumers is asked what price they think a product (either a general group or specific product) should be, and how much they actually paid the last time they purchased such a product, will give important forecasting data. Other pricing data can be obtained through price/value/quality relationship research of the complete sales proposition (not just the product) and through the determination of psychological and 'bargain' prices.

5. Sales and distribution

This area of forecasting research is concerned with the methods and channels of distribution, activities in retail stores, distribution coverage, the activities of the field sales force, before and after sales services, availability of stocks and the effect of transport facilities.

6. Advertising, sales promotion, and merchandising

Media research, pre- and post-testing of copy and artwork, research into sales promotional techniques, can produce data of importance to the forecaster, It can also broadly indicate the effect the communication media will have on the sales of a new product or the effect that a change in emphasis in the promotional mix will have upon the sales of the existing product range.

7. Industrial

The special problems of industrial marketing may often require additional research to be carried out. This would include research into market structure, characteristics, and growth as well as end-use analysis of products that are vertically integrated into a chain of manufacturing processes, analysis of customers and potential customers by 'trade use' or SIC (Standard Industrial Classification). It should also include an examination of specific industry buying policies and research into the 'originating' industries, if a company's product enters at some stage in the chain of manufacture. An example of the latter point is the metal container industry's concern with current crops of fruit and vegetables for forecasting purposes. These and other research areas appropriate to particular industries provide vital information for the special needs of the industrial forecaster.

8. Competition

An analysis of competitors' and potential competitors' profiles (production capacities, prices, corporate images, product development, promotional expenditure, future development plans, etc) in the light of a company's own future policies, can help the forecaster to make a more realistic prediction of market conditions and consequently of sales volume.

Methods of collection

The collection of data under these various headings is largely based upon sampling techniques, where a representative sample of consumers or users is surveyed. The main exceptions to this are in the case of competition (where competitors are relatively few) and where the number of consumers or users in a market is small, as in some industrial situations where the data can be collected about all competitors and from all users. Alternatively, data may be collected from key customers only, especially where they purchase a large proportion of a company's or industry's products. However, even with key customers, it can be dangerous to draw wide conclusions from data from small samples. Other key people who can provide information that can affect forecasts are to be found in most government departments, especially Public Relations Officers.

Sales and technical staff as information sources

Within a company both sales and technical staff can provide market information, although often their contribution is subject to certain limitations, due primarily to inherent bias and lack of market research training.

This tactical information, which should be the easiest to obtain, is usually the most difficult. Every salesperson should be trained to pass information back to headquarters. In fact, this intelligence-gathering quality should be developed to a high degree.

If it is important that salespeople are trained to note and report back information, it is equally important that someone is trained in the collation and interpretation of this information. Continuous study and analysis of salesstaff's reports can produce profitable information results.

Examples of customer 'grass-roots' forecasting information that salespeople can find out are:

— Manufacturing methods.
— Rate of production.
— Testing procedures.
— Need for finance.
— Quality requirements.
— Name of present supplier.
— Purchasing procedures.
— Competitive equipment in use or product stocked.
— Decision patterns.
— Budget period.
— Stockholding policy.
— Is the company a trendsetting or following company?
— Need for technical advice.
— Does the customer rely on demand derived from another industry?
— Seasonal demand.
— Has the customer a new, unusual or different application for your products?
— Investment plans.
— In which industry or consumer goods market does the customer operate?
— Product development plans.
— Competitive situation of customer.

This information from a particular company is important if a forecast of whether a large contract will or will not be obtained is required.

Field surveys

Surveys can involve the use of the personal interview, where the individual consumer/user is taken through a formal questionnaire, or the focused interview in which guide questions are asked to get the consumer to speak freely about a specific topic giving facts, opinions, feelings, etc. The success of these techniques depends on having a skilled interviewer, a sound questionnaire or adequate guide question list and a good response from a properly selected representative sample of consumers/users.

Telephone surveys

Another method is the telephone interview which relies upon asking consumers/users to recall some recent action (purchase, visits, viewing, etc) or where the consumer/user is asked about something that is happening or something that he is doing at that time (viewing television, listening to the radio, etc).

Postal surveys

Postal or mail surveys can be used to gather data, either based upon a mailing list where a questionnaire is sent to consumers/ users, or upon 'mail in' questionnaires in newspapers and magazines, or upon replies to questionnaires included in the packaging of products. These postal methods often require the use of incentives to motivate consumers/users to provide the information.

Panel or audit methods

There is a series of data-gathering techniques that can be classified as panel or audit methods. Product testing panels are used where the comments of a group of consumers/users are sought in relation to products and product acceptance. They can be used also to gauge the impact of packaging, design, brand names and advertising. The panel can operate as a group meeting at a central point or as individuals being interviewed on a continuous basis. Another type of continuous panel deals with consumer purchasing habits and patterns, and requires panel members to record in diaries details of purchases. Alternatively, pantry or 'dustbin' checks are made to obtain purchasing and usage data from a panel of consumers. Although panels are widely used in consumer goods fields they can also be used to obtain data for industrial marketing. The panel technique can be used directly for sales forecasting purposes. Some companies use a panel of experts or specialists, some from within the company (various executives) but mainly from outside the company (economists, statisticians, key customers and business consultants) to meet, discuss and come to an agreed forecast.

Audit services on a subscription basis have already been mentioned in the section dealing with desk research into published data. Occasionally, the retail audit method is used by single manufacturers on an ad hoc basis.

The laboratory shop is a further audit device where a shop or series of shops operating in normal market conditions and owned by a manufacturing company or agency is used to examine the purchasing patterns and movements of all manufacturers' products together with their point of sale material, price and discount offers, etc. Audit methods are particularly useful in obtaining 'over-the-counter' sales data where distribution lines are long and ex-factory deliveries to wholesalers do not reflect immediately the changes in consumer purchasing patterns.

Although panel and audit techniques could be described as 'pure' marketing research, the data obtained from them can have a direct bearing upon future sales and therefore should be used by the forecaster if the results are available or warrant the cost.

Observational methods

There are also observational methods of gathering information. These include observing additional information during a personal interview, observation by consent (stock audits and pantry checks are examples), observation of behaviour where the people concerned are not aware that they are being observed (eg observing the effectiveness of point-of-purchase promotional advertising material), observational counts of customers (purchasers of a product group or brand, passers-by, etc), and participant observation such as cookery, gardening, operating a machine, driving, or any other such activity.

Motivation research

In the appropriate market situation, consumer research as described above can be of direct use to the market and sales forecaster by indicating who buys what, where, how, when and how often, but it may be less successful in discovering 'why' consumers behave in the way they do and what motivates them. This has in recent years given rise to the use of indirect methods that probe beneath the surface of consumer or user behaviour to analyze those factors that influence the choice and attitude of the consumer. This is known as motivation research. Social psychologists and others have helped market researchers to evolve such techniques as group discussion interviews, depth interviews (in which persons interviewed are encouraged to 'talk themselves out' on a particular topic), perception tests, shopping list tests, picture or situation completion tests, word association tests, sentence completion tests, etc. All these techniques are designed to provide data and results that are expressed in qualitative terms as opposed to the quantitative results of conventional marketing and forecasting research.

Experimental marketing

Another method of gathering forecasting information externally is through marketing experiments. Test towns and/or test areas or industries are examples of obtaining information by controlled experiments. For example, a test town may be used to discover consumers' acceptance of product features (flavour, colour, design, performance, packaging, etc) and to measure the level of repeat purchases. A test area (perhaps a television region) may be used to study sales under realistic marketing conditions using the same weight of advertising and sales promotion per capita that the company intends to use during a national launch. The experiment becomes 'controlled' when two test towns or areas are used; one with certain features of the marketing proposition included and one without. Perhaps one is provided with special packaging, or special point of purchase display material, or special advertising, and the other is not. A comparison of the sales results of the two areas is then made and the effects on sales are assessed.

But test marketing forewarns competitors, and therefore in industries where security and surprise impact upon a market is important, the pilot launch technique may be used. With this method the company may research a market segment regarding particular consumer needs and develop a product in its laboratories to meet these needs. They then introduce the product, using the data obtained from this stage of the product life cycle, to make adjustments to the product, the overall sales proposition and the marketing mix as they proceed; this would include adjustments to the original forecast and possibly to forecasting methods.

Experimentation also includes split run advertisements in newspapers or magazines where different advertisements are run in national or regional media to gauge the effect of particular advertisements on sales in different areas.

The effect on sales of changes in factors relating to the sales force, is another area for experiments. A comparison is made of results in one area using salesmen plus a display team and in another using merchandisers; or in one area using the normal sales force and another using a special task force to obtain distribution coverage. Experiments using variations of call frequency and journey cycles, differing time allocation to various classes of customer, etc can also be used to study potential sales volume changes.

Use of field research in forecasting

Whether the sales forecaster will use any or all of these techniques of original external field research will depend upon how important the forecast is to the company, whether this type of research is to be carried out for other purposes and the results will be available anyway, and whether or not adequate information is available from desk research into internal records or published data. It will also depend upon the cost of obtaining the data through original field research in relation to the money available or the profit contribution such research findings will make. Lastly, it will depend upon the time available, the degree of accuracy required, and the type, size, and geographical spread of the markets to be surveyed.

4

Key market-related factors: identification, weighting and prediction

'Genius is 1% inspiration and 99% perspiration'
Thomas Edison

Although they are said to be the 'life blood' of an organization, sales do not exist as prime entities but are merely the consequence or the averaging out of the impact of a number of key market-related factors, both internal or external, to an organization.

These key market-related factors are frequently increasing or decreasing in volume, value or velocity, over a period of time. They will affect how the total 'deal' that an organization is offering (eg product, process, service, image, performance, quality, etc) will be received in a specific market place, ie whether it will be purchased, thereby becoming 'a sale'.

The ability to *identify* direct and indirect factors that affect an organization's sales performance in a particular market segment, *measure*, *interpret* and *predict* their future direction, intensity and velocity, and *integrate* their combined effects with the right amount of weighting, is crucial to effective forecasting.

Controllable, influencing and non-controllable factors

These key market-related factors were mentioned in Chapter 1 (controllable and non-controllable factors) where they were briefly considered in the context of the overall forecasting environment in general, and their relationship to the marketing mix in particular. In this chapter, the process is taken a stage further by examining methods of identifying, weighting and predicting them under the extended classification of controllable, influencing, or non-controllable (direct and indirect) factors.

For example, the key market-related factors affecting the market and sales (and therefore the sales forecast) in an international company that markets ethical pharmaceutical products could be selected from the following:

Controllable factors (company policy), eg primary demand development, expansion, quality change, retrenchment, new generic drug market entry, divestment in particular product type/market area, licensing and royalties arrangements, etc.

Controllable factors (other functional areas), ie policies, strategies and operating practices in production, purchasing, finance and accounting, personnel, etc.

Controllable factors (marketing, and sales), ie policies, strategies and operating practices in marketing research, product/service planning, pricing, branding, forecasting, advertising, public relations, sales promotion, packaging, display, methods and channels of distribution, personal selling and 'servicing'.

Factors that can influence market performance, eg the current stage of the product/service/industry life cycle, 'up-to dateness' of company owned patents, the degree of current market segmentation, market position, market share, patients' and doctors' attitudes and behaviour, company/product/service combination offered and its image, level of doctor education/knowledge/experience.

Non-controllable factors (direct), eg competition, price levels of drugs, branded versus generic trends, location of market segments, disease incidence and trends, mortality and morbidity rates, health care systems, number of doctors, availability of channels of distribution, government policies and controls, etc.

Non-controllable factors (indirect), eg the economic, social and political climate, cultural factors, the legal system, environmental factors, population and demographic characteristics, standard and cost of living, educational literacy level, rate of inflation, exchange rates, etc.

All or some of these key market-related factors will determine and/ or influence the ultimate sales outcome, and by implication, should affect a company's market and sales forecast. The problem is identifying which factors are currently most dominant, so that these can be selected/prioritized/weighted and their direction predicted so that their trend/influence can be reflected in projections of immediate past sales data.

Furthermore, there is a need to identify and distinguish between key market-related factors that have short-, medium- and long-term effects on sales and therefore on forecasts (see also chapter 2). There is a tendency for the short-term forecaster to leave, or be required to leave, the medium- and long-term considerations to others (eg corporate planners, specialist market analysts, etc).

Identification of key market-related factors

The identification of key market-related factors can be achieved by the individual forecaster or, more effectively, by brainstorming and/or interactive working by a mixed group of persons involved in marketing planning and those who have to use forecasts. Such brainstorming and/or group activities can be used to assess a factor's degree of relevance, to predict its anticipated effect and to apply the impact of key market-related factor forecasts to historic and current sales data, or to modify statistically derived market and/or sales forecasts.

These group activities can be used also to apply human judgement, experience and intelligence to the final forecast, and to reason whether it is feasible as well as desirable. Furthermore, such group activities can be used to train a particular group of individuals to become more effective forecasters in their own specific areas of the organization.

Ideally, the progress and direction of all the key market-related factors should be 'mapped' and 'tracked', but because of the size of such an operation in some cases, this may not be feasible in some organizations. One favoured approach is to identify the most dominant factors *at this moment in time*, but ackowledging that these may change in another time period. Hence the need to identify *all* the key market-related factors that have a potential to influence a company's sales performance. If possible, the data of the less dominant factors should be grouped together into 'favourable' and 'unfavourable' categories to get a subjective overall 'flavour' of their combined influence.

Weighting and rating of key market-related factors

A development of the above approach is shown in Figure 4.1 (it is also used in the later chapter on 'Subjective forecasting as a forecasting method'). Using this method, 'experts' (internally and/or externally) are asked to identify key influencing impact factors under each heading in the format, to rank them in order of importance, to grade them according to anticipated impact and then to indicate whether they consider the current state of a key market-related factor to be favourable or unfavourable to company sales. By assigning rank and weight to individual key factors, a quantitative dimension and degree of intensity is given to a qualitative/judgemental opinion.

Another approach to identifying the potential impact of key

Influence/impact factors	Rank in order of importance	IMPACT						Favourable	Adverse	Neither
		Considerable (5)	Some (4)	Average (3)	Little (2)	None (1)				
1) **International factors** a) b) c) d)										
2) **Economic factors** a) b) c) d)										
3) **Industry factors** a) b) c) d)										
4) **Market factors** a) b) c) d)										
5) **Company factors** a) b) c) d)										
6) **Consumer/user** a) b) c) d)										
7) **Competition factors** a) b) c) d)										
8) **Environmental** a) b) c) d)										
9) **Psychological factors** a) b)										

Figure 4.1 *Subjective key market-related assessment format*

market-related factors on markets and sales, and giving it some statistical 'shape', is shown in Figure 4.2.

Around each of the relevant key market-related factors identified in Figure 4.2, a scenario is written of possible stages and/or degrees of impact. A grading is given, either very good, good, average, poor, or very poor, in terms of its effect on sales. At the same time, a numerical rating is given to the judgemental grade to allow for comparisions of intensity to be made and to indicate the estimated influence of the current assessment of the factor.

Often the outcome of making comparisons between assessed factors, causes a re-assessment to be made by the forecaster and a more feasible degree of the current impact is determined.

In some companies, the first stage of a further refinement is the weighting in terms of influences of particular broad groups of market-related factors. In a second stage this weighting is applied to all relevant detailed characteristics of such factors when these are rated. An example of this is shown in Figure 4.3.

The next stage of this method is to list all the appropriate component aspects of these broad groups of market-related factors that are identified as having impact potential. Each would be given the weighting shown for the broad category in Figure 4.3. For example, the appropriate component parts of 'competition' would be listed and given a weighting of 3 and this would be applied to any 'component part' rating given. The key market-related component parts for assessing competition and a company's competitive position might be listed as follows:

- customer spread;
- price leadership;
- importance of brand name;
- broad product line;
- low cost producer;
- technological advantage;
- operating at optimum capacity;
- profitability;
- financial strength;
- integration (forward, backward or horizontal);
- degree of risk-taking;
- management and organization;
- ability of sales force;
- advertising capability;
- market share;
- market position;
- labour relations;
- quality;
- service.

Identified Key market-related factor	Very Good (3)	Good (2)	Average (1)	Poor (0)	Very Poor (−1)
Economic Climate	Products/Services will sell readily in times of inflation	Strongly resistant to changes in economic climate	Sales will show average sensitivity to economic change	Sensitive to economic change	Highly sensitive to economic change
Availability and Price of Raw Material	Inexpensive to purchase, unlimited supply	Can be purchased at reasonable price; many suppliers	Can be purchased at reasonable price; few suppliers	Can be purchased at relatively high price; few suppliers	Can be purchased at a very high price; one supplier one supplier
Market Trend	Market growing at rate considerably higher than total industry; more than 15%	Market growth somewhat greater than total industry; 5% to 14%	Market growth keeping pace with overall industry; less than 5%	Market not growing and in some areas experiencing slight decline	Market experiencing significant decline
Government Spending	High in all sectors	High in selected sectors	Marginally above average of last few years	Slight cuts in selected sectors	Curtailed due to the inflationary state of economy
Machine Tool Orders	High in the relevant sectors	Recovering from previous year	Average for last 3 years	10% decline over previous years	Essential replacement orders only
Factory Building Starts	High in the sectors relevant to company	Slow but steady upward trend	Average	15% decline over previous years	Little activity

Figure 4.2 *Describing and rating key market-related factor assessments*

Broad market-related factor	Weighting	×	Rating	=	Score
International pressures	1		These		
Economic factors	3		ratings		
Industry factors	2		are subjected		
Market factors	2		to the		
Competition	3		weighting		
New technology	1		in the		
Social and cultural factors	1		previous		
Legislation	2		column.		
etc . . .					

Figure 4.3 *Weighting and rating of broad groups of key market-related factors*

The ratings given to each are multiplied by the weighting and a score is calculated. It is this score that will identify those factors that will have the greatest impact on sales, when all the component parts of the broad groups of key market-related factors have been calculated.

Although the method of weighting and rating is in itself subjective, it does give some quantifiable shape to the perceived relative importance of each of the factors, and indicates by how much the purely statistical forecasts and projections should be adjusted. It also forces the individual forecaster to view a forecast more objectively, helping to overcome judgemental bias, often fashioned by past experience rather than by present realism.

Even so, the weightings and ratings are particularly personal and the method is more effective if it is 'individually' applied by members of a small forecasting team. The justification of each team member's key market-related factors, their chosen weightings and ratings, and ensuing discussions, are more likely to give a consensus approach to balanced and feasible final forecasts.

Obviously, more resources of time and money will need to be spent forecasting those key market-related factors that are heavily weighted and rated, and in some cases those that are not so significant can be grouped together.

Manipulating forecasting outcomes

Another practical application of weighting and rating is where factors in a market can be categorized as non-controllable and controllable. The latter can be weighted (in practice by giving them extra resources) to have a greater impact on, and perhaps to offset, problematic non-controllable factors.

For example, in a particular organization, non-controllable factors could be sub-divided into market forces and environmental forces. The factors over which a company has some control and/or decision-making, could be viewed as the company's marketing mix. The component parts of the marketing mix can be resourced in such a way as to create a more favourable response in selected non-controllable factors.

An example to illustrate this approach can be seen in its application to a company in the ethical pharmaceutical market as shown in Figure 4.4.

Non-controllable key market-related factors	Weighting	Rating	Score
Market Forces Patients' attitudes and behaviour Price level of drugs Doctor's attitudes and behaviour Branded versus generic drugs Competition Methods of availability of channels of distribution Company/Product image Level of advertising and promotional expenditure			
Environmental forces Population and demographic statistics Geography and location of market Disease incidence and trend Mortality and morbidity rates Social environment Cultural factors Awareness of new drug therapy Education and number of medical practice doctors Number of hospital beds Public versus private health care systems and organizations Legal controls Government intervention and controls			

Controllable key market-related factors			
Marketing Mix Marketing research Product/Service planning Intellectual property (patents, registered trade marks, etc) Pricing Branding Forecasting Advertising Public relations Sales promotion Personal selling Packaging Display Servicing Channels of distribution			

Figure 4.4 *Non-controllable and controllable key market-related factors applicable to a hypothetical company in the ethical pharmaceutical market*

It can be seen that the impact of a non-controllable market-related factor on sales (and therefore on the forecast) could be lessened and/or influenced by increasing the resources channelled into one or several of the controllable factors in the marketing mix, eg increased advertising and public relations activity could lessen the adverse effects of 'doctors' attitudes and methods' or information regarding the 'availability and awareness of new drug therapy'. Likewise, increased resources into 'personal selling' could diminish the effect of 'competition', etc.

Statistical methods of assessing factor/sales relationships

There are a number of statistical methods available for assessing, measuring and using the relationship between various key market-related factors and sales.

Sometimes the relationships between key market-factors and sales are directly proportionate, ie as the former increases or decreases, so sales move proportionately, eg when (in Figure 4.4) a particular 'disease incidence and trend' increases, so the demand for, and normally sales of, a particular drug increases. However, care must be taken not to depend too much on such a link, because the key market-factor mentioned is only one of the many influences on the sales of a particular drug.

Regression analysis and correlation (see page 152) can be used to measure and use such relationships as a forecasting tool. In the former, a function is developed mathematically, which expresses the relationship between a dependent variable (sales) and one or more independent variables (key market-related factors). Correlation and the correlation co-efficient used as a measure of association, on the other hand, is designed to measure the direction and intensity of the relationship.

There are degrees of correlation, where data is partially correlated (measured by the co-efficient of correlation, see page 158), and although care must be taken when using it as a technique to determine the importance of particular key-market factors (and as a forecasting technique, pages 155 to 166) it is, nevertheless, a very effective tool for the forecaster.

Furthermore, multiple regression is used when wishing to forecast sales or one market-related factor from several other variables that are thought to have a causal relationship with the dependent factor. The multiple regression method determines the existence of some form of functional relationship between a dependent variable, such as sales and combinations of a number of independent variables, such as key market-related factors shown earlier.

The two most commonly used multiple regression techniques are 'forced entry' and 'step-wise regression'. The former is where all variables contribute to a single predictive equation and the latter where each variable is listed in order of best predictive power.

The technique of multiple correlation is derived from multiple regression, using the co-efficient of correlation as a measure of association and intensity of the relationship between the dependent and the the independent variables. A worked example is shown on pages 166 to 168.

Factor analysis

Factor analysis is an 'umbrella' title for a particular approach, making use of a series of statistical tools. It can be useful in any situation where a large number of variables are involved initially and there is a need to reduce them to a smaller number of underlying dimensions.

Factor analysis has a wide range of applications; for example, it has been used in conjunction with economic factors, to derive a set of uncorrelated variables for further analysis, when the use of highly intercorrelated variables may yield misleading results in regression analysis.

Factor analysis assumes that the observed variables are linear combinations of some underlying (hypothetical or observable) factors. Some of these factors are assumed to be common to two or more variables and some are assumed to be unique to each variable. Because of the multi-dimensional nature and the number of variables involved, factor analysis has become more widely used in recent years, primarily due to the development of computer speed and capacity, and also the availability of specialized computer programs.

Cluster Analysis and Discriminant Function Analysis

These are related techniques that enable the forecaster to determine how individual situations/factors can be grouped or differentiated on the basis of scores on one or two variables.

Cross Impact Analysis

This technique is designed to study the effects on the probabilities of events of the interactions of those events with each other. It is used to analyze the numerous chains of impact that can occur (as one event affects a second event, which in turn affects a third event, and so on) and to determine the overall effect of these chains on the probability that each event with occur by a specified time.

Because of the flexibility of cross-impact analysis (it can be applied to a wide range of problems) and the ease of applying it, it has become widely used in forecasting/futures research. It has been used in studies of key market-related factors, economic and industry factors, and in many other areas.

All the above statistical methods have increased in use as computers have become more universally accessible and also because of the development of specialised computer programs, enabling wider and more rapid analysis of appropriate key market related factors.

Conclusion

Key market-related factors are frequently increasing or decreasing in volume or value or velocity, over a period of time. They will affect how the total 'deal' that an organization is offering (eg product, process, service, image, performance, quality, etc) will be received in a specific market place, i.e. whether it will be purchased thereby becoming 'a sale'.

The ability to *identify* direct and indirect factors that affect an organization's sales performance in a particular market segment, *measure*, *interpret* and *predict* their future direction, intensity and velocity, and *integrate* their combined effects with the right amount of weighting, is crucial to effective forecasting.

5

Basic Forecasting Considerations

'It is a capital mistake to theorize before one has data'
Arthur Conan Doyle

Assessment terms

It has already been acknowledged that forecasting is affected by the various environments in which a company operates. Broadly, these are the international economy, the national economy, and the individual market. Forecasts can therefore relate to these various market environments in addition to the particular company's sales forecast.

More specifically, there are quantifying terms that should be clearly defined before a forecast is made or compared, eg is the forecast relating to the market potential or to the actual market volume? The range of quantifying terms include the following:

1. *The overall market capacity* — this is the amount of product and/or service that could be absorbed in an overall market *irrespective of price* or market segmentation considerations. For example, the future potential overall market for cars of all types would include consumers who would like to own a car but are not able or willing to pay the existing price as well as those who are.
2. *Market segment capacity* is the amount of a product and/or service that could be absorbed in the future by a specialized segment of a market *irrespective of price* considerations.
3. *Market potential* — this quantifies the effective demand for a product and/or service at a *given price* within a specific market segment.
4. *The actual market volume* is the sum total of suppliers' sales made *at a given price* or price range to a specific market segment.
5. *The market prospective* is the quantity a company could sell in a particular market segment irrespective of company resources, eg a company could have a marketing opportunity to sell 500

units but has current production or financial resources to produce 350 units. It was indicated earlier that this situation requires management to consider alternatives (sub-contracting, acquisition, etc) to maximize the company's market opportunities.

6. *Actual company market share or sales* — a company's sales in a particular market segment are obviously an integral part of the actual market volume, of which they are often expressed as a percentage.

The relationship between the various assessment terms can be seen in Figure 5.1.

Units of measurement

To get a really comprehensive prediction of the future, forecasts should be based on three (possibly four) types of data. An ideal forecast is based on predictions using:

1. Current price sales volume data, ie sales volume valued by the prices *currently* prevailing during each time period. The disadvantage of this type is that inflationary current prices can give a misleading picture of sales.
2. Constant or base year price sales volume data, ie sales volume values that have been adjusted by relating them to the prices prevailing during a *particular* sales period. The particular period chosen is known as the base period and all sales volume figures of other sales periods in the series being considered are calculated at base year prices. The main advantage of this method is that it removes much of the inflationary influence on the forecast of increasing (or decreasing) prices over a span of time and gives a picture of the market measured in sterling values.
3. Commodity units, ie sales measured by the number of units sold: tons, yards, gallons or individual units. This method removes any problems of rising or falling prices, inflation, etc, but can only be used where companies sell only a few product types, or where product types are fairly uniform.
4. A fourth forecast type may be considered where appropriate: indirect taxation, ie VAT, excise duty, etc is included in the data. As changes in this factor will result from arbitrary decisions based on government policy to gather more revenue and/or to reduce or encourage demand, it will be more difficult to forecast.

It will be necessary to exclude any element of taxation from (1) and (2) above to determine trends, but it should be included when con-

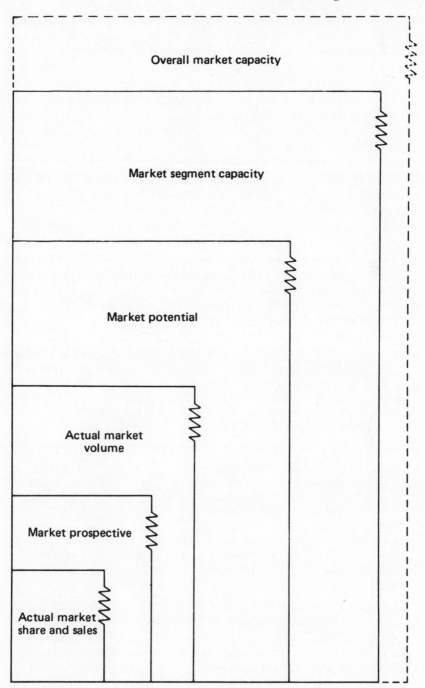

Figure 5.1 *A diagram showing the relationship between various assessment terms*

sidering overall demand for a product because changes in indirect taxation will affect price, and as a general economic rule, the higher the price the less will be demanded and vice versa.

A historic comparison of the three (or four) groups of data will highlight certain relationships, eg what happened to demand and the other factors when one variable changed? It will produce some useful facts that will influence forecasts.

Series of data under the above four headings can be made for total industries, general company sales, or specific product group types within a company. Table 5.1 is an example of the four groups of data relating to the sales of the brewing industry in the UK over a period of 11 years. Such a table could be developed for any industry/market but it must be remembered that it represents a total market/industry and not individual company movements.

The relationship of such data can be easily appreciated from Figure 5.1. It appears that, except for 1991, the UK market for beer is not very price sensitive, has high purchasing priority in relation to other products and defies the 'normal' economic rule that 'at higher prices less will be demanded'. The question for the forecaster is, did the market change fundamentally in 1991 or is this a 'one off' situation? The effects of a 5 per cent increase in indirect taxation from 1988 to 1989 appears to have caused only a .008 per cent fall in beer consumption. Whereas the effects of a 7.8

Table 5.1 *Sales and tax data relating to the UK brewing industry*

1 year	2 Consumer expenditure at market prices £m	3 Consumer expenditure based on 1985 prices £m	4 Taxes on expenditure £m	5 UK Beer consumption in thousand hectolitres
1981	155,412	196,011	42,465	62,317
1982	170,650	197,980	46,467	60,930
1983	187,028	206,932	49,500	62,232
1984	200,261	210,959	52,576	62,082
1985	218,947	218,947	56,592	61,507
1986	243,030	232,996	62,947	61,213
1987	267,523	245,823	69,074	61,973
1988	302,057	264,096	76,133	63,263
1989	330,532	272,917	79,963	63,212
1990	350,411	274,744	76,967	63,093
1991	367,853	269,033	83,023	60,844

per cent increase in indirect taxation from 1990 to 1991 appears to have caused a 3.56 per cent fall in beer consumption. Obviously, other factors that have an adverse effect on the consumption of beer, eg the 'Don't drink and drive' campaign, need to be taken into account.

What is important is the rate of increase in the four factors and the comparison between periods. Thus from 1981 to 1988, consumer expenditure at market prices rose by 94 per cent, consumer expenditure at 1985 prices increased by 68 per cent, taxation on expenditure rose by 79 per cent, but beer consumption increased by only 1.5 per cent. Whereas from 1988 to 1991, consumer expenditure at market prices rose by 22 per cent, consumer expenditure at 1985 prices increased by only 1.86 per cent, taxation on expenditure rose by 9 per cent, but beer consumption *declined* by −3.8 per cent.

The identification of the factors causing these different degrees of change between the various years would be helpful to a forecaster in making predictions, particularly if similar sets of circumstances could be expected to prevail in the future.

In any case, a projection into the future of the data lines shown in Figure 5.2 could be used as the basis for a forecast of each of the four types of data. In the brewing industry case, the relative stability

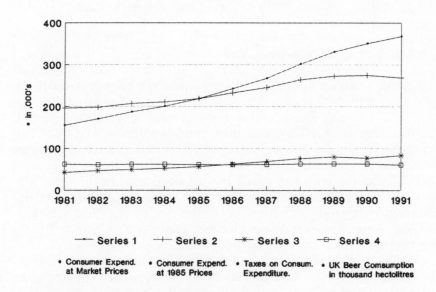

Figure 5.2 *Sales and tax data relating to the UK brewing industry*

of the beer consumption data emphasizes a basic rule in forecasting, ie base projections on unit volume data (rather than on value data), whenever possible, but especially in times of inflation.

A further technique is to plot the percentage increase/decrease values between the years and endeavour to project such data into the future, thereby predicting the next period percentage increase/decrease value.

The type of analysis using expenditure at current prices, at constant prices, indirect taxation and unit volume data may highlight a much more serious situation than that shown in the brewing industry case above. It could be possible for a company experiencing increasing sales revenue to discover that this has come about possibly from an increased price per unit (or even taxation), whereas unit sales volume could be steadily declining.

Chapter 7, 9 and 10 examine a range of basic methods of market and sales forecasting; so, for simplicity, only forecasting methods using one of the above types have been used. But, with each example given, it should be remembered that all three types of data (and, if appropriate, the fourth concerning taxation) should be considered and projected for effective market and sales forecasting. Further, it will be useful to calculate a forecast based upon the above-mentioned methods for each different type of market segment to get a true picture of the sales in different geographic or socio-economic groups. This means, where appropriate, separating the home market sales from the export, the teenage market from the 'more mature', urban dwellers from rural dwellers, etc.

Demand analysis, elasticity and price

Demand analysis discovers and measures the factors at work in the market place that affect sales. It is therefore a fundamental factor in forecasting. But effective demand (which is another way of considering sales) has certain implications when viewed from the point of marketing. Not only does effective demand mean that the potential customer has the money to pay for the product, but also that he has the power to make buying decisions and that he is a person who can receive satisfaction from the total sales proposition. Even in industrial marketing where the buying decision may rest with a group of people (the decision-making unit), a company can be said to receive satisfaction from the product or service.

The relationship of the amount demanded to the price of a product or service is a prime consideration of the forecaster because it is upon potential sales as well as on costs that prices are set.

In fact in economics the term elasticity is used to describe this relationship, and has been defined as the responsiveness of demand (sales) to relatively small changes in price. For example, in Figure 5.3a, demand for the product is said to be relatively inelastic, a slight change in price making little difference to sales. Where this market situation prevails, a price increase (from B to A) will cause only a slight decline in sales (from Y to X). Conversely, it is not a good market situation for using price reductions as a sales promotion tool, because a price reduction must be considerable to increase sales slightly.

In Figure 5.3b, demand for the product is said to be relatively elastic, a slight change in price making a disproportionately larger difference to sales. Where this market situation exists a price increase (from D to C) will cause a considerable decline in sales (from Q to P). Conversely, it is a good market situation for using price reductions as a sales promotional tool, since a slight decrease in price (from C to D) will cause a disproportionately large increase in sales. Knowledge of the effect that price changes will have on sales is vital to the forecaster.

The slope of any demand curve (ie its elasticity) will change over a whole range of prices and in practice it is difficult to set up demand schedules over a very large range of prices. However, the elasticity of demand can be determined by two arithmetical methods:

1. Proportionate change method where

$$\text{Elasticity of demand} = \frac{\text{Proportionate change in amount demanded}}{\text{Proportionate change in price}}$$

For example, if on a demand schedule (or from marketing research) the following two items occurred:

> @ £9 per unit 4,000 units were sold
> @ £8 per unit 5,000 units were sold

then using the above formula, elasticity could be expressed as:

$$\frac{\frac{1000}{4000}}{\frac{1}{9}} = \frac{\frac{1}{4}}{\frac{1}{9}} = \frac{1}{4} \times \frac{9}{1} = 2\frac{1}{4}$$

Where the result is more than 1, demand is relatively elastic; a fall of 1/9th in price causes an increase in sales of 1/4. Alternatively, if the two items from a demand schedule were:

113

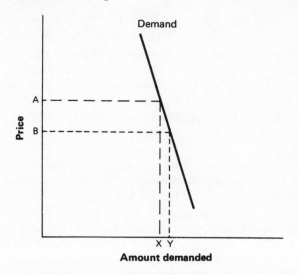

Figure 5.3a *A relatively inelastic demand curve — a price increase from B to A causes only a small decline in sales (from Y to Z)*

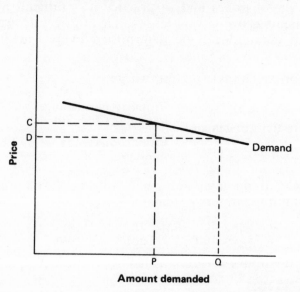

Figure 5.3b *A relatively elastic demand curve — a price increase from D to C causes a considerable decline in sales (from Q to P)*

@ £9 per unit   300 units were sold
@ £6 per unit   330 units were sold

then using the above formula, elasticity could be expressed as:

$$\frac{\dfrac{30}{300}}{\dfrac{3}{9}} = \frac{\dfrac{1}{10}}{\dfrac{1}{3}} = \frac{1}{10} = \frac{3}{1} = \frac{3}{10}$$

Demand is relatively inelastic as the result is less than 1. A price reduction of 1/3rd causes only a 1/10th increase in sales.

2. The outlay method of determining elasticity: this involves the examination of the outlay that customers are willing to make for a product, ie price × volume.
    For example:

    @ £9 per unit   300 units are sold = £2,700 consumer outlay
    @ £6 per unit   330 units are sold = £1,980 consumer outlay

By reducing price, the outlay (sales revenue) is less, even though the number of units sold has increased. This indicates that demand is relatively inelastic.

When considering the effect of a price change on sales revenue it is necessary to recognize that because of market circumstances, it is possible for the demand curve to slope the opposite way for part of its length, ie an exceptional or backward bending demand curve. This implies that at the current stage of the market, as price increases so will sales.

Between points A and B in Figure 5.4 sales increase as prices go up. This can happen in situations of shortage, or where further price increases are anticipated, or where consumers associate a range of prices with an expected quality or image. In the last case, if prices are increased, the product becomes associated with a different 'quality group', and if the demand is greater than in the former group, sales will tend to increase. Sales of many luxury and semi-luxury consumer products react in this way.

Pricing studies and income

Many products are either over-priced or under-priced, and in either case this has a direct effect on sales and therefore on sales forecasting. In fact, incorrect pricing has caused the failure of many new products. The under-priced product is not only losing sales revenue and profit, but it could also be losing sales because the price does not project the image expected by consumers. Alter-

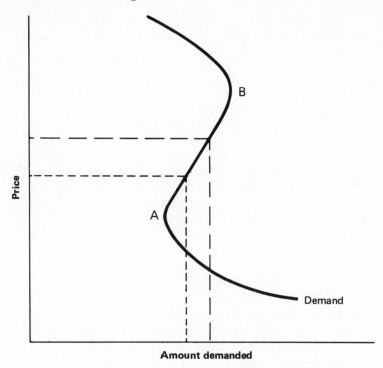

Figure 5.4 *An exceptional demand curve*

natively, the over-priced product, by restricting demand, is not only causing a loss of sales and perhaps a loss of sales revenue, but also a loss of profit by preventing fixed overhead costs from being spread over a greater sales volume.

The market-orientated approach to pricing is to charge what the market will bear in relation to the type and size of market, customers' needs and priorities, and the scale of the marketing company's operation. Price confrontation studies can be used in marketing research to help determine an effective pricing policy. A sample of potential buyers is confronted with a product and their reactions to a series of prices at which products of this nature could be sold are assessed. The reasons for willingness or unwillingness to buy at certain prices are analyzed and an optimum price, related to potential sales revenue and profit, is established.

Pricing policy and consumer/user reaction to price has a direct effect on sales and therefore is a prime consideration in sales forecasting.

But price is not the only factor that will affect demand. The consumer's demand for a product/service will be positively related to his income. If his income increases, he will tend to buy more of a number of products, although there are exceptions to this. Income elasticity can be seen by relating the proportionate change in income to the proportionate change in the amount demanded.

Information regarding demand can be obtained through published data and from marketing research. Information concerning prices can be obtained from official statistics and observation in the market; and details of consumer incomes analyzed by various groups can be gathered from official statistics and observation.

The market forecaster can relate present or projected price and income data to market demand, and can carry out statistical analysis of the effects of changes in price and consumer income on market demand. For example, it may be found that a 2 per cent increase in price caused a 1 per cent fall in demand and a 2 per cent increase in income resulted in a ½ per cent increase in demand.

The multi-technique approach

Although a number of forecasting techniques are mentioned in Chapters 6, 7, 8, 9 and 10 it is not suggested that any one technique should be used in isolation. Within the company constraints of acceptable costs, the limits of time, and the company's needs in the market, as many forecasting techniques as possible should be used. Each forecast obtained will be different but investigation of the variances between them will bring to the surface factors contained in one and not in another, that are increasing or declining in forecasting importance. In fact, analysis of such variances, horizontally across the board, will often bring to light new trends or the up-turn or down-turn in market or sales values.

In some cases it is possible to establish a vertical check by one forecast on a group of others. For example, the sum total of all salesmen's forecasts can be compared with area managers' forecasts. Why do they differ? Can one of the parties identify a factor that will influence the forecast, which has not been appreciated by the other party? A further stage is possible by comparing the sum total of area managers' forecasts with regional or national sales managers' forecasts.

Finally, a total forecast is obtained by assessing all the component forecasts; it is useful to have a forecasting committee, a panel of experts, or jury of executive opinion to do this. Complete agreement may not always be possible but this approach ensures that every aspect is critically examined.

The forecast may be a total forecast figure or be broken down into product, size, model, etc. Also it may take the form of a single figure or of maximum and minimum values, together with a percentage probability of achieving them.

At the final level of assessment of the component forecasts, techniques need not be highly sophisticated, for if the best possible, methods and data have been used to obtain the component forecasts, the final assessment is often a matter of enlightened averaging out.

6

The Measurement
of Change

*'Economic forecasting, like weather forecasting in England, is only valid
for the next six hours or so, beyond that it is sheer guesswork'*
M J Moroney

The measurement of change

It is necessary to measure the changes in certain general factors
outside a company's control which could affect the marketing
environment in which it operates. In fact, these external factors
were mentioned in Chapters 1 and 4, the major groupings being
shown as the general economic and political environment, technological factors, climatic factors, cultural forces, population factors,
standard of living factors, social forces, and appropriate international considerations.

The use of indicators

When statistics regarding one or part of these areas signal broad
movements in them, they are indicators in the forecasting sense.
Before using indicators the forecaster must consider what precisely
the indicator measures, what type of base period it uses, how it was
constructed, what unit of measure it uses, how valid it is, and
whether it could contain an element of bias. He or she must also
consider whether it shows a provisional or final figure, whether it
is seasonally adjusted, and the degree of relevance to the forecasting problem.

Economic change

Economic indicators measuring economic change are very good
examples of this method of forecasting and to explain their use
will show the application of indicators generally.

Earlier, in Chapter 3, the *Monthly Digest of Statistics* was mentioned. This publication provides numerous examples of economic
indicators in addition to the basic data for the compilation of
many more.

To qualify as an economic indicator, the data concerned should provide a yardstick against which periodic movements in the cost or volume of the economic factor concerned can be measured.

A good starting point for making a market forecast for various product groups is to use an indicator relating to the total economy, eg the gross national product. If this is linked with the percentage attributable to total consumer expenditure and the percentage of consumer expenditure attributable to the particular product and service, a very precise picture of the market is obtained.

Forecasts of such economic indicators are often made by government and private agencies, but in addition, indicators relating to economic trends in more advanced economies such as the USA, will often show the future pattern for these indicators in Britain.

Economic indicators refer to a wide range of economic and financial information showing changes and movement in various fields. For example, there are indicators of industrial production, employment and unemployment, machine tool orders, retail sales, wages rates, raw material prices, and many more. Such indicators can be presented either in absolute figures or values (eg the value of exports shown in pounds sterling), or presented as an index number where increases or decreases are shown as a percentage of the base year figure of 100. Whether actual values or index values are used, data can be further presented either on a period basis (eg the level of industrial production over the last three months), or on a basis of a particular moment in time (eg the total hire-purchase debt as at 31st December 19X3).

Data of UK Economic Indicators from the Annual Abstract of Statistics (published by the Central Statistical Office) show their current levels and recent history, which permits comparison with industry and/ or company sales and projection into the future. Examples of the main UK indicators (collated in the *Marketing Pocket Book 1993*, page 6) are shown in Table 6.1.

Since most economic indicators are, by their nature, general, they often have to be interpreted and evaluated to determine how changes in them will affect a particular company, industry, or market. Further, some indicators will be more appropriate for certain markets than others, and in most cases a combination of such indicators will be necessary to provide data to set up an effective composite indicator forecast for a particular company.

Various facets of the economy and the economic climate can be examined through economic indicators and often trends in them can be anticipated, permitting more realistic industry or market forecasts to be made.

Distribution system change

A channel of distribution can be described as a vertical sequence of levels of trading activities that bridge the overall gap between the manufacturer and the consumer. Thus the wholesaler is one level and the retailer another.

The choice of the channels of distribution is the prerogative of the individual company, but the channels available or acceptable will develop as part of the economic structure of a country. The freedom of choice by the individual company may not be as real as it appears, for in the last analysis, the economics of operation, the service offered by competitors and the level of service customers are willing to accept, will all be key factors when deciding the choice of channels.

Channels of distribution cannot be considered in isolation; they are interrelated with, and sometimes substituted for, other aspects of physical distribution: for example, if economical, local company warehouses may be substituted for wholesalers, or the appointment of a retail agent (exclusive dealership) may eliminate the need for wholesalers. Alternatively, powerful voluntary chain or group wholesalers, through whom a large number of small retailers can be reached effectively, may be substituted for a company local warehouse.

Changes in distribution systems can occur either through a conscious change of policy within the existing channels structure, or through the emergence of new channels. In actual fact these two alternatives represent the effect of the same factor, ie the dynamic nature of channels systems: they are constantly, though gradually, changing. This change can relate either to the nature of the particular channel level, ie the changing role of the wholesaler, or a change in the relationship of levels, ie the new relationship between retailer and wholesaler through the emergence of voluntary chains and groups.

In consumer goods markets the choice of alternatives of combinations of the various levels and types of channels of distribution available can be seen in Figure 6.1 In forecasting, the trends in the volume of business done through the various combinations of channels cannot be ignored. The decline of the share of business done by independent retailers reflects the trend towards 'giantism' in retailing in recent years and the reduction in the number of small retailers.

Often trends in distribution channel emphasis are caused by basic considerations such as lower cost or more efficient operation through one channel compared with another. But often factors emerge that have varying effects upon channel decisions; the development of supermarkets, hypermarkets, self-service and self-selection, the concept of one-stop shopping, the abolition of resale price maintenance, and the appearance of voluntary chains and groups, cash and carry

Table 6.1 *Examples of UK Main Economic Indicators: 1985–91*

		1985	1986	1987	1988	1989	1990	1991
Gross Domestic Product								
at current prices	£billion	356.1	382.9	421.2	467.9	512.2	550.3	575.6
	% change	+9.5	+7.5	+10.0	+11.1	+9.5	+7.4	+4.6
at 1985 prices	£billion	356.1	370.0	387.7	404.2	413.4	417.5	408.3
	% change	+3.6	+3.9	+4.8	+4.3	+2.3	+1.0	−2.2
Gross Domestic Product[1] per								
Capita at current prices	£	6.289	6.746	7.399	8.199	8.949	9.586	10.000
	% change	+9.2	+7.3	+9.7	+10.8	+9.2	+7.1	+4.3
at 1985 prices	£	6.289	6.519	6.810	7.084	7.223	7.271	7.093
	% change	+3.3	+3.7	+4.5	+4.0	+2.0	+0.7	−2.4
Consumers Expenditure								
at current prices	£billion	217.6	241.3	264.9	298.8	327.4	348.6	368.0
	% change	+9.1	+10.9	+9.8	+12.8	+9.6	+6.5	+5.6
at 1985 prices	£billion	217.6	231.2	243.3	261.3	270.6	272.8	268.0
	% change	+3.5	+6.2	+5.2	+7.4	+3.5	+0.8	−1.8
Retail Sales	Index	100.0	105.3	110.7	117.7	119.9	120.4	119.5
	% change	+4.6	+5.3	+5.2	+6.3	+1.9	+0.4	−0.7
Retail Prices	Index	100.0	103.4	107.7	113.0	121.8	133.3	141.1
	% change	+6.1	+3.4	+4.1	+4.9	+7.8	+9.5	+5.9
Population (Mid-Year Est.)	Million	56.6	56.8	56.9	57.1	57.2	57.4	57.6
Average Earnings	Index	100.0	107.9	116.3	126.4	138.0	151.3	163.5
	% change	+8.5	+7.9	+7.8	+8.8	+9.1	+9.7	+8.0
Industrial Production (Total)	Index	100.0	102.4	105.7	109.5	109.9	109.3	106.1
	% change	+5.5	+2.4	+3.2	+3.6	+0.3	−0.5	−3.0
Unemployment (% of Labour Force)[2]		10.9	11.1	10.0	8.1	6.3	5.8	8.1

Vacancies at Jobcentres[3]	Thousands	162.1	188.8	235.4	248.7	219.5	173.7	118.0
	% change	+7.9	+16.5	+24.7	+5.6	-11.7	-20.9	-32.1
Interest Rate (Bank Base Rate)[4]	%	12.25	10.90	9.74	10.09	13.85	14.77	11.70
Gross Domestic Fixed Capital Formation at 1985 prices	£billion	60.4	61.8	67.8	76.6	81.8	79.9	71.9
	% change	+4.0	+2.4	+9.6	+13.1	+6.8	-2.4	-10.1
Gross Fixed Investment by Manufacturing Industry at 1985 prices	£billion	10.1	9.4	10.0	11.2	12.4	12.2	10.2
	% change	+14.7	-6.9	+6.6	+11.4	+10.6	-1.9	-15.8
Gross Trading Profits[5] North Sea Oil Companies at current prices	£billion	18.5	8.4	9.5	6.9	6.6	7.0	6.3
	% change	-2.6	-54.5	+12.9	-27.6	-4.7	+7.3	-10.4
Other Companies at current prices	£billion	38.8	45.3	53.0	62.9	66.2	67.7	68.0
	% change	+30.9	+16.9	+16.9	+18.6	+5.3	+2.3	+0.4
at 1985 prices	£billion	38.8	43.8	49.2	55.6	54.3	50.8	48.2
	% change	+23.4	+13.0	+12.3	+13.0	-2.4	-6.5	-5.1
Balance of Payments at current prices	£billion	2.8	0.1	-4.5	-16.2	-21.7	-17.0	-6.3

Notes: All indices 1985 = 100
1. Gross Domestic Product is at market prices
2. Unemployment % is the total number of unemployed (excluding school leavers) expressed as a percentage of the number of employees in employment, unemployment, self-employed and HM Forces.
3. Vacancies at Jobcentres excluding Community Programme vacancies.
4. Selected Retail Banks Base Rate (average for period).
5. Net of stock appreciation.

Sources: CSO Economic Trends. CSO Monthly Digest of Statistics. CSO Financial Statistics.
Overall Source: Marketing Pocket Book 1993. Page 6; published by the Advertising Association, in association with NTC Publications Ltd.

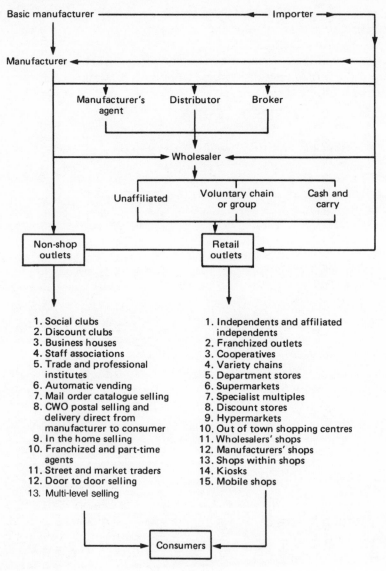

Figure 6.1 *The various levels and types of channels of distribution possible in consumer goods markets*

warehouses, discount stores and private labelling, would all have an effect on a channel decision.

In some industries, highly specialized channels develop, eg in pharmaceuticals some companies own their own outlets (Boots The Chemist) while others use specialist wholesalers. But most ethical drugs must be retailed by a qualified pharmacist. In industrial markets manufacturers mainly distribute direct to the customer, but in some cases specialist wholesalers are used.

The forecaster must consider what effect a change in distribution channel would have on company sales; or perhaps the medium-term effect of the increasing importance of one distribution channel compared with other current channels.

Sociological and consumer behaviour change

There are two basic approaches to the examination of consumer behaviour. One of them deals with the understanding of the behaviour of a variety of consumer groups, and the other concentrates on understanding the behaviour of the individual consumer. Group and individual behaviour will have a direct effect on sales and therefore on the sales forecast. It follows that the market and sales forecaster must be able to identify, measure and allow for sociological and consumer behaviour changes.

There are certain well-recognized sociological and psychological groups that are changing at different speeds. The nature of the groups and the speed of change will have varying impacts on different industries and markets. The broad groups are as follows:

1. Population.
2. Cultures and sub-cultures.
3. Social and socio-economic classes.
4. Reference groups, including face-to-face and family groups.
5. The individual.

1. Population

This refers to the degree to which a country or region is populated, usually expressed as the total number of inhabitants. It is a physical state and can be indicated by volume, location, urban or rural, region, sex, age groups, movement, etc. Changes in these and related factors (marriages, births, deaths, etc) affect consumer buying patterns. A main source of population information in the UK is the Office of Population Censuses and Surveys (OPCS). More information is given in Chapter 3 under the heading of Government Sources, population and households (page 75).

Demography, the study of population trends, permits comparison of data from period to period, or region to region and identifies patterns that are fundamental, when interpreted, to the forecasting of total markets and company sales.

Markets are people, and effective tracking of population trends and shifts is bound to increase the accuracy of forecasting one dimension of the environment in which a company operates.

2. Cultures and sub-cultures

These refer to particular forms, types, or states of manners, taste and intellectual development at a particular time or place. The whole form is intangible but the effect on consumer behaviour is real.

A cultural pattern emerges over a period of time and often through successive generations. It is a way of life developed through common ideals and the solving of common problems. It is often based on religion, race, region, patriotism, politics, or combinations of these.

As the population of a culture increases, the broad common ideals no longer satisfy certain minority groups and sub-cultures emerge. They have different problems and ideals, and place a different emphasis on various cultural factors compared with the majority: for example, a Moslem culture in a basically Christian country, the negro culture in the US, a Communist culture in a capitalist society. Sub-cultures affect consumer behaviour by influencing the formation of attitudes and are important indicators of the standards and values of the individuals making up the groups.

A relaxation of change in the 'rules' or basic concept of sub-cultures could be of importance to researchers forecasting human behaviour. These changes, and indeed the cultures and sub-cultures, may be difficult to quantify, but even a qualitative assessment is better than no assessment at all.

3. Social and socio-economic classes

Social classes emerge because consumers are brought together through certain common characteristics or states either inherent or acquired. Such social grouping factors include status, occupation, job performance, wealth and ownership, skill, power and identification. Often combinations of these factors fashion particular social groups, eg the linking of status with occupation or wealth.

Indicators of social class change are more equal educational opportunity, greater social mobility, the impact of modern communication and mass media, etc, and they cause some blurring of rigid social divisions and attitudes.

Numerous class structures have been identified and listed, and one example is shown in Table 6.2 Here, by linking social and occupational data to percentages of the population, market segment sizes can be determined, inter-social grade movement measured and a trend obtained.

Table 6.2 *Social and occupational data linked to percentages of the households in the UK*

Head of Household			
Social Grade	**Social Status**	**Occupation**	**Percentage**
A	Upper middle class	Higher managerial, administrative or professional	3
B	Middle class	Intermediate managerial, administrative or professional	11
C1	Lower middle class	Supervisory or clerical, and junior managerial, administrative or professional	23
C2	Skilled working class	Skilled manual workers	31
D	Working class	Semi and unskilled manual workers	23
E	Those at lowest levels of subsistence	State pensioners or widows (no other earner), casual or lowest-grade workers	9

In Table 6.3, the UK population is analyzed by social grade, sex, and 'main shopper'; all in terms of size and percentages. In Table 6.4, Regional Adult Population are analyzed in terms of social class.

By research it is possible to determine the buying motives and the purchasing and consumption habits of a particular class. The movement upwards in social classes often means that consumers spend more money on what the lower groups consider to be non-essentials. The consumer in the higher class groups will not be motivated by the same basic needs of consumers at subsistence level, but will often be searching for such satisfaction as esteem, convenience, prestige, uniqueness, approval of others, etc. Often the attainment of these satisfactions can be expressed in the purchases of certain types of products such as status cars, large

Table 6.3 *Population of UK aged 154, classified by sex, social class and main shopper*

Social Grade	All Adults 15+		Men		Women		Main Shoppers* (Female)	
	000's	%	000's	%	000's	%	000's	%
A	1.307	2.9	673	3.1	634	2.7	542	2.8
B	6.799	15.0	3.432	15.7	3.366	14.4	2.787	14.4
C1	10.970	24.2	5.007	22.9	5.963	25.5	4.993	25.8
C2	12.278	27.1	6.443	29.5	5.835	24.9	4.773	24.7
D	7.939	17.5	3.946	18.1	3.993	17.0	3.195	16.5
E	5.958	13.2	2.330	10.7	3.628	15.5	3.066	15.8
Total	45,250	100.0	21,832	100.0	23,418	100.0	19,355	100.0

Note: These social grades are based on grades of head of household.
*Main shoppers are identified as those who personally select half or more of the items bought for their household from supermarkets and food shops. This member may be male or female:

	000	%
Female main shopper	19.355	71.7
Male main shopper	7.627	28.3
All main shoppers	26,982	100.0

Source: National Readership Survey, July 1991–June 1992.

Overall Source: Marketing Pocket Book 1993 (page 11), published by the Advertising Association, in association with NTC Publications Ltd.

houses, extreme fashions, leisure pursuit products and even in the reading of particular newspapers and magazines.

Leisure pursuit products often indicate a consumer's identification (real or imagined) with a particular social group. As consumers' affluence increases and they have more disposable income, their demand for more sophisticated leisure products increases.

In Table 6.5. trends (1980–1990) in some aspects of leisure spending are shown. Although Consumer Expenditure at market prices have risen in all cases, some significantly, the percentage of consumer expenditure spent on them has either remained the same or has changed only marginally. The intervening years' expenditure could be obtained from the source indicated, to identify cyclical patterns, and a forecast into the future could be obtained.

Table 6.4 *Regional adult population in terms of social class*

Thousands of adults

	Total	A	B	C1	C2	D	E
GB	45,199	1,126	6,230	12,265	11,380	8,776	5,422
North & N. East	6,517	116	661	1,493	1,847	1,458	942
Midlands	7,367	122	819	1,937	2,041	1,564	884
London & S. East	15,860	623	2,728	4,897	3,592	2,532	1,488
S. West & Wales	6,115	98	869	1,640	1,693	1,204	611
N. West	5,248	98	625	1,313	1,243	1,125	844
Scotland	4,091	68	528	985	964	893	653

Source: 1991 JICNARS/RSL Marketing Data Book.

Overall Source: Marketing Pocket Book 1993 (page 24), published by the Advertising Association, in association with NTC Publication Ltd.

The existence of social classes and the way they express themselves in purchasing and consumption indicates differences in attitudes, values and priorities, and has important implications for the setting of marketing objectives and the forecasting of total markets and company sales.

Together with other variables, a person's socio-economic standing is often reflected in the residential neighbourhood in which they live. Several systems have been developed that assume an association between the kind of housing people occupy, their socio-economic status and their purchasing behaviour; the main systems using these methods of classification and analysis are ACORN and MOSAIC.

ACORN (A Classification Of Residential Neighbourhoods) uses information taken from the Government's Census of Great Britain. It is based on 38 'residential neighbourhood' types, their share of the GB population, and the 11 ACORN groups they form. Examples of ACORN types are 'B6 New detached houses, young families, 2.9 per cent of population', 'G24 Council estates with some overcrowding, 1.5 per cent of population', 'I 31 Multi-let big old houses and flats, 1.5 per cent of population', 'J 35 Villages with wealthy older commuters, 2.9 per cent of population', etc. This classification is linked to many other variables such as household size, cars per household, family size, etc. The main concept is that persons can be profiled according to the type of area in which they live, analyzed for sales potential, identified (and reached) by post code.

MOSAIC also operates on the residential neighbourhood concept, but is made up of a series of databases that cover

Table 6.5 *Trends in some aspects of leisure spending in the UK and their proportion of Consumer Expenditure*

Leisure Market	Consumer Expenditure		Percentage Consumer Expenditure in		Percentage Point Change
	1980 £m	1990 £m	1980	1990	
Books, newspapers and magazines	2,154	5,410	1.5	1.5	—
TV, radio and other durables	1,590	3,854	1.1	1.1	—
Records, tapes and musical instruments	522	1,592	0.4	0.4	—
Toys and games	617	1,142	0.4	0.3	−0.1
Photography	624	1,420	0.4	0.4	—
Beer	5,320	10,920	3.6	3.0	−0.6
Wine, cider and sherry	2,013	5,218	1.4	1.5	+0.1
Spirits	2,689	4,462	1.8	1.2	−0.6
Eating Out	4,848	12,747	3.3	3.5	+0.2
Gardening Products	779	2,012	0.5	0.6	+0.1
Gambling (Losses)	1,520	3,219	1.0	0.9	−0.1
Holiday (4 nights)	5,920	15,700	4.0	4.4	+0.4
Cinema	127	198	0.1	0.1	—
Air Travel	1,818	4,485	1.2	1.2	—

Source: MINTEL FACSFINDEL

demographic data, housing data, financial and credit data, and census statistics, and is based on 58 different residential groupings, analysis by other socio-economic variables and provides analysis by post codes.

4. Reference groups

This includes face-to-face and family groups. Consumer buying motives, brand choice, purchasing and consumption patterns are often influenced by what other consumers say or buy, especially those people with whom they compare themselves or whom they use as reference groups. Such groups can be classified as:

(a) *Membership groups.* These are groupings of people to which a person belongs and is recognized as belonging by others. It usually implies identification with the group's ideals, values, tastes, and behaviour. Groups such as the family, a club, company, church, college, political party, etc, can all fit into this category.

(b) The opposite to (a) is the *dissociative group* with whom an individual does *not* want to be identified or associated. Reference in this case is to the ideals, values and behaviour he finds acceptable. The group types are the same as for (a).

(c) *Aspirational groups*. These refer to groupings of people to which the individual would like or aspires to belong. The individual's buying behaviour is influenced by how he or she thinks the group behaves or purchases. Reference groups of this type are often made up of TV, film or radio stars, sportsmen or women, astronauts, millionaires, or even particular social sets.

(d) *Face-to-face groups*. These are groups of people small enough for the individual to communicate with face-to-face. This type of group has the most direct influence on an individual's ideals, tastes, values, and behaviour. This type includes the family, close friends, neighbours, fellow workers or students.

In many cases the greatest influence on the individual in forming and maintaining ideals, attitudes, tastes, values, etc, is the family group. Sometimes the result of the reference is positive, ie the individual does the complete opposite to express himself. The forecaster must be alert to the various behavioural and attitudinal patterns that dominate families in particular market segments and to the current trends and how they are expected to change in the future.

The purchases of certain products are more subject to reference group influence than others. For example, branded beer, cigarettes, clothing, cars, toilet soap, etc, are products that are associated strongly with reference group influence. Customer communication (advertising, etc) in this area will be most successful if it stresses the types of people who buy the product, particularly if it is designed to encourage the learning/educational process of product application or usage and is exhibited in media where those who refer to the group form the main audience.

Where reference group influences are weak, the marketing strategy is to stress product innovations and characteristics, functional advantages and performance, price, etc.

An appreciation of the influence of reference groups on consumer buying behaviour is an essential for forecasters in consumer goods markets, or for those carrying out end-use analysis for products being sold into industrial product markets.

5. The individual

A basic approach to the study of consumer buying behaviour is at the level of the individual. It has been said that:

> Social influences determine much but not all of the behavioural variations in people. Two individuals subject to the same influences are not likely to have identical attitudes, although their attitudes will probably converge at more points than those of two strangers selected at random. Attitudes are really the product of social forces interacting with the individual's unique temperament and abilities.
>
> Furthermore, attitudes — in buying as in anything else — do not automatically guarantee certain types of behaviour. Attitudes are predispositions felt by buyers before they enter the buying process. The buying process itself is a learning experience and can lead to a change in attitudes.[1]

It is necessary to understand why the individual consumer behaves as he does so that changes in ideals, tastes, values, etc, of groups of consumers can be anticipated and predicted.

It was shown in Chapter I that individuals do not buy products but groups of satisfactions or benefits to satisfy logical and psychological needs. But the individual will only purchase a product if he can perceive (hence the concept of perception) that it will satisfy his needs. Perception can be aided by physical stimuli including the actual product. But the effect of physical stimuli will be modified and interpreted by the individual's tastes, ideals, temperament, experiences and memory. Often the individual perceives only what he or she wants to perceive, and therefore the physical stimuli must be appropriate and appealing to satisfy logical and psychological needs.

Individual behaviour in purchasing and consumption is to a certain extent a learned response and as such can be influenced and changed. For example, the consumption of branded, ready-to-eat breakfast cereals in Britain and North America has been 'learned' over a period of time, in many cases replacing porridge, which needed preparation. Also the type of diet, way of life, etc, acceptable in one society may be repugnant in another, and is a learned response.

There are numerous learning theories that seek to explain consumer buying behaviour. They include stimulus response theories that are based on the concept of reward for each correct response; many sales promotional devices are based on this approach.

Other learning theories are based on the concept of cognition.

1. P Kotler *Marketing Management, Analysis, Planning and Control* p 93. Prentice-Hall, NJ, USA.

While acknowledging the stimulus response approach, cognitive theories imply that buying behaviour is influenced by habit based on memory, achievement, seeking, and insight based on reasoning. Basically, acceptance of the concept of a cognitive decision-making process implies an endeavour by the consumer to reduce risks. By repeat purchasing of a particular brand, or the repeated assessment of available information, the consumer is trying to avoid taking undue risks. Cognitive concepts are founded on habit and consistency, and are fundamental to brand loyalty and repeat purchasing.

Inconsistency in cognitive systems has been described as cognitive dissonance. Thus the person who purchases and consumes fattening foods when he is on a health diet, experiences dissonance (ie psychological discomfort) and often tries to reduce the dissonance and achieve consonance by rationalizing his actions.

Some other learning theories are founded on the personality of the individual and on the probability of the repetition of past purchasing behaviour. Such theories are based on the premise that if an individual's personality can be understood, ie his underlying organization of characteristics and behaviour patterns, then it should be possible to understand also the reasons for that person's behaviour, and what the reasons are for some of the superficial inconsistencies that occur in his behaviour. Based on these assumptions, it should then be possible to predict with greater random success how a given individual is predisposed to respond to given circumstances and suggestions.

A wide range of other factors affect the individual consumer's buying behaviour: attitudes, knowledge, faith, opinion, beliefs, economic motivation, rationality, etc. Every sale is a reflection of a decision to buy. This decision will be based on the consumer's perception (influenced by the other factors mentioned above) of the proposal related to value, utility, and ability to satisfy needs. If the initial impression is unfavourable, it will need to undergo a change before a positive buying decision is made. The consumer's perception depends on his or her attitude to the subject being considered.

All these theories relating to the individual seek to measure and predict the future response and pattern of consumer buying behaviour. As such, at least a broad appreciation of them is necessary for effective market and/or company sales forecasting.

This section on sociological and socio-economic factors can be summarized thus:

> The statement 'No man is an island' has empirical support. No man exists who does not reflect interaction with other people. Values, learning patterns, and symbolism are some of the results of the society in which a consumer develops. Sometimes social influences are negative rather than positive influences, but always they are influences.

Man evaluates his self against the behaviour of others and the values he has learned from others on previous occasions. He depends on others as a source of new information about product decisions and as a reference for evaluating the information.

Organizations seeking to influence consumer behaviour should realize that they must communicate not only with an individual but also with a social system.[1]

Industrial change

In industrial marketing one way of measuring change and of discovering the total market potential and the amount of business done by supplying industries with various user industries, is through input/output analysis.

Market forecasting using input/output analysis is based on the concept that in industrial marketing situations, the output of one industry is the basic input product/material of another. Input/output tables show the extent to which one segment of industry (defined by a broad Standard Industrial Classification category) obtains its basic materials/products from other segments, and in turn reflects the pattern in which the next stage of industries products are sold to a third set of industries; this has obvious forecasting implications.

Input/Output tables for the United Kingdom are published by the Central Statistical Office, based on the interrelationships of industrial and/or commodity groups. Amongst many tables providing information for the market forecaster, one provides '. . . commodity analysis of purchases by industry from domestic production . . .'. An extract from this table is shown in Table 6.6; the complete table, a 'use matrix', contains 102 'sales by commodity group' items and a complementary 102 'purchases by industry group' items, covering the whole of UK industry.

In Table 6.6, the columns represent industry group purchases of domestic production *from* the commodity group shown at the beginning of each row. For example, the industry group agriculture (column 1) purchased £2,296 million from within its own production, £82 million from No 8 water, £602 million from No 21 fertilizers, £9 million from No 25 pharmaceuticals, £14 million from No 26 soap and toiletries, etc.

Segmentation analysis of industry sales can be traced by examining the various rows in Table 6.6. For example, the commodity group, special chemicals (row 24) sold £412m to No 1 Agri-

1. Engel, Kollat, & Blackwell *Consumer Behaviour* p 615, Rinehart and Winston, New York, USA, 1978.

culture, £6m to No 3 coal, £6m to No 4 oil and gas, £29m to mineral oil processing, £37 million to No 10, iron and steel, etc.

When the data in Table 6.6 is linked with another table which 'provides an analysis of purchases of imports similarly classified by industry and final demand destination', it provides the forecaster with 'a complete analysis of the total purchases by each industry of goods and services used in current production and by each form of final demand, cross-classified by commodity group'. By analysis, products and services (and therefore markets for them) can be traced and qualified from original producer to ultimate end-user.

Input/output tables therefore permit the forecaster to make more accurate forecasts of a market or segments of it, by making comparisons with existing market forecasts obtained from other sources. Investigation of differences between two market forecasts often reveals unexploited marketing opportunities and new potential segments not previously apparent.

Input/output tables establish a user industry pattern that can be used on total industry data. Comparison between the data in several publications of official input/output tables would also indicate emergent trends. The effects of changes in one industry can be traced backwards through any chain of inter-industry relationships and forecasts made of variations in demand that will result.

International change

The indicators (and methods of using them) shown in the previous sections will apply also in this section; in essence the international environment is the sum total of all economies, cultures and social classes in the world.

Obviously some of these indicators are more relevant to forecasters in particular companies than others. Just as there are market segments in the home country which a company would not contemplate entering, so there are total markets or market segments abroad in which a company would not be interested, either from the viewpoint of profits or some other factor. Alternatively, there may be markets abroad where a company could make more profits than in the home market. The problem is finding such markets, measuring them and forecasting their future.

One initial stage could be to place countries into certain broad categories, and decide with which groups it is desirable to trade. By noting changes in these countries and their gradual movement from one category to the next, international change can be measured.

Indicators that can be used as a basis for measuring change in the international environment are many. They include: the gross

Table 6.6 *An extract from input/output tables of the UK*

Sales by commodity group	Purchase by industry group									£ million		
	1 Agric	2 For&fish	3 Coal	4 Oil&gas	5 Min oil	6 Electric	7 Gas	8 Water	9 Met ores	10 Steel	11 Alumin	12 Oth met
1 Agriculture	2.296	—	—	—	—	—	—	—	—	—	—	—
2 Forestry and fishing	—	4	—	—	—	—	—	—	—	—	—	—
3 Coal extraction etc	2	—	87	—	0	1.147	1	0	0	345	6	15
4 Extraction of oil and gas	—	—	—	862	7.135	—	1.938	1	—	—	—	—
5 Mineral oil processing	293	22	15	—	1.072	3.233	10	3	3	14	5	3
6 Electricity etc	99	12	262	—	58	873	16	114	15	213	58	59
7 Gas	89	3	7	—	2	69	211	1	5	115	16	20
8 Water	82	5	—	—	27	78	—	48	0	34	6	5
9 Extraction of metal ores etc	—	—	—	—	—	—	—	—	4	85	38	33
10 Iron and steel etc	5	—	195	21	—	11	16	7	1	1.600	2	179
11 Aluminium etc	12	—	—	—	—	2	0	0	—	35	188	12
12 Other non-ferrous metals	12	—	—	—	—	3	0	0	3	54	7	69
13 Extraction of stone etc	4	—	—	—	—	—	—	0	3	5	1	—
14 Clay products	12	—	—	—	—	—	9	—	—	0	—	—
15 Cement etc	23	—	—	—	—	—	—	—	—	17	—	—
16 Concrete etc	17	—	—	—	—	9	8	10	0	8	—	0
17 Glass	6	2	—	—	0	2	1	0	0	1	—	—
18 Refractory and ceramic goods	5	—	—	—	—	2	—	—	—	36	3	1
19 Inorganic chemicals	—	—	0	—	73	6	2	0	11	30	9	21
20 Organic chemicals	—	—	17	3	26	1	1	0	1	3	8	1
21 Fertilizers	602	—	—	—	—	—	—	—	—	—	—	—
22 Synthetic resins etc	—	—	1	—	0	1	2	0	0	3	—	0
23 Paints, dyes etc	13	—	6	2	1	1	4	0	0	21	4	0
24 Special chemicals	412	—	—	6	29	6	8	14	2	37	0	3
25 Pharmaceuticals	9	—	—	—	0	—	—	0	0	0	—	—

26 Soap and toiletries	14	—	1	—	0	1	5	1	0	0	0	0
27 Chemical products nes	—	—	—	—	—	—	—	—	—	—	—	—
28 Man-made fibres	14	—	—	—	—	—	—	—	—	—	—	1
29 Metal castings etc	—	—	8	29	0	26	10	14	0	59	0	—
30 Metal doors, windows etc	—	—	—	—	—	—	1	0	—	0	0	—
31 Metal packaging products	—	—	0	—	27	17	—	—	0	5	—	3
32 Metal goods nes	36	—	2	14	1	13	29	8	1	33	5	5
33 Industrial plant & steelwork	—	7	18	71	29	34	15	—	0	55	—	5
34 Agricultural machinery etc	23	—	—	—	—	—	—	—	—	—	—	—
35 Machine tools	—	—	—	—	—	0	0	—	—	7	2	4
36 Engineers small tools	9	—	1	6	1	5	5	2	1	0	1	2
37 Textile etc machinery	—	—	—	—	—	—	—	—	—	—	—	—
38 Process machinery etc	—	—	1	—	10	9	10	10	—	26	8	6
39 Mining etc equipment	—	—	310	—	1	6	3	—	13	15	3	3
40 Mech power transmission equip	—	—	1	107	—	—	—	—	—	7	4	1
41 Other machinery etc	—	12	34	517	9	19	24	9	2	57	12	10
42 Ordnance etc	—	—	—	—	—	—	2	4	—	6	—	—
43 Office machinery, computers etc	—	—	6	—	1	4	1	—	—	—	0	0
44 Insulated wires and cables	4	—	18	—	0	50	15	1	—	7	—	—
45 Basic electrical equipment	—	—	9	—	0	44	2	1	0	9	0	0
46 Industrial electrical equipment	1	1	0	—	0	1	2	1	0	16	2	2
47 Telecommunication etc equipment	—	3	6	—	3	20	127	—	—	—	—	—
48 Electronic components	—	—	15	—	—	13	—	3	—	—	—	—
49 Electronic consumer goods etc	—	—	—	—	—	—	—	—	—	—	—	—
50 Domestic electric appliances	—	—	—	—	—	—	—	—	—	—	—	—
51 Electric lighting equipment	2	—	—	—	1	4	7	4	—	4	—	1
52 Motor vehicles and parts	16	15	3	—	1	5	7	4	1	—	1	1
53 Shipbuilding & repairing	—	19	—	236	—	—	—	—	—	—	—	—

national product; income per capita; population change; urban/ rural structure; analysis of socio-economic groups; size of market; levels of unemployment; availability of raw materials; sufficiency of food supply; availability and cost of energy; foreign trade and balance of payments position; the home country share of total country imports; the home country share of total country exports; type and stability of government; degree of state ownership; degree of industrial concentration; transportation services and facilities; recent attitude to the home country; exchange control and restrictions; facilities for the transfer of profits, royalties, interest, etc; the ratio of industry to agriculture.

Many of these are expressed as a statistic, eg the home country share of total country imports is 15 per cent. Others are qualitative, eg recent attitude to the home country, but can be partially quantified by expressing them in degrees of intensity, eg openly friendly, tolerant, critical, bitter.

Change can be measured by comparing the value of an indicator in one period against its value in another.

Another method of measuring international change is by the comparison of a series of appropriate indicators in different countries. From such analysis has emerged the concept of *comparative marketing* which can be defined as the identification, analysis, and measurement of common factors and differences in structure, systems and techniques among various countries and regions.

This approach can help companies to decide which are the most advantageous and favourable international markets to enter. But it is of particular use to market forecasters through the technique of historical analogy. This is based on the concept that in like circumstances similar market situations and sales volumes could emerge, often with a time lag between them. For example, certain similarities in market situations observed in the USA have been seen to happen in Britain five years later. If the right combination of indicators can be found to indicate an appropriate market situation, a certain size of market volume can be anticipated in various countries.

Problems in measuring international change arise from the difficulty of obtaining reliable measurable data to form indicators and from the problems of effectively quantifying intangible national characteristics and traditions. Some sources of international data are listed on page 82.

To summarize, the use of indicators and their projection through extrapolation, historical analogy, lead and lag techniques, or assessment methods can all help the forecaster to assess changes in the international environment.

Technological change

Just as there is a need to examine the conditions in a market and to give an overall forecast before attempting to make an individual company forecast, there is also a need to examine existing technology used in an industry and to forecast the future development of sales of a product, but in the long term a fundamental factor will be the range and type of products that technology generally has evolved.

Many companies attempt to forecast future developments in technology because of their obvious effect on the development of new products, and also because of their impact on market forecasting in general and on individual company product forecasting in particular.

It is not only the innovating type of company that needs to forecast technological developments, but also the company that follows the lead set by the innovators. Further, it is needed by the company that modifies a basic product concept to the needs of a specific market segment, and also by the company with the same product as others but which offers a different overall combination of customer satisfactions. All operate in the technological environment and will be affected by it.

Technological forecasting can be highly sophisticated or very elementary in its methods: but the fact that it is considered at all will cause executives to examine, consider and plan their own product range more effectively.

Generally, technological forecasting is concerned mainly with trends, not precise predictions. For example, it would be extremely useful for some companies to know how power sources such as engines will develop over the next 20/30 years. Technological forecasting would be able to produce predictions about the general trends and concepts in various power source areas but would not expect to establish the precise design specification likely to be used.

Some of the most popular methods of technological forecasting are as follows:

1. Morphological research

This is an exploratory approach which seeks to divide the problem into its basic areas through a detailed analysis of the parameters relating to an existing product. An example of this technique was featured by Erich Jantath[1]: 'It is possible to show that a simple, chemical jet engine characterized by 11 basic parameters can be

1. *Science Journal* October 1967. London.

constructed in 25,344 combinations of these 11 parameters. Some of these represent quite novel devices which might not have been conceived without the kind of rigorous analysis which morphological research provides.'

By considering each component of a product in terms of all the possible alternatives (chemical formulations, design, materials, etc) it is possible to examine the assembly of various combinations of alternatives so that suggestions as to the future development of a product, concept, or technology are evolved.

2. Systems analysis

This approach makes a highly detailed examination of the components and factors of existing systems. From the current operations areas of potential growth, development or innovation are suggested when existing technology from other fields is applied. For example, the application of plastics in a situation where metal was formerly used, or the application of computerization to complex machinery that had previously been manually controlled.

3. Normative relevance tree techniques

Techniques in this area are based on establishing desirable goals and objectives in products, concepts, technology, etc. This is followed by a detailed evaluation of the alternative actions, resources, developments or ways by which the target objective can be reached. The term 'tree' is derived from the pattern of the model (see Figure 6.2). The main trunk is the objective or goal, the alternatives are the branches and these are extended to the twigs, the ends of which represent the shortcomings and deficiencies in existing technology that prevent or discourage the alternatives being used to reach the objective.

One major approach is to consider systematically the possible impact of any probable developments in technological knowledge, or the probable evolution of new concepts, on future developments.

Another major normative approach is to identify a range of potential problems in a technology, product, or concept that is likely to be met in the short, medium and long term. The various technologies and developments to resolve these problems are then identified either objectively or subjectively.

The major advantages of the normative method are that it forces a company to set objectives, recognize future technological problem areas and carry out effective planning for the future. Further, it can help to forecast future demand in relevant product areas and can also indicate to a company opportunities for new product develop-

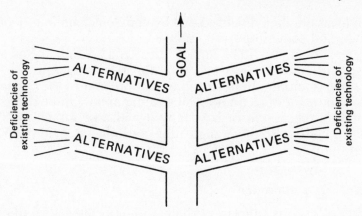

Figure 6.2 *A diagram giving a broad description of the normative relevance tree concept*

ment. Normative relevance tree techniques linked with cost/benefit analysis, critical path analysis and PERT (programme evaluation and review techniques) can be very effective in causing a more efficient application of capital expenditure, in establishing more appropriate priorities in company programmes, in reducing costs and in keeping a company ahead of competitors in appropriate technological areas.

4. Brainstorming

This technique is not strictly a technological forecasting device, but can be used in such a way as to have a useful role in technological prediction. It is a group technique for stimulating and developing creative ideas in a company: it has been said that, with brainstorming, high calibre ideas can be deliberately brought to the surface.

The method is to get together a small group of 10 to 15 persons who are appropriate to the technology/new product area, such as research and development engineers, designers, marketing researchers, consultants, high-level salesmen, etc, then start them thinking about the development of new technology or products in a specific area, eg power sources. As ideas are put forward rapidly they are written down, preferably where they can be seen by the group so that, by combining them with other ideas and improving them, new ideas are sparked off. It is necessary to develop a momentum and not to interfere with the 'ideas-getting' process by discussion or criticism at this stage. Quantity is required as this increases the probability of obtaining non-standard ideas and the 'ideas period' goes on until the group dries up, although care must be taken not to end prematurely.

The ideas are then discussed one by one, some eliminated, others retained and some improved upon.

The next stage should be carried out after a break in the meeting, to give participants a rest and time for ideas to germinate. This final stage is another brainstorming session on how the barriers to the development of technology in specific areas can be overcome, and then a discussion of how long it will take to achieve these breakthroughs. Usually, range time periods, eg 1995–2005, are agreed upon.

5. *The Delphi approach*

A panel of experts from immediate and associated scientific and technological areas is set up. Although they never meet, the effect is an advanced version of the brainstorming technique. A number of rounds are played. First, the members of the panel are asked individually to predict the future course of a technology or product development. The results are analyzed and this initial survey is followed by another which is based on the distilled results of the first, perhaps on the first 10 predicted technological revolutions. The second survey questionnaire may ask the experts to state specifically levels of probability of achieving the first 10 new concepts and/or technology. They may also be asked to rank their individual expertise or competence to deal with a particular concept area. The resulting list would show potential technology breakthroughs in order of probability. This list would again be circulated to the panel of experts and they would be asked to indicate both the time and probability of the distilled list of potential developments.

The Delphi technique does not make a precise forecast or explicit assumptions, but it does produce a suggested time period during which a potential breakthrough could take place, eg 'automated interpretation of medical symptoms, 1995–2005' and 'remote facsimile newspapers and magazines printed at home, 1995–2025.'[1]

The Delphi approach is founded on the intuitive thinking of experts based, after the first round, on information that is the distilled result of the panel as a whole. While it may not be precise, it has a very definite effect on company goal-setting in the research and development area.

6. *Scenario writing approach*

This method also depends on intuitive thinking, describing in a logical sequence of events how, starting from the present day, tech-

1. *Science Journal*, October 1967, London.

nology in a specific area will develop step by step. From this sequence, problems are listed that are associated with the required breakthroughs needed to achieve the ultimate objective.

This method of forecasting identifies areas of difficult development but also systematically examines the branches or direction of potential technological change or development and the possible courses of action at each key decision point in the future.

7. Technological trend extrapolation

This method is based on the collection of historic and present data regarding a technology, product, or product concept, which is then projected into the future.

It is a useful exploratory approach, but the high degree of uncertainty surrounding the range of parameters that can be chosen and the possible number of interpretations of the resulting trends tend to reduce the forecasters' level of confidence in it.

Technological trend extrapolation is particularly applicable to pace-setting data, speed, efficiency, strength, performance, etc, but becomes less effective and accurate in highly complex, fast-moving situations of high reaction or interaction. Further, in situations where the normative approach (starting at some point in the future and working back to the present) forces the pace of development, trends based on historic data are less likely to be relevant.

Direct extrapolation. This is merely a case of taking an existing trend and projecting it to some future point in time. It ignores the possibility of radical breakthroughs in technology and its findings may have to be modified by some other approach such as the Delphi technique.

The vector approach. Where a total concept, product, set of resources, etc, is being considered it is possible to calculate average growth or development rates over the recent past and show them on a vector diagram. This has the effect of ranking the average growth rates. Consideration can then be given to the effect of extrapolating these average growth rates into the future.

The line of best fit approach (Figure 6.3). By this method the various stages of the development of a total concept or product are plotted on a time scale at the point where they were introduced, in relation to the increase in efficiency or performance they cause. For example, the diagram could show the pattern of discovery of computer technology measured in terms of speed of handling data or decision-making. The historic development pattern could be plotted and a line of best fit added and projected into the future. This projection would indicate the speeds of handling data or decision-making that could be expected in the year 2005.

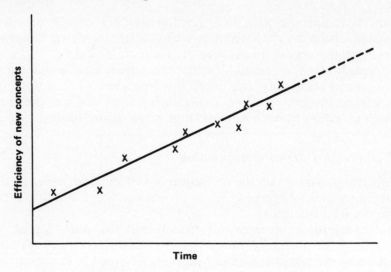

Figure 6.3 *The line of best fit approach*

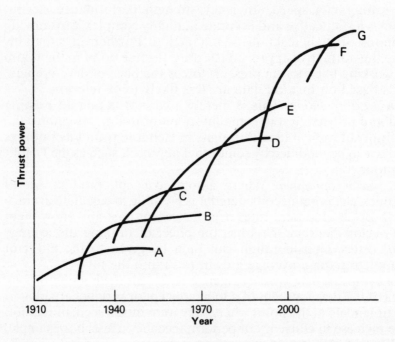

Figure 6.4 *Envelope curve extrapolation — the hypothetical development of aero engine types*

Envelope curve extrapolation (Figure 6.4). This is a development of the last method, of considering new developments in a technology. Not only is the initial point in time plotted together with the efficiency or performance level, but also the whole pattern of development of each aspect of the overall concept. For example, if the development of the efficiency of power sources, ie engines and motors of different types, were considered, a curve of development related to time would evolve from plotting the efficiency development and improvement pattern of each type, ie the steam engine, petrol engine, electric motor, diesel, turbine, diesel electric, jet engine, rocket motor, etc. The current pattern, plus the known discoveries that have yet to be fully exploited, can be projected into the future. It is a means of forecasting the impact of anticipated developments without specifically determining the technology by which it will be reached.

'S' curve trend comparison (Figure 6.5). In many technologies, their developments in terms of improved efficiency, speed, performance, etc takes the shape of a misshapen letter S. There is the discovery, followed by the gradual improvement in efficiency as time passes, which in turn is followed by a 'take off' period where the technology suddenly develops and performance increases rapidly over a relatively short period of time. This is later followed by a lower development growth rate. Later still, at saturation level a plateau can develop where it becomes impossible to develop the technology further. Extrapolation in this case means completing the S shape pattern for existing technology. Also when existing S curves are tending to level out it suggests that a new development in technology will emerge to take the overall concept forward. It might also indicate to innovating companies areas ready for technological development.

The long-/short-term performance graph (Figure 6.6). This is not so much another technique as a variation on the S curve trend comparison above. It recognizes the S shape development, but poses a situation where two technologies have developed to perform the same or similar functions. Consider an area in the technology of pneumatics, the compression of air as a power source.

There are two main ways of efficiently compressing air. Expressed simply, one is the *reciprocating method* where air is compressed by means of cylinders and pistons. The *rotary vane method* is the second approach, where a vaned rotor is rotated at speed, forcing air up through a tube. The reciprocating method came first and the S pattern developed as improvements to design improved efficiency. In 1949 the rotary vane method was introduced, commencing another S pattern, particularly in the area of the mobile compressor unit. Both methods perform the same task and, as

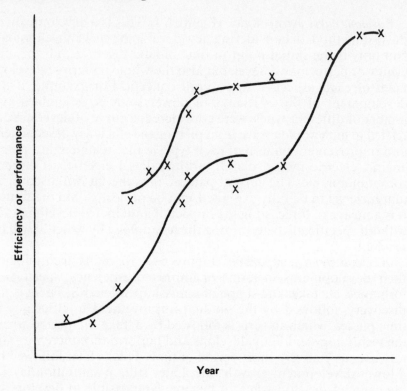

Figure 6.5 *S curve trend comparison*

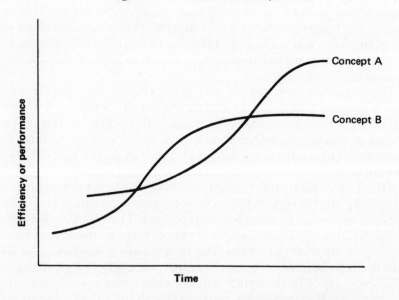

Figure 6.6 *Long-/short-term performance*

developments in each of the two methods emerge, a comparison of efficiencies is possible. Also by the long-/short-term performance graph it is possible to extrapolate the S pattern into the future. This might indicate, as in the graph, that the method that is giving the greatest level of performance in the short term may be overtaken in the long term by the other method, when remotely possible developments occur.

It will be seen that the technological forecasting methods listed tend to be rather more subjective than objective, and as such may tend to be less precise than some others. The methods shown are either attempting to link the development of technology with its effect on the market, or are information feedback systems. The information derived makes it possible to anticipate and identify possible future technological developments and assess the various alternatives.

Technology is one of the market environments in which a company operates and will have a direct effect therefore on sales forecasting. While not all companies have the resources to embark upon highly sophisticated technological forecasting, any attempt, no matter how elementary, is better than no prediction of future technology at all.

In fact, the techniques of technological forecasting fall into two categories, *exploratory* and *normative*. These have been defined thus: 'exploratory forecasting consists in using our present knowledge of science potentialities and technical trends for projection purposes under a *ceteris paribus* assumption which generally neglects all other possible structure changes. On the contrary, normative forecasting works backwards from the future to the present; it implies a coherent examination of future needs in a future society, which helps define first socio-economic objectives and then purely technical research objectives and the best way to achieve them.'

7
Objective Methods of Forecasting

'Statistics must be as the lamp post is to a drunken man, one of support rather than illumination'

Anon

Objective methods of forecasting

Forecasting methods can be either objective (predictions and projections), subjective (conclusions) or a combination of both. Objective forecasts tend to be of a statistical/mathematical nature and subjective forecasts tend to be intuitive, based on the application of experience, intelligence and judgement.

The ideal forecast is a combination of both types. It is made up of a number of individual forecasts, some objective and some subjective. The degree of emphasis on either type will depend on a number of factors. These include the type of industry. A composite forecast in a fashion industry will tend to need a higher subjective content than a forecast in a basic raw materials industry. The absence of appropriate quantitative data may force a company to rely more heavily on subjective methods. Further, the cost in terms of time and money of obtaining a sophisticated statistical forecast may cause a company to use mainly intuitive techniques. In some cases (perhaps with a product completely new to the company) the appropriate experience and the informed intuition may not be available and emphasis will tend to be on statistical techniques.

But even with the individual objective statistical forecast there is a case for subjecting it to the appraisal, judgement and intuition of practical marketing men. Mechanical forecasting by statistical researchers who are far removed from, or out of touch with, the market place can often result in naive projections of future sales. In some companies the results of statistical projections are referred to as forecasts and after they have been subjected to informed intuition they become predictions. Although perhaps apparently pedantic, such an approach does emphasize the importance of the dual forecasting approach.

Not all techniques can be precisely defined as objective or subjective; therefore, they have been assigned either to this chapter (objective methods) or to Chapter 9 (subjective methods), on the basis that their nature is predominantly one or the other.

Tied indicators and derived demand

For some products, published statistics upon which to base a market forecast are scarce. In such a case there may be other products which sell in an identifiable relationship, and which are better documented, with readily available data.

Where sales of one product may be related to the sales of other products the latter would be termed a *tied indicator* and demand is derived. This relationship can be seen where products are incorporated into others, eg the demand for fractional horsepower motors might be linked with the sales of washing machines, vacuum cleaners, dish washers, and refrigerators. Forecasts of the latter products would be useful to forecast the sales of specific motor types.

Sometimes a 'double tie' can be identified and used. For example, if a company manufacturing metal cans identifies a specific end-product market it may forecast the sales of its own product by using the tied indicator of the demand for tinned peas. But also the forecast of the market for the sales of cans for that specific product could be ascertained by considering the acreage of peas which are contracted for sowing by the leading canning companies.

End-use analyses of the ultimate market, together with tied indicators, make useful forecasting devices where a company's products are merely one stage in a line of product stages for ultimate consumer or user purchase.

Lead and lag techniques

One of the most popular approaches for the use of independent variables such as economic indicators is the *lead/lag method*. This method involves finding one or more economic indicators that tend to assume a similar pattern to the data being forecast, but which increase or decrease ahead of it. By observing movements in the leading indicator, forecasts can be made, as these movements will repeat themselves later in the lagging data. This is done ideally by the use of graphs as well as tables of figures, for although the units of measurement of the indicators compared may be different (eg £s, index numbers, tons, etc), directional changes, upwards or downwards, will be clearly indicated. An example is shown in Figure

7.1. There, the wholesale price index (the leading indicator) is three months ahead of the cost of living index (the lagging indicator).

There are many types of independent variables, such as economic indicators, that have a direct lead/lag effect on sales; it is necessary for forecasters to discover those most appropriate to a particular company's needs and situations.

In some cases it is possible to establish a more long-term lead/lag relationship: movements in the birth rate will affect the demand for school clothing five years later. This lead/lag relationship can be useful not only in forecasting but also in indicating marketing opportunities.

The main advantage of the lead/lag technique is in determining potential directional increases or decreases in market situations or sales, eg a turn down or turn up on a total consumer expenditure graph. But it is unlikely to provide information regarding the extent of the directional change.

Lead/coincident and lag method

A refinement of this method is the introduction of midway or coincident indicators. The indicators used, although only indirectly related to the lead and lag indicators, tend to coincide, and therefore help to reinforce or modify conclusions arrived at from the leading indicators. Some examples will illustrate this method:

Leading	Coincident	Lagging
Average hours worked	employment position	retail sales
Government 'below the line' expenditure	gross national product	employment position
Industrial production	retail stocks	retail sales
Raw material prices	wholesale prices	cost of living
New orders for durable goods	machine tool orders	level of industrial production
Bank advances	home building starts	building society advances
Wage rates	new orders for durable goods	hire purchase debt
Machine tool orders	level of industrial production	corporate profits
Factory building approvals	machine tool orders	index of industrial production

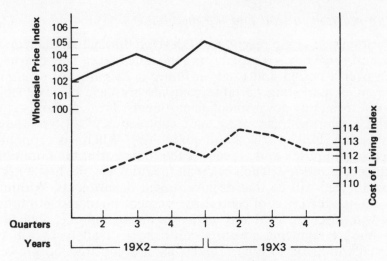

Figure 7.1 *An example of lead/lag indicators; wholesale prices leading the cost of living*

The coincident indicator is useful in checking the validity of using a pair of indicators as one leading another. Consider item one in the above list where average hours worked lead retail sales. The use of the employment position indicator will show how retail sales will be affected. If average hours worked increases and the employment position remains unchanged, then this will reflect overtime working by the existing labour force. This in turn will affect the retail sales of luxury or semi-luxury products or services as more disposable income is available above the basic required for general living. But if average hours worked increases and the employment position improves during a period of medium or high unemployment then the tendency will be for retail sales to increase in sectors dealing with basic items of food and clothing.

Where both leading and coincident factors increase or decrease and the lagging one does not move or moves in the opposite direction, investigation will often show the emergence of a new factor. For example, in the above case, if average hours worked increased together with an improvement in the employment situation, retail sales did not increase or increased only slightly, a new factor such as increased saving might be found.

When using lead and lag techiques it is advisable to use a number of pairs of indicators as some can be used to check the validity of others. It will be noticed that in the above list of indicators the same indicator can appear in different columns depending on what information is needed. Lists of appropriate lead and lag indicators can be evolved for various market situations.

Chain reaction in lead and lag methods

Occasionally, a chain reaction will develop throughout the market segments served by a company, and the time lags can be measured often over a period and used on future occasions. For example, companies marketing portable compressors have basically four market segments: government departments, local authority and service authorities (gas, water, etc), contractors of all types (civil engineering, builders, etc) and plant hire. When an economic squeeze is imposed and is seen by the indicator of the minimum lending rate and restriction of credit facilities, etc, the first market to be affected will be that of government departments. Within a few months the effect of central government financing and influence will affect the local and service authorities' market segments. The market segments covering contractors of all types will be affected within six to nine months, as new construction projects are postponed or curtailed. However, some projects must go on and when, because of the economic squeeze, capital for equipment is either unobtainable or too costly, there tends to be a considerable increase in business in the plant hire sector from three months after imposition of restrictions.

Economic lead and lag indicators can be used not only to forecast sales but also to indicate in advance the segments of the market upon which the company should be concentrating its sales promotional efforts.

Sometimes the lagging effect can be measured relatively accurately. In many areas of the capital goods market the effect of an economic indicator, the minimum lending rate, has a direct lagging correlation, ie a 1 per cent increase in the minimum lending rate will cause a 3 per cent to 4 per cent decrease in sales in six months' time. Conversely, when the minimum lending rate decreases by 1 per cent, sales tend to increase 3 per cent to 4 per cent in six months' time as the new minimum lending rate permeates the economic system. Relationships such as these are extremely useful in forecasting and individual companies will need to develop their own lead/lag values, as economic changes affect different companies in different ways.

Correlation and regression analysis

Two widely used forecasting techniques are regression analysis and correlation. In the former, a function is developed mathematically which expresses the relationship between a dependent variable (sales) and one or more independent variables. Correlation, on the other hand, is designed to measure the direction and intensity of this relationship. Normally, only those variables showing a significant level of correlation are subjected to regression analysis.

If two or more quantities or factors vary in sympathy, so that movements or changes upwards or downwards in one tend to be accompanied by movements of a corresponding nature in the other, they are said to be correlated. But the forecaster must ensure that the correlation is not spurious, as it is possible to get a high numerical correlation where two series have increased continuously, without there being any necessary cause and effect relationship at all.

Correlation can be direct or positive with both series of data moving in the same direction, increasing or decreasing, or it can be inverse or negative with the two series moving in opposite directions, ie as one increases the other decreases and vice versa.

Correlation between two series of data can be completely absent, in which case it could be said that the two series were completely independent of each other.

There are degrees of correlation, where data is partially correlated, and although care must be taken when using such data to forecast, it can still be used with qualification as a very useful method of prediction.

Market correlation with economic indicators

Taking two economic indicators from the *Annual Abstract of Statistics* (published by the Central Statistical Office), 'consumer expenditure at market prices' and 'consumer expenditure on footwear', a very definite correlation between the two indicators can be seen over a period of time (see Table 7.1). That is, as consumer expenditure increases, the amount spent on footwear increases almost proportionately; the percentage declining only marginally (column 4).

Consumer expenditure in the UK is regularly forecast by government economists (and others) and if a relationship can be established, such as the one in the footwear industry shown in Table 7.1, a forecast for both the industry and a company within the industry could be made. Alternatively, the forecaster could project a trend from the consumer expenditure data to obtain a forecast for the next year, in this case 1992. Assuming that the 1.012 per cent share of consumer expenditure continued or the share continued to decline on the pattern of recent years, a prediction for the sales of footwear could be obtained.

Furthermore, there would be a relationship between the sales of a company in the footwear industry and the size of the market measured by 'consumer expenditure on footwear', ie its market

Table 7.1 *The relationship of consumer expenditure on footwear and total consumer expenditure in the UK*

Year	Consumer expenditure at market prices (£m)	Consumer expenditure on footwear (£m)	Footwear as a percentage of consumer expenditure (£m)
1981	155,412	1,842	1,185
1982	170,650	2,068	1,211
1983	187,028	2,296	1,227
1984	200,261	2,512	1,254
1985	218,947	2,780	1,269
1986	243,030	2,998	1,233
1987	267,523	3,085	1,153
1988	302,057	3,210	1,062
1989	330,532	3,400	1,028
1990	350,411	3,679	1,049
1991	367,853	3,725	1,012

Source: Annual Abstract of Statistics 1993, C.S. Office.

Table 7.2 *The relationship of consumer expenditure on footwear to a company's sales producing its market share*

Year	Consumer expenditure on Footwear (£m)	Company Sales (£m)	Market Share %
1986	2,998	119.920	4.0
1987	3,085	138.825	4.5
1988	3,210	160.500	5.0
1989	3,400	161.500	4.75
1990	3,679	183.950	5.0
1991	3,725	186.250	5.0

Source (Column 2): Annual Abstract of Statistics 1993, C.S. Office

share. This relationship is reflected in the hypothetical situation shown in Table 7.2.

Suppose a forecast of consumer expenditure at market prices was made either by government economists or by in-company projection and this prediction for 1992 was £382.500m. A company forecast could be made as follows:

£382,500m × 1 per cent (Table 7.1, column 4) = £3,825m predicted expenditure on footwear.
£3,825m × 5 per cent (Table 7.2, column 4) = £191.25m predicted company sales.

The validity of such a forecast would depend upon market factors remaining much as they have been over the last five years, or at least changing at an existing rate.

The company may hope to increase its share of the market, or competition being experienced at the present time may be such that the company may have to make a great effort to maintain its 5 per cent share of the market. In both cases marketing, advertising and other promotional expenditure may have to be expanded considerably to increase or maintain the market share.

In the above example, total consumer expenditure has been taken as the economic indicator, but others may be chosen that are more appropriate to a market or a company. For companies in the consumer durables market, total consumer disposable income might be more appropriate as it takes account of the amount consumers may be inclined to save as well as spend. Total capital formation would be an indicator appropriate to companies in industrial machinery markets, etc.

Correlation and company sales

One of the most important stages of the correlation technique is to determine the degree of correlation, and this can be done graphically, or, more precisely, by statistical methods. Supposing research has shown, or it has been noticed over a period of time, that movements in the size of a particular economic indicator (although it could be any independent variable) tend to coincide with the sales of (and consequently the demand for) a particular product — product A. The two series of data could be listed as in Table 7.3.

If the data in Table 7.3 is plotted on a graph with the economic indicator on one vertical axis, the sales of product A on the other, and time along the horizontal axis, the result would be as shown in Figure 7.2.

It will be noticed that although the lines on the diagram are not in exact unison, they tend to have a similar basic pattern.

If the two series of data were shown in a different way, with the economic indicator on the horizontal axis and the sales of product A on the vertical axis and the pairs plotted, a scatter of plot marks will be obtained as in Figure 7.3.

The first plot mark in Figure 7.3 will be found by observing 322

Table 7.3 *Two series of data which are to be examined for correlation*

Year	Economic indicator (£m)	Sales of product A (£000s)
19X3	322	25.7
19X4	320	27.7
19X5	311	30.0
19X6	329	33.6
19X7	358	36.9
19X8	363	38.2
19X9	379	39.6
19Y0	390	38.6
19Y1	430	42.7
19Y2	446	43.7
19Y3	466	48.1
	11)4114	11)404.8
	374 average	36.8 average

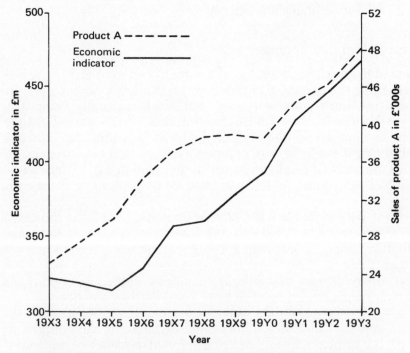

Figure 7.2 *The values of the economic indicator in £m and the sales of product A in £000's plotted on a time series diagram*

on the horizontal and 25.7 on the vertical axis, and marking where these two values intersect on the graph; and so on for all the pairs of data. In the foregoing table both columns were totalled and then divided by 11 to give the average in both cases. The average pair can be plotted (marked 0 in Figure 7.3) and a trend line inserted through the average mark and as near the centre of the scatter of all the other marks as possible.

This method of fixing a regression line is rather rough, as a slight movement of the line on the pivot of the average plot mark will alter the reading considerably at the ends of the line. It is a guide to the degree of correlation, but if the regression line is intended as a basis for forecasting other anticipated values, it would be advisable to adopt a more precise way of fitting a regression line, perhaps by the least squares method shown later in this chapter. In fact the line of best fit has been added to the data, between points A and B as calculated on page 184.

It will be noticed that there is a tendency for the plot marks to form an irregular pattern from low left to high right. This indicates that there exists a degree of positive or direct correlation. If the scatter was so wide that no overall trend could be distinguished, this would indicate the absence of correlation, and the fact that after change in the value of one set of data, a sympathetic change could not be anticipated in the other series. The implication in the

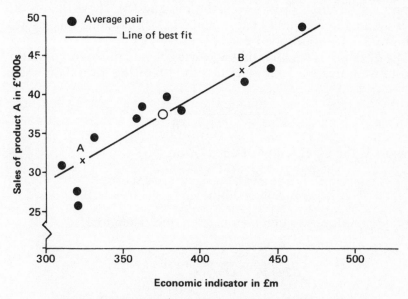

Figure 7.3 *A graph of two sets of data plotted in pairs and indicating a high degree of correlation*

above example is that if the value of the independent variable, ie the indicator, moved upwards, the sales of product A would tend to do the same.

If it is easier to obtain a forecast of an independent variable such as an economic indicator than to project the sales level itself, or if a lead/lag relationship exists, then forecasting by this method is relatively easy. The forecast of the appropriate economic indicator is used and the forecast of the other value is read from the regression line on the scatter diagram. In the last example, if the forecast of the economic indicator was £450m, reading from the diagram, the sales of product A could be expected to be around £46,000; perhaps in x months' time if there was a lagging effect.

The degree of correlation is very important when using a linear regression line in sales forecasting. It is possible to take the data from the previous example (Table 7.3) and, using statistical methods, determine how closely correlated these two sets of data really are. Further, it can be calculated just how much confidence can be placed in concluding that a movement in one series of data would anticipate a movement in the other series.

The data in Table 7.3, showing values of the economic indicator and the sales of product A, can be listed and, using the symbols x and y respectively, a table can be evolved to provide data leading to a coefficient of correlation (Table 7.4). Columns 3 (x_{dev}) and 6 (y_{dev}) in Table 7.4 show the deviation each value is away from the appropriate average (bottom of columns 2 and 5). These figures are then squared in columns 4 ($x_{dev}2$) and 7 ($y_{dev}2$). Column 8 represents column 3 (x_{dev}) multiplied by column 6 (y_{dev}).

The question is whether the two series of data move in sympathy and to what degree. To answer this the following formula is used.

$$r = \frac{\Sigma(x_{dev}y_{dev})}{\sqrt{[(\Sigma x_{dev}^2)(\Sigma y_{dev}^2)]}}$$

where r is the co-efficient of correlation.

Σ is a summation sign (the sum of),
so $\Sigma x_{dev}2$ is sum of all the $x_{dev}2$ values, ie 29,056

The other values are taken from the table. Therefore:

$$r = \frac{3533.6}{\sqrt{(290.56 \times 485.66)}} = 0.9542$$

To visualize the implications of this value (0.9452 co-efficient of correlation), consider the following scale:

Table 7.4 *An analysis of the values of the economic indicator and sales of Product A to permit the calculation of the co-efficient of correlation*

1	2 Economic indicator (£m) x	3 x_{dev}	4 x_{dev}^2	5 Sales of product A (£000s) y	6 y_{dev}	7 y_{dev}^2	8 $x_{dev} \times y_{dev}$
19X3	322	− 52	2,704	25.7	−11.1	123.20	+ 577.2
19X4	320	− 54	2,916	27.7	− 9.1	82.81	+ 491.4
19X5	311	− 63	3,969	30	− 6.8	46.24	+ 428.4
19X6	329	− 45	2,025	33.6	− 3.2	10.24	+ 144.0
19X7	358	− 16	256	36.9	+ 0.1	0.01	− 1.6
19X8	363	− 11	121	38.2	+ 1.4	1.96	− 15.4
19X9	379	+ 5	25	39.6	+ 2.8	7.84	+ 14.0
19Y0	390	+ 16	256	38.6	+ 1.8	3.24	+ 28.8
19Y1	430	+ 56	3,136	42.7	+ 5.9	34.81	+ 330.4
19Y2	446	+ 72	5,184	43.7	+ 6.9	47.61	+ 496.8
19Y3	466	+ 92	8,464	48.1	+11.3	127.70	+1,039.6
	11)4,114	− 241 + 241	29,056	11)404.8	−30.2 +30.2	485.66	+3,550.6 −17 +3,533.6
	Mean 374			Mean 36.8			

159

Perfect direct correlation	**Independence**	**Perfect inverse correlation**
Value $+1$ — $+0.75$ — $+0.5$ — 0 — -0.5 — -0.75 — -1		

The nearer the correlation co-efficient is to unity (± 1) the better the degree of correlation, and a zero (0) co-efficient indicates that there is no correlation between the two series. Values falling between these limits suggest degrees of dependence and correlation between any two series of data being considered. Thus, in the example where $r = 0.9452$ (a positive figure) it could be concluded that there is a considerable correlation or connection in changes and movements between the two sets of data. The nearer the co-efficient (r) falls to the independence value of 0, the lower will be the degree of reliability that can be placed on using one series of data to anticipate or forecast the movements of the other. A value of less than 0.5 would not be considered reliable but a value over 0.75 would be taken to indicate a highly reliable correlation.

Testing the significance of the co-efficient of correlation

It would be quite wrong, however, to take the co-efficient of correlation without some qualification. It does not necessarily provide conclusive evidence that there is correlation to the degree that future predictions for the movement of one variable factor can be based upon the movements of another. In the last example a sample of 11 years was taken, and the size of the values for these 11 years may, or may not, have been caused by sheer chance, or may not be representative of values that could be normally expected. The fewer observations made, or the shorter the range of time over which they are made, the greater will be the chance of obtaining non-typical values by sheer chance. In order to accept the co-efficient of correlation without qualification it is necessary to check its significance or reliability, and to take into account the number of observations (n) made. Further, it is generally assumed that the degree of correlation is not satisfactory unless the odds against a particular correlation co-efficient being obtained by chance alone are less than 5 in 100. That is, in only 5 cases out of 100 could the observed value for r have been obtained accidentally in the absence of correlation. Any probability value between 0.05 (5 cases in 100) and 0.01 (one case in 100) is significant and reliable. Any value less than 0.01 is highly significant or reliable. Thus, 0.001 as a value would occur by chance or accident only once in 1,000 cases. The significance of the correlation co-efficient can be checked by using a table of the type shown in Table 7.5.

The number of *degrees of freedom* to be used to check the signifi-

Table 7.5 *A table for checking the significance of the co-efficient of correlation*

1 Degrees of freedom	2 Co-efficient of correlation 0.05	3 0.01	4 0.001
1	0.997	1.000	1.000
2	0.950	0.990	0.999
3	0.878	0.959	0.992
4	0.811	0.917	0.974
5	0.754	0.874	0.951
6	0.707	0.834	0.925
7	0.666	0.798	0.898
8	0.632	0.765	0.872
9	0.602	0.735	0.847
10	0.576	0.708	0.823
11	0.553	0.684	0.801
12	0.532	0.661	0.780
13	0.514	0.641	0.760
14	0.497	0.623	0.742
15	0.482	0.606	0.725
16	0.468	0.590	0.708
17	0.456	0.575	0.693
18	0.444	0.561	0.679
19	0.433	0.549	0.665
20	0.423	0.537	0.652

cance of a co-efficient of correlation is determined by deducting 2 from the number, n, of items used ie $(n - 2)$. In Table 7.4, 11 items were used, therefore

$$n - 2 = 11 - 2 = 9 \text{ degrees of freedom.}$$

Having determined the degrees of freedom (9), it is necessary to read across Table 7.5 until the value of the co-efficient of correlation being examined is found, or at least a value close to it. At the top of columns 2, 3 and 4, the measures of significance are shown. Column 2, headed 0.05, indicates 5 chances in 100. Column 3, headed 0.01, indicates 1 chance in 100. Column 4, headed 0.001, indicates 1 chance in 1,000: additional measures of significance columns are given in books of statistical tables.

The co-efficient of correlation in the last example was 0.9452 with 9 degrees of freedom. Reading across Table 7.5 at 9 degrees of freedom it can be seen that such a value (0.9452) is beyond the last column, ie is more than 0.847, which represents the probability of 1 chance in 1,000. Thus, it can be said that the co-efficient of correlation of 0.9452 with 9 degrees of freedom is highly significant and reliable, as the chance of it being obtained accidentally is less than 1 in 1,000 times.

The importance of taking an adequate number of observations, that is, an adequate size of sample, can be seen if the co-efficient of correlation of the last example (Table 7.4), 0.9452, is examined under different circumstances. If this value was obtained using only three observations, the degrees of freedom would be $3 - 2 = 1$ degree of freedom (ie $n - 2$). Referring to the table, it can be seen that the chances of such a value being obtained by accident is much higher; in fact more than 5 in 100. That is, at 1 degree of freedom it is not high enough to enter column 2 (0.05) which has a value of 0.997. As the chance of such a value occurring by accident should be less than 5 per cent (ie 5 in 100) for the value to be significant, that is for the two series of data to be correlated to a reliable degree, it could be said that where $r = 0.9452$ with one degree of freedom, it is not significant. The implication is that the values of the two sets of data being tested for correlation could, based on three observations, have been freak values obtained purely by accident. The obvious thing to do in such circumstances would be to increase the number of observations, thereby increasing the degrees of freedom, and again calculate the chances of such a value occurring by accident.

Table 7.6 *Two series of data that are to be examined for an inverse correlation relationship*

Observation	Outdoor temperature in degrees	Demand for electricity in MWatts
1	14	20
2	13	3
3	17	26
4	9	48
5	8	35
6	6	80
7	5	60
8	4	50
9	1	98
10	3	90
	10)80	10)510
	8 Average	51 Average

Inverse or negative correlation

So far, circumstances have been considered where movements in one series of data tend to be accompanied by *sympathetic* movements *in the same direction* in another series of data, ie direct or positive correlation. However, in some cases it will be found that *inverse* or *negative correlation* will permit forecasts to be made; ie where the values contained in one series of data increase, the values in the other series tend to decrease, and vice versa. Consider as an example an increase in the demand for, and consequently the sales of, electricity as the outdoor temperature changes. By taking an imaginary part of the country and making 10 random observations, the two series could be evolved as in Table 7.6

If the values in Table 7.6 are shown in a graph with the demand for electricity on the vertical axis, and the outdoor temperature on the horizontal axis, a scatter diagram would be obtained. By determining the average plot mark, ie plotting the averages of the two series of data, 8°C and 51 MWatts, it would be possible to draw a line through the centre of the plot marks thereby giving a regression line (see Figure 7.4). Alternatively, a more precise way of fitting a

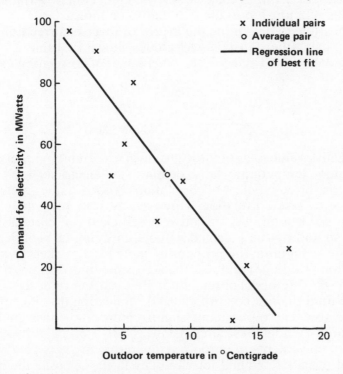

Figure 7.4 *An inverse correlation diagram showing that as one variable increases in value of the other decreases*

163

regression line would be by the least squares method (see page 184).

Notice how the pattern of the scatter diagram tends to fall from high left to low right, indicating the presence of a degree of inverse correlation. Whether the regression line is roughly fitted by pivoting a ruler on the 'average' pair or whether it is more precisely fitted statistically, perhaps by the least squares method, the diagram can be used for forecasting.

Again, if it is easier to forecast an independent variable, such as a climatic factor in the last example, than to project the demand level itself, or if a lead/lag relationship exists, then forecasting by the inverse correlation method is relatively easy. Using Figure 7.4, when a weather forecast is made indicating the outdoor temperature, eg 10 degrees Centigrade, the forecast of demand for electricity can be read from the regression line, ie 40 MWatts.

Weather forecasts are usually readily available, so although the relationship is contemporary, ie changes in both series happen at the same time, a forecast of demand for electricity can be made. But where forecasts of the independent variable are not readily available, forecasting is easier when the independent variable has a lead/lag relationship to the demand to be forecast.

It is possible to determine the degree of inverse correlation precisely by using the statistical techniques shown in Table 7.7

Using data from Table 7.7, the co-efficient of correlation can be calculated:

$$r = \frac{\Sigma(x_{dev}y_{dev})}{\sqrt{[(x_{dev}^2)(\Sigma y_{dev}^2)]}} = \frac{-1259}{\sqrt{(246 \times 8808)}} = -0.86$$

The negative value (−0.86) indicates inverse correlation; that is, as the outdoor temperature falls, demand for electricity increases. The nearer the co-efficient of correlation (r) is to −1, the greater the degree of inverse correlation. However, as seen previously with positive correlation, the negative co-efficient of correlation r =−0.86 should not be accepted without checking its significance. Therefore, examining the probability table used to check positive correlation (Table 7.5) and reading across the line, degrees of freedom 8 (ie the number of observations 10−2=8), the value 0.86 is not reached until the last column, ie 0.001, indicating that it could be expected to occur by accident slightly more than once in 1,000 observations. Under these circumstances, r=−0.86 is highly significant, and movements in outdoor temperature are very good indicators of potential demand for electricity in the opposite direction. Linked with weather forecasts from the Meteorological Office, fairly accurate forecasts for the sale of electricity could be made.

Table 7.7 *An analysis of the values of the demand for (sales of) electricity and the outdoor temperature to permit the calculation of the co-efficient of correlation*

1	2	3	4	5	6	7	8
Observation	Outdoor temperature in degrees Centigrade x	x_{dev}	x_{dev}^2	Demand for electricity in MWatts y	y_{dev}	y_{dev}^2	$x_{dev} \times y_{dev}$
1	14	+6	36	20	−31	961	−186
2	13	+5	25	3	−48	2,304	−240
3	17	+9	81	26	−25	625	−225
4	9	+1	1	48	−3	9	−1
5	8	0	0	35	−16	256	0
6	6	−2	4	80	+29	841	−58
7	5	−3	9	60	+9	81	−27
8	4	−4	16	50	−1	1	+4
9	1	−7	49	98	+47	2,209	−329
10	3	−5	25	90	+39	1,521	−195
	10)80	0	246	10)510	0	8,808	−1,263 +4
	8 average			51 average			−1,259

There are many cases where economic indicators can be found that tend to move in the opposite direction to industry or company sales, ie where some degree of inverse correlation exists.

Correlation and regression analysis techniques are useful in market and sales forecasting not only with economic and industry indicators but with any type of independent variable that appears to be linked with the sales of a product, although the two unit values may not be the same, eg in the last example demand for electricity in MWatts and the outdoor temperature in degrees Centigrade. Small or medium sized companies that have a negligible or relatively small market share could establish a correlation series with independent variables outside their immediate industry, thus making their forecasting more effective.

Multiple correlation or multivariate analysis

The last section considered the situation where movements in one set of data are accompanied by 'sympathetic' movements in another series. Sometimes a number of variable factors are correlated to the particular series under consideration, eg market or company sales. This is known as *multiple correlation*.

Obviously, the greater the number of variables, the more complex is the calculation, and it becomes the ideal problem to be handled by a computer. As the number of variables increases, the exercise becomes one of market simulation and model building and this is discussed later.

The basic principle of multiple regression and correlation can be illustrated by an elementary example:

Table 7.8 *An analysis of data to permit the calculation of the degrees of multiple correlation between variables*

Period	Units demanded			Deviations from mean							
	X	Y	Z	x	y	z	x^2	y^2	xz	xy	yz
1	4	6	12	-2	-4	3	4	16	-6	8	-12
2	5	8	11	-1	-2	2	1	4	-2	2	-4
3	5	9	8	0	-1	-1		1			1
4	7	12	8	1	2	-1	1	4	-1	2	-2
5	8	15	6	2	5	-3	4	25	-6	10	-15
Totals	30	50	45	0	0	0	10	50	-15	22	-32
Means	6	10	9								

There are five sets of items $\therefore n = 5$

There are three commodities, X, Y and Z, and it is believed that the demand for Z is partly dependent upon the demand for X and Y.

The relationship can be examined by using a multiple regression equation:

$$\hat{Z} = A + BX + CY$$

where $\hat{Z}$ is the predicted or best estimated number of units demanded of the dependent variable; X and Y are the respective units demanded of the independent variables, and A, B and C are constants to be determined from the data in Table 7.8.

After the analysis in Table 7.8, 'normal' equations can be set up, in terms of deviations from the arithmetic means instead of from zero origin:

(i) $\Sigma z = nA + B\Sigma x + C\Sigma y$
(ii) $\Sigma xz = A\Sigma x + B\Sigma x^2 + C\Sigma xy$
(iii) $\Sigma xz = A\Sigma y + B\Sigma xy + C\Sigma y^2$

Where Σ = sigma, the sum of, ie a summation sign.

Therefore:

(i) $0 = 5A + B0 + C0$
(ii) $-15 = A0 + 10B + 22C$
(iii) $-32 = A0 + 22B + 50C$

Notice how the use of deviations from the arithmetic means of the variables eliminates many expressions in the 'normal' equation, eg $A\Sigma x$ = zero.

Solving these equations in the conventional way, ie by the use of determinants or simple substitution

$$B = -2.875 \text{ and } C = 0.625$$

The above calculations were based on deviations from the arithmetic means, and it is necessary to restore them to zero as the origin, therefore

$$
\begin{aligned}
Z - Z \text{ (mean)} &= -2.875(X - \overline{X}) + 0.625\,(Y - \overline{Y}) \\
Z - 9 \text{ (mean)} &= -2.875(X - 6) + 0.625\,(Y - 10) \\
Z &= 9 - 2.875X + 17.250 + 0.625Y - 6.25 \\
Z &= +\ \ 9 \\
&\quad + 17.25 \\
\hline
&\quad + 26.25 \\
&\quad -\ \ 6.25 \\
\hline
&\quad 20 - 2.875X + 0.625Y
\end{aligned}
$$

This gives the required multiple regression of Z on X and Y, as

$$\hat{Z} = 20 - 2.875X + 0.625Y$$

The 'fit' is as follows:

	Actual values of Z	Predicted values of Z
	12	12.25
	11	10.625
	8	8.375
	8	7.375
	6	6.375
Totals	45	45

It may be verified that

regression sum of squares $(\hat{Z} - Z)^2$ $\quad = 23.125$
and error sum of squares $(Z - \hat{Z})^2$ $\quad = 0.875$
and total sum of squares $(Z - Z)^2$ $\quad = \overline{24.000}$

The multiple correlation co-efficient is accordingly

$$\sqrt{\left[\frac{23.125}{24.000}\right]}$$

approximately perfect negative correlations, ie $r = -1$.

The example shows that the demand for commodity Z decreases as the demand for commodities X and Y increases. Conversely, the demand for Z increases aš the demand for X and Y decreases.

The above formula can be proved by using the arithmetic means, ie where $X=6$ and $Y=10$, therefore the predicted or best estimate of Z:

$$20 - 2.875 \times 6 + 0.625 \times 10 = 9$$
(which is, in fact, the arithmetic mean of Z)

Using this formula, a forecast can be made for Z; for example, where $X=8$ and $Y=12$:

$$Z = 20 - 2.875 \times 8 + 0.625 \times 12$$
$$20 - 23 + 7.5 = 4.5 \text{ forecast for } Z$$

Least squares method — a regression line technique

The least squares method is a relatively simple mathematical technique that ensures that the calculated functional linear equation is the one with the best fit of the data. A line is said to be the best fit line when it minimizes, in relation to all other possible lines, the sum of the squares of the vertical deviations of the observations from that line. Its drawback is that if the sales data used is too erratic, the straight line will only represent a broad directional

Table 7.9 *Analysis of sales data to calculate a trend by the method of least squares*

1	2	3	4	5	6	7
Year & quarter	Sales in £000s	Deviation of each quarter from assumed mean quarter	Dev²	Sales × deviation	Trend ordinates	Trend
19X3 2	34	– 4	16	– 136		31.86
3	29	– 3	9	– 87	35.3 – (4 × 0.86) =	32.72
4	35	– 2	4	– 70	35.3 – (3 × 0.86) =	33.58
19X4 1	36	– 1	1	– 36	35.3 – (2 × 0.86) =	34.44
2	37	0	0	0	35.3 – (1 × 0.86) =	35.30
3	31	1	1	31	35.3 + (1 × 0.86) =	36.16
4	37	2	4	74	35.3 + (2 × 0.86) =	37.02
19X5 1	40	3	9	120	35.3 + (3 × 0.86) =	37.88
2	39	4	16	156	35.3 + (4 × 0.86) =	38.74
n =	9)318		60	+381		
				– 329		
	35.3 = arithmetic average			52 ÷ 60 = 0.86		

169

trend, and if the data is very smooth there will be no need for a trend line. If a series of quarterly sales is taken, a simple way to find the trend by the least squares method is shown in Table 7.9.

In Table 7.9 columns 1 and 2 represent the sales volume in the various quarters; the quarterly sales are totalled and the arithmetic mean is found (35.3).

As quarter 2 of 19X4 is the middle quarter of the nine quarters considered, this quarter has been chosen as the assumed mean or middle quarter and column 3 shows the deviation + or − away from the assumed mean.

In column 4 the deviations have been squared (thereby eliminating the minus signs) and then totalled. In column 5, sales (column 2) are multiplied by the unsquared deviations (column 3); the minus total is subtracted from the plus total and the answer is divided by the total of the deviations squared, ie the total of column 4. The resultant figure (ie 0.86) will show by how much the trend line will change in each quarter: in fact, it represents the slope of the line and is the increment by which the trend line increases. In column 6 the arithmetic mean of the sum of the quarterly sales figures (ie 35.3) is used, and by adding or subtracting according to the item's position either side of the assumed mean, the number of quarters (column 3) is multiplied by 0.86. The answer in each case is the plot mark for the trend line and is shown in column 7. In practice, as it is a straight line trend, it is necessary only to calculate the top and bottom values in column 6 and join them, checking that the line runs through the arithmetic mean. The original sales data and the trend line are shown in Figure 7.5.

It will be seen in Figure 7.5 that the trend line can be projected into the future (from point A) with sales forecasts being obtained from the projection. This projection will be of use for medium- or long-term forecasting but not for short-term prediction as it does not allow for the seasonal pattern clearly indicated on the graph.

Short- and long-term comparisons

Later in this section, a method of seasonally adjusting this straight line projection will be considered. However, it has a short-term use, as it is often advantageous to observe a change in trend in a recent, relatively short period, compared with a longer period. Figure 7.5 showed the sales curve for nine quarters and a trend line fixed accordingly. However, if the data for the last five quarters is taken, and a trend line obtained, as in Table 7.10, it would give a short-term picture of current trends.

This process of comparison (Table 7.9 with Table 7.10) could be used over any time span series, eg nine years (compared with the

Table 7.10 *An analysis of sales data from recent periods giving a short-term picture of current events*

Year & quarter	Sales in £000s	Deviation of each quarter from assumed mean quarter	Dev²	Sales × deviation	Trend ordinates	Trend
19X4 2	37	−2	4	−74	36.8 − (2 × 1.3) =	34.2
3	31	−1	1	−31	36.8 − (1 × 1.3) =	35.5
4	37	0				36.8
19X5 1	40	1	1	40	36.8 + (1 × 1.3) =	38.1
2	39	2	4	78	36.8 + (2 × 1.3) =	39.4
n =	5)184		10	118 / −105		
	36.8 = arithmetic average			13 ÷ 10 = 1.3		

171

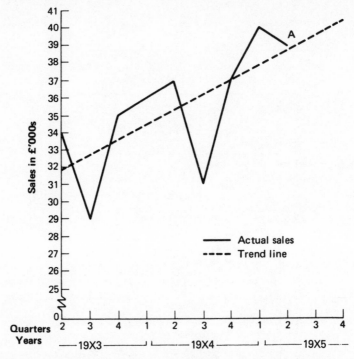

Figure 7.5 *Quarterly sales volume curve with least square trend line superimposed*

nine quarters in the example) indicating a long-/medium-term business cycle pattern. Superimposed on the previous graph, the trend line just obtained in Table 7.10 would indicate the presence of new short-term influences that were either not present throughout the period covered by the long-term data or were hidden or modified by other influences in the opposite direction (see Figure 7.6).

Figure 7.6 shows that the conditions being experienced in the short-term are causing the trend of sales to be higher (C to D) than the long-term sales trend (A to B). It is the analysis of the differences in these predictions that will warn the forecaster of fundamental changes in conditions in the market. Then it must be decided whether such differences are only temporary, in which case there may be a reversion to the long-term trend, and there might be a case for removing the causal item from the sales total. Alternatively, if the conditions are likely to recur, allowance must be made for them in future predictions. Where the short-term trend line fits the long-term line exactly, it is wise to suspect the apparent confirmation that things are the same in the short and

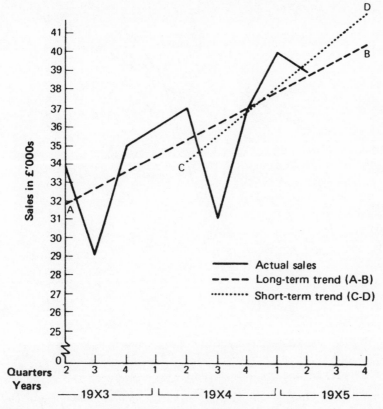

Figure 7.6 *Quarterly sales volume curve with two least squares trend lines —
A-B long-term, and C-D short-term*

long periods; there are often compensatory factors outweighing
each other, thereby giving the same trend line as before.

Least squares method — even number of items

In the previous two examples, series containing an odd number of
items were used and the 'assumed mean quarter' in column three
was not difficult to identify, ie item five in the first series and item
three in the second series. However, occasions arise when only an
even number of items are to be considered (eg 12 months) and/or
where a better indicator of trend is obtained by using an even
number, eg where quarters are considered it is obviously more
accurate to work in units of four (four, eight, 12, etc).

When an odd number of items is considered it is possible not
only to identify the middle year or quarter but also the middle

173

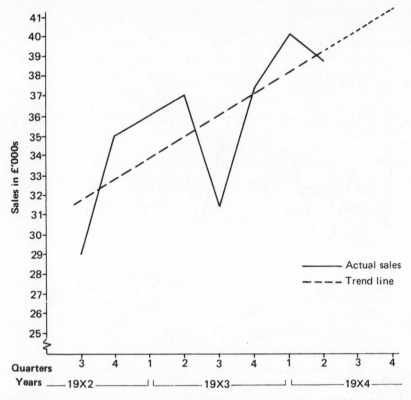

Figure 7.7 *A quarterly sales volume curve with least squares trend line based on an even number of items*

point in that item, eg midnight 30 June for a year, or in the case of a series of quarters, midday of the middle day or midnight between the middle two days. Therefore with an even number of items in a series the method is to work in half years or half quarters. Thus if a series was as follows (eight items) the former least squares method would be adapted as in Table 7.11 and Figure 7.7.

Least squares method with confidence limits

There is a slightly different method of obtaining a line of best fit by the least squares technique. This alternative method permits the forecaster to exploit the available data further by calculating probability control limits within which the *actual* sales will tend to be located in ensuing periods. All this assumes that the basic factors underlying business conditions do not radically change. An example of this method is shown in Table 7.12.

Table 7.11 *The calculation of the highest and lowest trend points using the least square method with an even number of items*

1 x Year Quarter	2 y Sales in £000s	3 x dev in ½ quarters	4 x dev²	5 Sales y × x dev	6 Trend ordinates and trend
19X2 3	29	− 7	49	− 203	$35.5 - (7 \times 0.55) =$
4	35	− 5	25	− 175	31.65
19X3 1	36	− 3	9	− 108	
2	37	− 1	1	− 37	
3	31	+ 1	1	31	
4	37	+ 3	9	111	
19X4 1	40	+ 5	25	200	
2	39	+ 7	49	273	$35.5 + (7 \times 0.55) =$
n =	8)284		168	+ 615	39.35
				− 523	
x̄ =	35.5			92 ÷ 168 = 0.55	

The least squares method is based upon an equation. The equation of the trend line is expressed so:

$$\hat{y} = a + bx$$

where $\hat{y}$ is the estimated value, given the value of an independent variable, x

where a is the intercept of the trend line on the vertical axis and is, therefore, a constant

where b is the slope of the trend line indicating the mean increment of sales and is, therefore, a constant.

Therefore, the mean quarterly increment of sales will give the slope of the trend line:

$$b = \frac{\Sigma(x_{dev} y_{dev})}{\Sigma x_{dev}^2} = \frac{1560}{28} = 55.71$$

(where Σ is the sum total or summation sign)

Therefore 55.71 represents the value of the incremental increase of the slope of the trend line in each time period.

The bottom value of the trend is found by taking the average and the appropriate number of increments.

$$243 - (3 \times 55.71) = 75.87$$

The upper position of the trend line is fixed by calculating:

$$243 + (3 \times 55.71) = 410.13$$

These two points can then be joined by a line and this will give a line of best fit to the data.

Probability control limits can now be calculated to discover the extent of error that the estimated trend could experience. This is done by using the formula:

$$\text{standard error} = \sqrt{\left[\frac{\Sigma y_{\text{dev}}^2 - b(\Sigma x_{\text{dev}} y_{\text{dev}})}{n - 2}\right]}$$

where n is the number of items, ie 7

$$\sqrt{\left[\frac{93143 - 55.71\,(1560)}{7 - 2}\right]} = \sqrt{\left[\frac{93143 - 86907.6}{5}\right]}$$

$$= \sqrt{(1247)} = 35.31$$

Later, in the section dealing with probability (page 187), measures of dispersion or the scatter of data about an arithmetic mean are considered. It is stated that one standard error either side of the arithmetic mean, on data having a normal frequency distribution, would include 68.3 per cent of the values (see page 189). Further, two standard errors either side of the arithmetic mean would include 95.4 per cent of the values. Considering the trend line in the last example, as the arithmetic mean and by calculating two standard errors ($2 \times 35.31 = 70.62$) either side of the trend line, it could be confidently predicted that in approximately 95 cases out of 100 the future sales will fall between these two limits when they are projected into the future. By taking actual sales and the trend shown in Table 7.12, confidence control limits of the trend can be fixed by taking the trend reading for January as 75.87 ± 70.62. Therefore,

$$75.87 - 70.62 = 5.25 \text{ is the lower limit line}$$
$$75.87 + 70.62 = 146.49 \text{ is the upper limit line}$$

Similarly, if the value of the of the line of best fit at July is taken, the control lines can be fixed accordingly:

$$410.13 \pm 70.62.$$

Therefore,

$$410.13 - 70.62 = 339.51 \text{ is the position of the lower limit}$$
$$410.13 + 70.62 = 480.75 \text{ is the position of the upper limit}$$

Probability confidence lines could then be drawn, superimposed on the sales curve and line of best fit and projected into the future as shown in Figure 7.8.

Table 7.12 *Analysis of monthly sales data to establish a trend line and to set probability confidence limits*

1 X Months	2 y Sales in £000s	3 x dev of each month from assumed mean month	4 y dev from rounded sales average	5 x dev² (col 3 squared)	6 y dev² (col 4 squared)	7 x dev × y dev (col 3 × 4)
Jan	50	− 3	− 193	9	37,249	579
Feb	190	− 2	− 53	4	2,809	106
March	180	− 1	− 63	1	3,969	63
April	200	0	− 43	0	1,849	0
May	300	1	+ 57	1	3,249	57
June	370	2	+127	4	16,129	254
July	410	3	+167	9	27,889	501
	7) 1700			28	93,143	1560
	242.8 Rounded to 243					

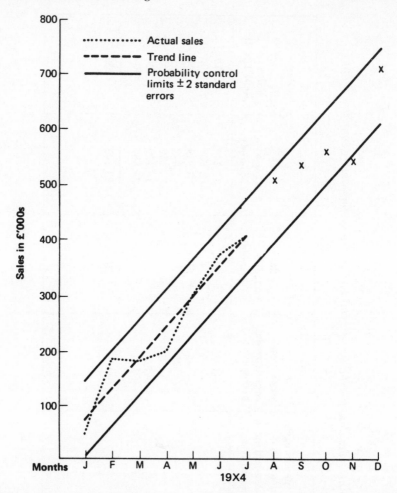

Figure 7.8 *A graph of monthly sales, a least squares trend line and confidence limits set 2 standard errors either side of the trend and projected into the future. The actual sales figures for later months are marked as X*

When setting probability confidence limits it would be possible to use three standard errors ± the trend line, but such limits are generally too wide to be of use. It is a question of balancing usefulness and convenience with the degree of accuracy required. The control limits of two standard errors are usually used in this type of calculation, because a 95 per cent degree of accuracy is adequate: ie in only five cases in 100 is there the possibility that the actual sales volume achieved will fall outside these limits. The probability control lines will become further apart as the degree of fluctuation of sales increases.

In some forecasting situations the control lines are used as maximum and minimum levels for production scheduling, purchasing levels etc.

In Figure 7.8 the actual sales figures for August, September, October, November and December have been inserted and show that with the exception of November they are contained within the projected probability control limits. The November sales figure is marginally below the lower limit line (sales £550,000 as opposed to limit line value of £555,000), but based on past figures such an exception would be expected to occur only in five cases in 100, ie 95 per cent probability of inclusion within the limits.

Seasonal adjustments to straight line trends

Seasonal adjustments of the projected trend line would be useful in the former case (Figure 7.7) and would make it a more effective forecasting tool. Sometimes when the probability confidence limits are set at only ± 1 standard error (that is with 68.3 per cent confidence) they will be so wide apart, because of seasonal influences and non-typical residual factors, that they will be of little use in making a sales forecast within *reasonable* probability limits. Therefore, it will be of great use to the forecaster when considering historic data to determine actual sales deviations away from the trend and then to analyze these deviations, determining how much is due to average seasonal factors, and how much is due to non-typical factors. Thus, it is possible to draw up a table indicating by how much, plus or minus, the actual sales figures are away from the trend. This is shown in Table 7.13.

In Table 7.13 columns 1, 2 and 3 show the quarterly sales figures, and also the trend line values as calculated in the previous example (Table 7.9). Column 4 denotes *actual* deviation values of sales away from the *appropriate trend* value. In column 5 these values have been converted into percentages of the *trend*. Column 6 shows mean quarterly seasonal deviation, the values of which were found by gathering all the percentage values for each quarter and finding the mean quarterly seasonal average, as in Table 7.14.

By repeating the averages shown in Table 7.14 for the appropriate quarters (column 6), they can be subtracted from the percentage sales deviation (column 5 in Table 7.13) to establish how much was due to average seasonal factors and how much was due to other random causes (column 7 in Table 7.13). It is particularly useful to establish these values as percentages rather than absolute values (although this could be done as well), because it permits more effective proportionate comparisons between periods. Although actual sales volume in one quarter might be down, the seasonal percentage value could still be correct in relation to other quarters'

Table 7.13 *Analysis of sales data by trend, mean seasonal deviation and random factors*

1	2	3	4	5	6	7
Year and Quarter	Sales in £000s	Trend	Sales away from the trend	Sales dev (as a % approx)	Mean quarterly seasonal dev as a % approx	Other random factors (as a %) (5 – 6)
19X3 2	34	31.86	+ 2.14	+ 6%	+ 4%	+ 2%
3	29	32.72	– 3.72	– 11%	– 13%	+ 2%
4	35	33.58	+ 1.42	+ 4%	+ 2%	+ 2%
19X4 1	36	34.44	+ 1.56	+ 5%	+ 5.5%	– 0.5%
2	37	35.3	+ 1.7	+ 5%	+ 4%	+ 1%
3	31	36.16	– 5.16	– 15%	– 13%	– 2%
4	37	37.02	– 0.02	0%	+ 2%	– 2%
19X5 1	40	37.88	+ 2.12	+ 6%	+ 5.5%	+ 0.5%
2	39	38.74	+ 0.26	+ 1%	+ 4%	– 3%

*Table 7.14 Showing the method for obtaining the
mean quarterly seasonal average*

Year	Quarters			
	1st	2nd	3rd	4th
19X3	–	+ 6%	– 11%	+4%
19X4	+ 5%	+ 5%	– 15%	0%
19X5	+ 6%	+ 1%	–	–
	2) + 11%	3) + 12%	2) – 26%	2) + 4%
	+ 5.5%	+ 4%	– 13%	+ 2%

seasonal percentage values in the rest of the year. This is particularly so of luxury or semiluxury items for which consumers may reduce their purchases if incomes fall, rather than staple or necessity items which will be the last to suffer a cut in demand. Further, there is often a need for a company to maintain its share of a market. Therefore, if the market is contracting, it is obviously wise to consider the percentage the company holds in two different periods rather than absolute amounts. The same applies to the percentage sales deviation, percentage mean quarterly average and other random factors as a percentage. It becomes possible to compare these values *of the trend* no matter what the basic absolute values happen to be.

The quarterly seasonal percentage values are also of use in further predictions of sales where the probability control limits ($\pm$ 2 seasonal deviations) are rather wide because of seasonal fluctuations. For example, it is possible to convert the mean quarterly percentages, + 5.5 per cent, + 4 per cent, – 13 per cent, + 2 per cent (Table 7.14) into their relationship to the trend. If the trend line is considered as 100 per cent, then the 1st quarter seasonal percentage being + 5.5 per cent can be read as 105.5 per cent of the trend line value. The 2nd quarter seasonal percentage being + 4 per cent can, therefore, be read as 104 per cent; the 3rd quarter seasonal percentage being –13 per cent can be read as 87 per cent of the trend line (ie 100 per cent – 13 per cent); and the 4th quarter seasonal percentage being + 2 per cent can be read as 102 per cent of the trend line. This is shown graphically in Figure 7.9. Notice here that the vertical axis is a percentage of trend; the trend being shown horizontally at 100 per cent.

Taking the trend line as shown in Figure 7.5 and projecting it into the 3rd and 4th quarters of 19X5 and on to the 1st and 2nd quarters of 19X6, it is then possible to seasonally adjust and plot estimated sales by multiplying by the appropriate quarter seasonal

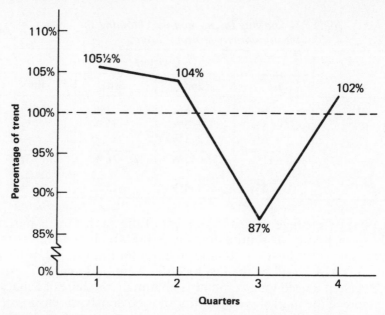

Figure 7.9 *Mean quarterly seasonal averages shown as percentages of a trend line*

percentages shown in Figure 7.9. The relationship of the actual sales, actual and projected trend line and the estimated seasonally adjusted sales are shown in Figure 7.10.

The seasonally adjusted projected sales trend is calculated as shown in Table 7.15.

Table 7.15 *Calculation of seasonally adjusted trend line*

1	2	3	4	5
		Projected trend reading	**Quarterly seasonal percentage**	**Seasonally adjusted sales trend (3 × 4)**
Year	**Quarter**			
19X5	3	38.75	87	33.7
	4	40.6	102	41.4
19X6	1	41.5	105.5	43.8
	2	42.5	104	44.2
	3	43.25	87	37.6

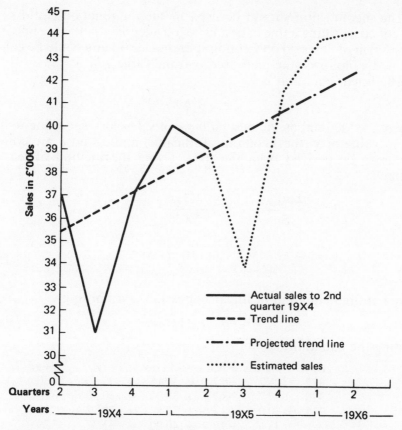

Figure 7.10 *The seasonally adjusted projected trend line after the mean quarterly seasonal averages have been applied*

This method of seasonal adjustment can be applied to any method of straight line projection, eg moving averages shown later in Figures 7.32 and 7.33.

Least squares method using non-time-constrained data

In the section on correlation and regression analysis (page 155), a least squares regression line was fitted to a scatter diagram (Figure 7.3, Line A-B). On the vertical axis was the dependent variable, ie 'Sales of Product A' and on the horizontal axis was the independent variable 'Economic Indicator'; thus the data was not of the time series type as in the examples of the least squares method used so far. The absence of the time factor means that the device of the 'assumed mean quarter' or other time period used to calculate the regression line in the examples so far cannot be used.

The method that should be used in such a situation could be described as 'fitting a line of best fit' to a scatter diagram or the linear regression of Sales (y) on Economic Indicator (x) and could be calculated as follows (the data used is from Table 7.3).

The linear equation is:

$$\hat{y} = a + bx$$

where $\hat{y}$ is defined as the best *estimate* of sales corresponding to a given value of x (the Economic Indicator) and a and b are constants to be derived from the data. Using the method of least squares:

$$b = \frac{\Sigma(x_{dev}y_{dev})}{\Sigma x_{dev}{}^2} = \frac{3533.6}{29056} = 0.1216$$

and

$$a = \bar{y} - b\bar{x} = 36.8 - (0.1216)\,(374)$$
$$= -8.7$$

The required equation of linear regression is accordingly:

$$\hat{y} = -8.7 + 0.1216x$$

Fitting the equation:

x	y	-8.7	$+0.1216x =$	$\hat{y}$	$(y-\hat{y})^2$
322	25.7	−8.7	+ 39.15 =	30.45	22.56
320	27.7	−8.7	+ 38.90 =	30.20	6.25
311	30.0	−8.7	+ 37.82 =	29.12	.77
329	33.6	−8.7	+ 40.00 =	31.30	5.29
358	36.9	−8.7	+ 43.53 =	34.83	4.28
363	38.2	−8.7	+ 44.14 =	35.44	7.6
379	39.6	−8.7^2	+ 46.08 =	37.38	4.9
390	38.6	−8.7	+ 47.42 =	38.72	.0144
430	42.7	−8.7	+ 52.29 =	43.59	.79
446	43.7	−8.7	+ 54.23 =	45.53	3.34
466	48.1	−8.7	+ 56.66 =	47.96	.01
11)4114	404.8*	−95.7	+500.22	= 404.52*	55.8
374					

*These two totals should agree, but there is a small error caused by the calculation process.

If the basic data is expressed graphically by plotting the relevant pairs, a scatter diagram is evolved. A line of best fit can then be added by picking a value of $\hat{x}$, eg 322, and identifying the corresponding value $\hat{y}$, ie 30.45, and plotting it; in the diagram that is shown as point A. It is then necessary to pick another value of x at the other end of the series, eg 430, together with its corresponding value of $\hat{y}$, ie 43.59, and again plotting it; in the diagram this is shown as point B. Points A and B are then joined, resulting in a line of best fit to the basic data (Figure 7.3).

It is worthwhile going forward to calculate the 'standard error of the regression'. First find the 'error sum of squares'. This is defined as

$$(1 - r^2)\,(\Sigma y_{dev}^2)$$
$$= (1 - 0.945^2)(485.66) = 51.77$$

The 'regression sum of squares' is accordingly

$$485.66 - 51.77 = 433.89$$

The 'analysis of variance' may be illustrated by the familiar 'Pythagoras' diagram as follows:

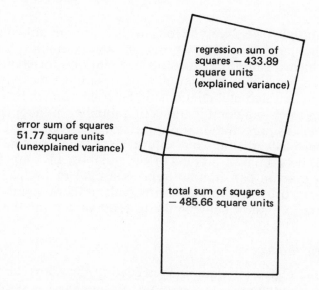

regression sum of squares — 433.89 square units (explained variance)

error sum of squares 51.77 square units (unexplained variance)

total sum of squares — 485.66 square units

The standard error of the regression equation is then found as

$$\sqrt{\left[\frac{\text{error sum of squares}}{n-2}\right]} = \sqrt{\left[\frac{51.77}{11-2}\right]} = 2.4\,\text{units}$$

The standard error is used in the following way:

If x is, say, 430, the best estimate of y is 43.59 (see table on page 184). But this is an estimate only, subject to a standard error of 2.4 units (distributed normally) and following the convention of 2 standard errors, for a value of x of 430 the value of y lies within the limits of 43.59 plus and minus (2×2.4), ie between 38.79 and 48.39, with approximately 95 per cent probability (the 19 in 20 chance).

Regression — summary

Simple regression

It will be seen from examples on pages 152–166 that simple regression is effected where a linear relationship of the form $y = a + bx$ is assumed and the parameters of a and b are constants (estimated). The factor x can be any variable including time (see page 168) which makes it a time series, or an economic indicator (see page 153) which makes it a causal model. On the other hand, y represents the variable to be forecast, eg sales, costs, profits, market share or some other factor where the outcome depends upon some variation in x.

Multiple regression

By using multiple regression the forecast is based not only on past values of the item being forecast, but on other variables that are thought to have a causal relationship (see multiple correlation on page 174). The multiple regression method determines the existence of some form of functional relationship between a dependent variable such as sales and combinations of a number of independent variables such as gross national product, total consumer expenditure, company advertising expenditure, retail sales, prices, price differentials between own product prices and those of competitors. Multiple regression can handle trend, seasonal or cyclical type data, and can provide confidence intervals, tests of significance and measures of best fit between the forecast values and the data.

Econometric models

Basically, the regression equations needed in the above methods are part of econometrics. An econometric model is a system of simultaneous regression equations which by their nature depend upon each other and therefore their parameters need to be estimated in a simultaneous manner. Thus an econometric model that a company might develop of its industry/market would include several equations to be solved simultaneously. Econometric models are primarily used for forecasting macro-economic series such as gross national product, total consumer expenditure, prices, investment, etc, but they can also be used effectively to forecast the sales of large organizations whose very size influences (to some extent), and is directly influenced by, the activity of a national economy.

The use of probability in forecasting

It is often advisable to calculate the statistical probability of any forecast being correct. But the use of probability linked with the device of sampling is a further statistical sales forecasting tool.

The logic of sampling follows from the law of statistical regularity, which states that a sample group chosen at random from a larger group will tend to have similar characteristics. Sampling is based upon (a) the principle of probability, determining the possible margin of error as to whether the sample is typical of the whole population; (b) the principle of random numbers, that is, to be representative of the whole population the sample must be unbiased and the randomness of the sample ensured; (c) the law of the inertia of large numbers, which shows that the larger the sample the greater the chance of cancelling out errors and minute changes, and thus the average group tends to remain the same.

The tendency to 'normal' distribution

In dealing with consumer populations it must be remembered that, although each individual has his or her own characteristics, preferences and dislikes, there will be, in a large population, a grouping around a central point indicating common opinions or behaviour patterns, preferences and dislikes. The tendency for the distribution of certain data to be grouped around a central point gives a regular, bell-like, symmetrical pattern, or frequency distribution curve, that indicates what is termed a 'normal' distribution. In the ideal normal distribution situation the data either side of the central position varies from the actual mean or middle value by chance alone and, therefore, tails off equally on either side. For example, the heights of a group of men chosen at random tend towards the normal frequency curve pattern when set out by height values (Figure 7.11).

The vertical axis in Figure 7.11 shows the frequency at which values occur and on the horizontal axis the values themselves — height, or it could be weight, costs, opinions, survey data, etc. The point of central tendency, giving the peak of the curve, is a particular statistic that represents the middle or central value of a whole series of observations and consequently, due to the intensity or number of the values around this point, dominates the whole series. There are various measures of central tendency — the median, the mode, the geometric mean, the harmonic mean, but the one that is relevant in sampling is the *arithmetic* mean.

The arithmetic mean is the average value (x) found by dividing

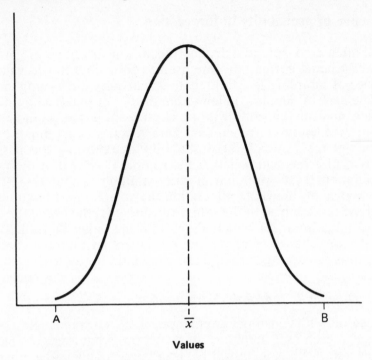

Values

Figure 7.11 *A hypothetical normal distribution curve*

the sum total of the values of items by the number of items. It is the most commonly used because it is simple to derive, it is relatively reproducible, it lends itself readily to further mathematical treatment, and represents the most simple arithmetic link between the total of a series of items and the number of items involved. It has the disadvantage that it can be influenced by non-typical extreme items, but in spite of this it is the most useful measure of central tendency for the examination of consumer populations and samples taken from them.

Returning to the normal frequency curve which is an ideal, theoretical distribution, a data series is often assumed to be of this pattern in examining markets when the overall distribution is not known but appears to be influenced by chance factors alone. Alternatively, this assumption may be made when the data series is derived from a number of similar sized but unconnected factors. In both cases the validity of the assumption may be assessed by contrasting the frequency distribution in question with the ideal normal frequency curve. It will be noted that except for the items that fall exactly on the mean (x) a number of items in decreasing frequencies fall at distances either side, and thus deviate from the mean to form such a curve. On the graph these were contained within the limits of A-B. The scatter of these items about the mean is important — because of their make-up and frequency they may indicate why they are not average. It is also important when considering a market, to know how many persons in the selected population (ie potential customers) are not average and how often they are likely to occur.

The standard deviation and probability

The arithmetic mean has been termed 'a measure of central tendency'. A single statistic describing the scatter of the different items either side of the mean is termed 'the measure of dispersion'. The most commonly used measure of dispersion is the standard deviation indicated by the sign σ (sigma). A particularly useful feature of a normal distribution is that, if its arithmetic mean and the standard deviation are known, it is possible to predict the percentage of that distribution expected to fall between certain limits thereby enabling a forecast to be made (Figure 7.12).

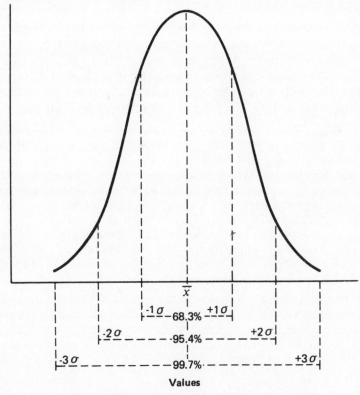

Figure 7.12 *A hypothetical normal distribution curve analyzed in terms of the dispersion of standard deviation around the mean*

From a normal distribution of the type shown in Figure 7.12, it can be seen that:

68.3 per cent of the items lie within the range ± 1 σ about the mean
95.4 per cent of the items lie within the range ± 2 σ about the mean
99.7 per cent of the items lie within the range ± 3 σ about the mean

Similarly for an actual sample, if it is truly representative of the whole population, items falling beyond ± 1 σ would occur approximately five times in every 100; and items falling outside the ± 3 σ limits only three times approximately in every 1,000 items, when projected to cover the whole statistical population.

If the forecaster can build up a sample that is representative of the whole statistical population or universe, it will be possible to make decisions and reach conclusions about the measurements (if it is a continuous series such as the heights of men or sizes of shirts), or the opinions, habits, behaviour and reactions of the whole population.

Relevant frequency distributions

A number of samples chosen at random from a particular population will each have its own arithmetic mean, and, if plotted on the same graph, all the sample means will tend to have the normal frequency distribution described above. The three types of frequency distributions with which the examination of markets is concerned in statistical sampling have been summarized[1] as follows:

(a) Universe, the total of all measurements; that is, the total population. Since the frequency distribution of the universe is not known, it is approximated by a
(b) Random sample, which is a small-scale representation of the universe, with characteristics (such as mean, median, or standard deviation) approximately the same as those of the universe. If many random samples are drawn from a given universe, the frequency distribution of the means of all these samples would be a
(c) Distribution of sample means. This distribution tends to be normal, even though the other two are not normally distributed, and it has less dispersion than the other two.

The standard deviation indicates the spread or dispersion of the individual items in a distribution about their mean. The distribution of sample means has a standard deviation of its own which is different from the standard deviation of the universe and the standard deviation of an individual sample. In order to distinguish it from the others,

1. McNair, Brown, Leighton & England *Problems in Marketing* 2nd ed 1957. McGraw-Hill Book Co. USA.

this standard deviation of the sample means is called the standard error. The standard error is used to estimate the probabilities associated with inferences made concerning the universe. These probability statements are based on the known fixed relationships for a normal distribution.

Calculating the standard deviation

However, before considering the standard error in detail it would be useful to examine the standard deviation and its application. The standard deviation is a root-mean-square deviation, that is, it is found by taking the square root of the sum of the squares of the deviations from the mean divided by the number of items.

The standard deviation is given by the formula:

$$\sigma = \sqrt{\left[\frac{\Sigma (x - \bar{x})^2}{n}\right]}$$

where
$\sigma =$ standard deviation
$\Sigma =$ summation sign (the sum total of)
$x =$ value of the item
$\bar{x} =$ arithmetic mean
$n =$ number of items

The above formula is precise when the values for the whole population are available. However, when the standard deviation of the population has to be estimated from the frequencies of a sample, the direct application of this formula introduces a bias; then the best estimate of the population standard deviation is derived by using $(n - 1)$ as the divisor. Thus the formula would read:

$$\sigma = \sqrt{\left[\frac{\Sigma (x - \bar{x})^2}{n - 1}\right]}$$

Where n is greater than 30, n and not $n - 1$ is used as the divisor. To give a simple example, supposing certain values (heights, sizes, etc), that for the sake of simplicity can be called 1, 2, 3, 4 and 5, were found to occur four times, eight times, twelve times, eight times and four times respectively in a given sample, the data for calculating the standard deviation would be found by setting up a table: Table 7.16.

Using the data from Table 7.16:

$$\sigma = \sqrt{\left[\frac{\Sigma f(x - \bar{x})^2}{n - 1}\right]} = \sqrt{\left[\frac{48}{36 - 1}\right]}$$

$$= \sqrt{\left[\frac{48}{35}\right]} = \sqrt{(1.371)} = 1.17 \text{ approx}$$

Table 7.16 *An analysis of data to permit the calculation of the standard deviation*

x Values	f Frequency	$(x-\bar{x})$ Deviation from mean	$(x-\bar{x})^2$ Deviation squared	$f(x-\bar{x})^2$ Frequency multiplied by deviation squared
1	4	-2	4	16
2	8	-1	1	8
3	12	0		
4	8	1	1	8
5	4	2	4	16
5)15	36			$48 = \Sigma f(x-\bar{x})^2$
$\overline{3} = \bar{x}$				

If the sample was representative of the population, it will be found that values falling outside the range $\pm 2\sigma$ in this case the arithmetic mean of $3 \pm (2 \times 1.17)$, ie outside the values of -0.96 and 6.4 are likely to occur only five times in every 100 values observed.

Such a statistical technique is of use in marketing research, forecasting and in marketing generally. It has many applications where the data to be processed is measured in units, lengths, costs, weights, or sizes, etc. For instance, it can be used in forecasting to decide how many of each size of a product to manufacture within a range. For example, it can be used in the manufacture of shirts, so that the range of sizes marketed and the numbers in each size will cover anticipated consumer demand. Further, it can be used in stock control to ensure that the correct proportions of a range of sizes are carried in stock. Also it can be used in complaints analysis and in connection with the expected life of a product in product development analysis, ie to make a prediction for the size of a replacement market, and in many other forecasting areas.

The make-up of the normal distribution curve

The normal distribution curve is sometimes referred to as a probability curve because it is possible to calculate from it the probability of obtaining a given number of items within a specified 'values' range in an actual statistical population.

In other words, the area under the whole of the actual frequency or probability curve is considered equal to 1 if working in decimal fractions (or 100 per cent if using percentages), and it is possible to calculate for what probable fraction of the statistical population

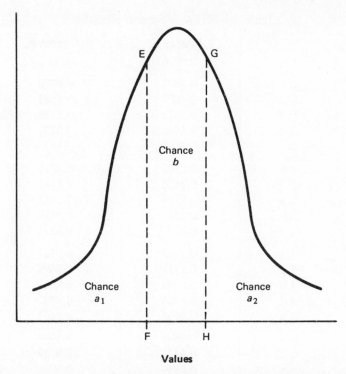

Figure 7.13 *A normal distribution curve showing the relationships between a1, a2 and b values*

certain values occur. For example, in the case of a shirt manufacturer, it could be predicted how any of his potential customers would be catered for if he marketed only sizes 15½ to 16½. The technique is to calculate the fractions or parts of the area of the normal frequency curve between the stated limits.

It should be noted that the lines E-F and G-H in Figure 7.13 are movable inwards towards the mean or outwards away from it, according to the size of the area required. Further, it must be realized that as the lines E-F and G-H are movable, the more they move towards the centre (the mean), the smaller chance b will become whilst chance a_1 and a_2 will become larger, simply because $b + a_1 + a_2 = 1$ or 100 per cent. Normal frequency probability tables have been compiled to indicate the variations in the size of b, a_1, a_2 in relation to the number of standard deviations from the arithmetic mean (Table 7.17).

In Table 7.17 z = the number of standard deviations from the arithmetic mean. Chance b = the probability of a value falling between given limits (z standard deviations) either side of the arithmetic mean. Chance a = the probability of a value falling to

193

Table 7.17 *Table of normal probability*

z	Chance *a*	Chance *b*
0.0	0.5000	0.0000
0.1	0.4602	0.0798
0.2	0.4207	0.1585
0.3	0.3821	0.2358
0.4	0.3446	0.3108
0.5	0.3085	0.3829
0.6	0.2743	0.4515
0.7	0.2420	0.5161
0.8	0.2119	0.5763
0.9	0.1841	0.6319
1.0	0.1587	0.6827
1.1	0.1357	0.7287
1.2	0.1151	0.7699
1.3	0.0968	0.8064
1.4	0.0808	0.8385
1.5	0.0668	0.8664
1.6	0.0548	0.8904
1.7	0.0446	0.9109
1.8	0.0359	0.9281
1.9	0.0287	0.9426
2.0	0.0228	0.9545
2.1	0.0179	0.9643
2.2	0.0139	0.9722
2.3	0.0107	0.9786
2.4	0.0082	0.9836
2.5	0.0062	0.9876
2.6	0.0047	0.9907
2.7	0.0035	0.9931
2.8	0.0026	0.9949
2.9	0.0019	0.9963
3.0	0.0013	0.9973
3.1	0.0010	0.9981
3.2	0.00069	0.99862
3.3	0.00048	0.99903
3.4	0.00034	0.99933
3.5	0.00023	0.99953
3.6	0.00016	0.99968
3.7	0.00011	0.99978
3.8	0.00007	0.99986
3.9	0.00005	0.99990

the right or left of the mean and z standard deviations away or the probability of a value falling outside the chance b limits. It refers to only half the total chance a value as a_1 falls to the left of chance b, and a_2 to the right of it.

It was stated earlier that the measure of dispersion, ie the standard deviation, is measured along the horizontal axis (values). The column in Table 7.17, shown as z, represents the number of standard deviation from the arithmetic mean, and it should be noticed that parts of it can be considered, as well as whole standard deviations. The column 'Chance a' refers to the measurement of either chance a_1 or a_2 or beyond the number of standard deviations ($z \times \sigma$), away from the mean. The column 'Chance b' represents the probability of a value falling within the area b, ie between the two lines shown on the diagram (E-F and G-H).

With Table 7.17 the validity of some of the previous statements made can be checked. Previously it was stated that on a normal frequency curve there are, between ± 1 standard deviations away from the mean, 68.3 per cent of the values (ie 34.15 per cent to the left of the mean, and 34.15 per cent of the values to the right of it). Consult the normal frequency probability tables in column z, where $z = 1$ (ie 1 standard deviation ± the mean), and by reading across to column 'Chance b' the decimal fraction 0.6827; expressed as a percentage this becomes 68.27 per cent and this figure rounded to one decimal place will give a value of 68.3 per cent. Notice that chance b is relevant here (ie the central area of the curve) to show what percentage of the values occur between ± 1 standard deviation about the arithmetic mean.

Consider the chance a_1, a_2 and b values in Figure 7.14 and using the data shown earlier in Table 7.16 which examined the method of finding the standard deviation, the arithmetic mean was the value 3, and a standard deviation of 1.2 was calculated. Measuring along the horizontal 1.2 either side of the mean, the vertical line E-F and G-H in Figure 7.13 can be inserted. The chance b reading at $z = 1$ is 0.6827, the chance a reading for chance a_1 is 0.1587, and again for chance a_2 0.1587. Therefore, if these values are added the total will equal 1:

$$
\begin{array}{r}
0.6827 \\
0.1587 \\
\underline{0.1587} \\
\underline{1.0001}
\end{array}
$$

The odd 1/10,000th above 1 is due to the arithmetical make-up of the tables, and is justifiably small enough to round the overall value off and call it 1.

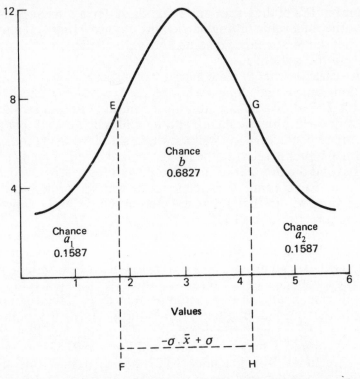

Figure 7.14 *A normal distribution curve with the chance b value considered as one standard deviation either side of the mean*

Forecasting demand using probability

A practical application of this technique could be seen if a possible forecasting problem of a shirt manufacturer is considered; it could apply, however, in any situation where a range of products is involved. The manufacturer may want to know the probability of demand for various sizes of shirts. Suppose he intends marketing a high quality and highly priced shirt. Because of the price, the demand for this type of shirt may be limited, but he has defined a group of potential customers (possibly by income group) to whom he knows this quality product will appeal, discovered possibly through a field survey. Suppose his potential market (total statistical population) is 100,000 men, and having taken a balanced sample of, say, 4,300 he discovers that the mean or average size is 16, and that there is a standard deviation of 0.5 (ie a ½-size in shirts). How many of his potential 100,000 customers will he cater for if he makes only the popular shirt sizes 15½, 16 and 16½? Thus, he will want to discover chance *b* as these sizes occur immediately around

196

the mean (16), one ½-size above the mean (16½), and one ½-size below the mean.

The formula required to answer this question is:

$$z = \frac{x - \mu}{\sigma}$$

where *x* is the value away from the arithmetic mean which is being considered and *z* is the standard normal deviate.

z and σ have already been defined (pages 189 and 193 respectively). Consider first size 16½:

$$z = \frac{16.5 - 16}{0.5} = \frac{0.5}{0.5} = 1$$

On the normal frequency tables it will be seen that where *z* = 1, chance *b* is 0.6827. But sizes 16 to 16½ represent only half the area of the total chance *b* value (15½, 16, 16½), therefore 0.6827 ÷ 2 = 0.34135.

Similarly, size 15½ also represents 0.34135 by the same calculation, and by adding the two halves the total chance *b* value is 0.6827 or 68.27 per cent.

It could be concluded that by making sizes 15½, 16 and 16½ the manufacturer will be catering for about 68 per cent of the 100,000, ie 68,000 men.

Situations arise where the chance *b* values do not fall evenly either side of the mean as above (sizes 15½, 16 and 16½). For example, retaining the same mean size, 16, and the same standard deviation, 0.5, suppose the same shirt manufacturer wanted to know how many more of his potential 100,000 customers he would cater for if, in addition to sizes 15½, 16, 16½, he added size 17 to his marketing range.

Chance *b* for size 15½ to the mean size 16 has
already been calculated as   0.34135

Chance *b* for the area covered by sizes 16, 16½
and 17 will be:

$$z = \frac{17 - 16}{0.5} = \frac{1}{0.5} = 2$$

On the table where *z* = 2, chance *b* = 0.9534.
This figure must be divided by 2 as 16 to 17
represents only ½ of the chance *b* value   0.47725

Total chance *b* for sizes 15½, 16, 16½ and 17   0.81860

Thus the size of his potential market when he makes sizes 15½, 16, 16½ and 17 will be 81.06% of 100,000, in other words	81860 men
The size of his potential market (taken from the previous example) when he makes sizes 15½, 16, and 16½ will be 68.27% of 100,000	68270 men
The number of extra potential customers by adding size 17 to his range will be	13590 men

Throughout this and the previous example, four places of decimals have been used and exact conclusions made (eg 13,590 extra potential customers) and this may be seen to give this technique a degree of precision that it would not possess in practice. It has been done to illustrate the method and the use of probability tables, and in the last part of the above example it might be more practical to use rounded values, ie 82,000 minus 68,000 indicates that there will be about 14,000 additional potential customers when the manufacturer adds size 17 to his range. This rounding of values allows for the fact that the practical curve can only approximate to the exact figures for the ideal theoretical normal curve. A further limitation of these hypothetical examples is that neck sizes of shirts are near-normal in their statistical distribution or pattern, whereas many marketing variables are not and therefore need different treatment.

Forecasting replacement demand with probability

The use of this technique can be developed further. Consider the situation where a manufacturer is concerned with the life of his product. He may need to forecast a replacement demand, or forecast the frequency at which consumers purchase the product, or assess the size of stocks required (either his own or his wholesalers or retailers). He may also need to consider (in relation to complaints-analyses) whether the number of reports concerning the life duration of the product are within the limits he should expect. The life of a product is often a good selling point, and favourable statistics regarding a product's durability make suitable advertising and sales promotion material. Further, the manufacturer may be concerned with the life of his product in relation to his product development policy. He may be considering improving the quality and consequently the life of the product, or competition may be forcing him to look at the existing product range. The usefulness of the statistical techniques concerning probability, the normal frequency curve and the standard deviation, can be gauged from the following example.

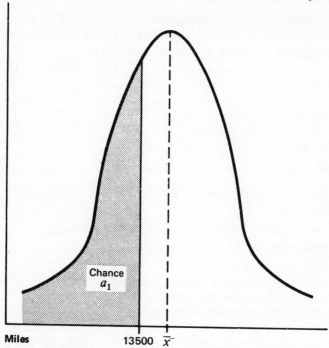

Figure 7.15 *Distribution curve showing the chance a_1 position on a normal distribution curve relating to the number of tyres that will fail before 13,500 miles*

A company manufacturing and marketing car tyres expects a mean running life per tyre of 15,000 miles with a standard deviation of 1,400 miles.

Of a batch of 10,000 tyres just produced how many can be expected to:

(a) fail before 13,500 miles?
(b) last beyond 17,000 miles?
(c) last between 14,000 and 16,200 miles?

Using the formula $z = \dfrac{x - \mu}{\sigma}$ The standard deviation has already been calculated as 1,400 miles. Therefore,

(a) How many fail before 13,500 miles? This will represent a chance a_1 as indicated in Figure 7.15.

$$z = \frac{15000 - 13500}{\sigma} = \frac{1500}{1400} = 1.071$$

On consulting the normal frequency tables it can be seen that the value 1.071 does not appear in column z. However, as value 1.071 is between 1.0 and 1.1 it is possible to discover the difference between the two in terms of chance a values, and 0.071 of this figure can be determined.

Where $z = 1.0$ chance $a =$	0.1587
(according to the tables)	
Where $z = 1.1$ chance $a =$	0.1357
By subtracting we find the difference	0.0230
Chance a value where $z = 1.0$ has already been found to be	0.1587
The chance a value of 0.071 where the difference between 1.0 and 1.1 is 0.0230, is 0.071 of 0.0230 =	0.016
Subtract as chance a values are falling between 1.0 and 1.1, and as 1.071 is 0.071 away from 1.0 the answer is bound to be smaller	0.1427

It can be predicted that 0.1427 or 14.27 per cent approximately of batch of 10,000 tyres, ie roughly 1,427 tyres, will fail before 13,500 miles.

(b) How many will last beyond 17,000 miles? This will be indicated as chance a_2 in Figure 7.16.

The value is calculated by determining how far 17,000 is away from the mean of 15,000, ie 2,000. Therefore,

$$z = \frac{17000 - 15000}{\sigma} = \frac{2000}{1400} = 1.428$$

Again this value does not appear in column z in the normal frequency probability tables. However, it is between 1.4 and 1.5:

Where $z = 1.4$, chance $a =$	0.0808
Where $z = 1.5$, chance $a =$	0.0668
Difference	0.0140
It has been shown that 1.4 has a chance a value of	0.08080
Further 0.028 of the difference 0.0140 is	0.0004
By subtraction (as the table values are falling) where $z = 1.428$, chance $a =$	0.0804

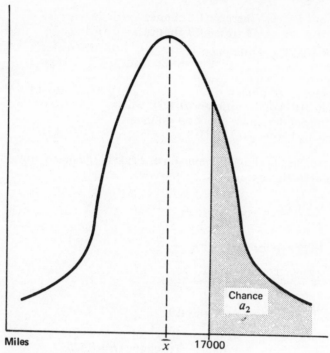

Figure 7.16 *Distribution curve showing the chance a_2 position on a normal distribution curve relating to the number of tyres that could be expected to last beyond 17,000 miles*

It can be predicted that 0.0804 or 8.04 per cent approximately of batch of 10,000 tyres, ie roughly 804 tyres, will last beyond 17,000 miles.

(c) How many tyres will last between 14,000 miles and 16,200?

To find this, chance *b* value is required, that is an area in the centre of the normal frequency curve, as indicated in Figure 7.17. But it will be noticed here that the values 14,000 and 16,200 are spread unevenly either side of the mean of 15,000 miles; and therefore the process will be in three stages. First, find the chance *b* value for the area to the left of the mean (14,000 to 15,000) and halve it, as it represents the chance *b* value below the mean only; secondly, find the chance *b* value for the area to the right of the mean (15,000 to 16,200) and then halve it; and thirdly, add the two halves, so:

(i) Therefore where $z = \dfrac{x-\mu}{\sigma}$

$$z = \frac{15000-14000}{\sigma} = \frac{1000}{1400} = 0.714.$$ This value is between 0.7 and 0.8

Where $z = 0.8$ chance $b = 0.5763$
Where $z = 0.7$ chance $b = \underline{0.5161}$
Difference $\qquad\qquad \underline{0.0602}$

It has been shown that $z = 0.7$
has a chance b value of $\qquad\qquad\qquad$ 0.5161
Further, 0.014 of the difference 0.0602 will be $\quad$ 0.0008
This time add because chance b values are $\qquad\quad \underline{}$
increasing between 0.7 and 0.8 $\qquad\qquad\quad$ 0.5169

However, as the chance b value on one side of the mean only is required, this figure must be halved:

$$\frac{0.5169}{2} = 0.2584 \text{ or } 25.84\%$$

(ii) Therefore where $z = \dfrac{x-\mu}{\sigma}$

$$z = \frac{16200-15000}{\sigma} = \frac{1200}{1400} = 0.857$$

this value is between 0.8 and 0.9

Where $z = 0.9$ chance $b = 0.6319$
Where $z = 0.8$ chance $b = \underline{0.5763}$
Difference $\qquad\qquad \underline{0.0556}$

It has been shown that $z = 0.8$
has a chance b value of $\qquad\qquad\qquad$ 0.5763
Further 0.057 of the difference 0.0556 will be $\quad$ 0.0031

Add because chance b values are increasing $\quad \underline{}$
between 0.8 and 0.9 $\qquad\qquad\qquad\qquad$ 0.5794

However, as the chance b value on one side of the mean only is required, this figure must be halved.

$$\frac{0.5794}{2} = 0.2897 \text{ or } 28.97\%$$

(iii) Stage three is to add together the results of parts (i) and (ii) above, so:

(i) $\quad$ 25.84%
(ii) $\quad \underline{28.97\%}$
$\qquad\quad \underline{54.81\%}$

It can be predicted that 54.81 per cent of the batch of 10,000 tyres, ie approximately 5481 tyres, will last between 14,000 and 16,200 miles.

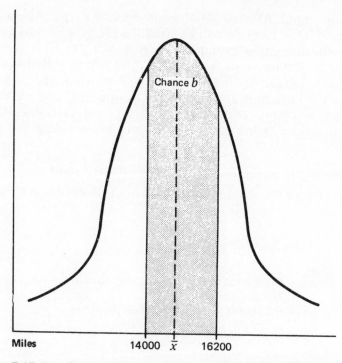

Figure 7.17 *Distribution curve showing the chance b position on a normal distribution curve relating to the number of tyres that could be expected to last between 14,000 and 16,200 miles*

The use of standard error

The usefulness of the measure of dispersion, the standard deviation, has been illustrated in the foregoing examples, but its usefulness is limited for purposes of sampling in marketing research and market and sales forecasting. To extend the usefulness of the standard deviation, the earlier statement regarding the standard error must be considered. It was stated that a number of samples chosen at random from a particular population will each have its own arithmetic mean, and if these means are plotted on the same graph, they will tend to assume the shape and distribution of a normal frequency curve, and will have their own arithmetic mean. This averaging method removes the bias that may be given by extreme items to the arithmetic mean of only one random sample. Obviously, the greater the number of sample means, the more accurately it will reflect the characteristics of the statistical population as a whole. The standard error therefore is the standard deviation of the normal curve obtained from plotting the arithmetic means of a number of sample distributions. The formula used for the calculation of the standard error will depend upon the type of data being considered. One formula will be used for the type of data considered in the foregoing examples, heights of men, sizes of shirts, mileage life of tyres, costs, weights, etc, and will be called *measured or continuous data.* Another formula will be used when the data concerned relates to proportions such as opinions and answers to questions, or counts and observations, in field survey work, and this data will be called *enumerated or proportional data.*

Calculating the standard error from measured data

The formula for the standard error (*SE*) of the distribution of sample means is:

$$SE\,(m) = \frac{\sigma}{\sqrt{n}}$$

Where *SE* (*m*) = the standard error of the distribution of the
sample means
σ = the standard deviation of all the items
in the population
n = the size of the sample

Often the standard deviation of all the items in the population is not known and in such a case the standard deviation of the individual sample is used as the nearest estimate. Consider a forecasting situation where the height of men was important. Suppose from a large population of men a sample of 100 was taken, and their heights measured. An average height of 70 inches was calculated and the standard deviation was 5 inches.

$$SE\,(m) = \frac{\sigma}{\sqrt{n}} \quad = \frac{5}{\sqrt{(100)}} = \frac{5}{10} \quad = \frac{1}{2}\,\text{inch}$$

If other samples of 100 men and women are taken from *the same population,* their averages would tend to be normally distributed about the mean of the whole population with a standard error of ½ inch. It could be concluded, therefore, that the *sample mean* of 70 inches had a 68.3 per cent chance (see Figure 7.14) of being within ± ½ inch (one standard error) of the *population mean* and a 68.3 per cent chance that the population mean would be within the range of 69½ inches to 70½ inches (70 ± ½ inch). Further, there would be a 95.4 per cent chance that the population mean would be within the range of 69 inches to 71 inches (ie ± 2 standard errors), and a 99.7 per cent chance that it would be within the range 68½ inches to 71½ inches (ie ± 3 standard errors) or conversely it would be likely to fall outside these latter limits only three times in 1,000 samples.

Calculating the standard error from enumerated data

The previous formula would be of little use where the data to be processed represents a choice of two alternatives as opposed to a series of continuous measurements. Market research techniques are often necessary in forecasting where there is an absence of historic data or where projections from historic data need to be confirmed. For example, in field survey work using questionnaires or observational techniques the collected data will in many cases fit into one of two alternatives. For example, the answers to survey questions may be 'yes' or 'no'; 'I would buy it' or 'I would not buy it'; 'I use it' or 'I don't use it'; 'I use brand X' or 'I use other brands'; 'good' or 'bad', etc. Market research and forecasting is often concerned with proportions or percentages of populations and samples, where those interviewed answer one way or the other. Where the data can only be one of two alternatives, one would be designated as p and the other as q; p indicates the existence of a certain opinion, attribute, action, habit, or characteristics, etc, q indicates the absence of it. The probabilities of getting either answer can be estimated and certain calculations are based on these probability values. Probability can be expressed on a scale 0 to 1 (or 0 per cent to 100 per cent); 0 implying that the event is certain not to occur (or that all the answers to a survey question will be 'no'), and 1 (or 100 per cent) implying that the event is certain to occur (or that all the answers will be 'yes'). Therefore, the formula $p + q = 1$ (or 100 per cent) will apply where a certain number (p) of respondents answer in one way and the remainder (q) answer another way. For example, if the answer to an interviewer's question was either 'yes' or 'no', and 60 per cent of his sample answered 'yes' (p) and 40 per cent answered 'no' (q), 60 per cent plus 40 per cent would equal the total sample, therefore $p + q$ must always equal 1 or 100 per cent.

It was stated earlier that the standard error is the standard deviation of the means of a number of samples, and obviously if the data was assembled from a number of different samples taken from *the same population*, it could not be expected that the proportions would be exactly the same in each case. However, supposing there was a need to forecast product acceptance. A product testing survey was carried out using a sample of 3,000 housewives and 1,800 said they would use the product being tested. Further, if many samples of 3,000 were taken from the same population it would be found that the percentage of the sample answering 'yes' would fluctuate, and the data could be listed as in Table 7.18.

Table 7.18 *The distribution of sample results around their own mean*

	Percentage answering 'yes'	Frequency (no of times occurred)
	63%	2
	62%	4
	61%	6
mean =	60%	8
	59%	6
	58%	4
	57%	2

If the data in Table 7.18 were plotted on a graph it would be found that it would approximate to the pattern of the normal frequency distribution curve. In fact, the greater the number of times that the population was sampled, the more definite would become the pattern of the normal curve. But to carry out such a great number of samplings would cost much in time and money, and in any case is unnecessary, because by determining the standard error of the sample, the proportions of the sample can be projected to the population as a whole within certain stated limits. It can be seen, therefore, that even when using proportions or percentages, the rules of normal frequency probability will apply because, in practice, random samples will tend to approximate to the normal frequency distribution curve. These rules can be used and applied to the individual case.

The standard error for enumerated or proportional data is given by the following formula:

$$SE\,(p) = \sqrt{\left[\frac{pq}{n}\right]}$$

where $SE\,(p)$ = the standard error of the proportion
p = the proportion of items indicating the existence of a certain opinion, attribute, action, habit, etc
q = the proportion of items where the above characteristics are absent

To illustrate this formula, take a simple situation where there is a total statistical population of 1,000 persons. The forecaster could be interested in these particular people because they have a unique combination of characteristics (age, sex, status, income, etc) which possibly makes them potential customers for a company's product.

On making up a representative sample of 180 and interviewing them, 30 answer 'yes' and 150 answer 'no' to a particular question on product use. How many persons in the total population could be expected to say 'yes' and what degree of error is likely?

$$SE\,(p) = \sqrt{\left[\frac{pq}{n}\right]} = \sqrt{\left[\frac{30 \times 150}{180}\right]} = \sqrt{(25)} = 5 = SE$$

If the extreme case is taken and 3 × standard error is calculated, so that it is possible to predict with confidence that in only three cases out of 1,000 will items fall outside these limits (see Figure 7.12), it will be found that 3 × standard error is 3 × 5 = 15. The number of persons in the sample of 180 who answered 'yes' was 30. As the sample is subject to fluctuation and bias, this must be allowed for by expressing the number as plus or minus 3 × standard error, ie 30 + 15. If 3 × standard error is considered in relation to the population it will be found:

$$\frac{1000\ (\text{ie size of population})}{180\ (\text{ie size of sample})} \times 15\ (\text{ie } 3 \times SE) = 83$$

It could be predicted, therefore, that the number of people in the whole population saying 'yes' would be:

$$\frac{30}{180} \times 1000 = 167 \pm 83$$

Therefore, it could be expected that the number of persons in the population answering 'yes' to the question could be as high as 250 and as low as 84 with 99 per cent confidence.

An application of the standard error in forecasting

Take a further example of a forecasting situation where a company is product testing a new toothpaste in an area where there are 50,000 housewives (the specialized statistical population). A random sample of 3,000 housewives is taken and they are given free samples which they are asked to use. Out of the sample, 1,800 housewives say they will buy the product. What is the smallest number of housewives in that area likely to buy the product?

$$SE\,(p) = \sqrt{\left[\frac{pq}{n}\right]} = \sqrt{\left[\frac{1800 \times 1200}{3000}\right]} = \sqrt{(720)} = 26.83$$

ie approximately 27

$$3 \times SE = 3 \times 27 = 81$$

This should be 'grossed up' to cover the whole statistical population, ie

$$\frac{50000 \text{ (ie total population)}}{3000 \text{ (ie sample)}} \times 81 = 1350$$

The value $3 \times SE$ in relation to the population would be:

$$\frac{1800}{3000} \times 50000 = 30000 \pm 1350$$

It therefore follows that it would be possible to say with 99.7 per cent confidence that, providing basic conditions do not alter, the number of housewives likely to buy the product could be as high as 31,350 and as low as 28,650.

Occasions arise in marketing research and forecasting, due to psychological factors, when the results obtained in the last example might not be true, due to consumer bias in answering whether they would buy the toothpaste or not. This might well be due to a subconscious human reaction — having received a gift (the sample), they want to do something in return for their benefactor and so pronounce in favour of the product, but later have no intention of buying it. An unbiased method of testing must, therefore, be found. Further, it might also be desirable to compare the product with those of competitors. Both these points might well be satisfied by a 'blind test', where samples of the new product and those of competing companies are placed in blank containers and lettered for identification. Taking the same sample size as before, 3,000 housewives, it might be found that:

Sample coded X (a competitor's) preferred by 1,000 housewives.
Sample coded Y (our new product) preferred by 1,400 housewives.
Sample coded Z (a competitor's) preferred by 600 housewives.

In which case it would be necessary to calculate, as before, for each sample (there may be more than three), to obtain an unbiased judgement, to determine the strength of competition (at relatively little extra cost) and to obtain the potential maximum and minimum sales in each case, so:

$$X = \sqrt{\left[\frac{1000\,(Y + Z)}{3000}\right]}$$

$$Y = \sqrt{\left[\frac{1400\,(X + Z)}{3000}\right]}$$

$$Z = \sqrt{\left[\frac{600\,(X = Y)}{3000}\right]}$$

By carrying through the calculation as in the previous example, it would be possible to determine for each brand the highest and the lowest number of housewives likely to demand it.

Time series analysis and historical analogy

Examination of relationships of variables that make up sales data over a period of time is referred to as time series analysis. A good starting point for company sales forecasting is the plotting of sales data on a time series graph. By doing this the stark mass of figures assume a visual shape; seasonal patterns and general trends can can be discerned and consequently deviation from them investigated. For example, the sales history of a particular product could be listed as in Table 7.19.

When plotted on a time series graph, the data in Table 7.19 would assume the graphical shape shown in Figure 7.18. Unless something happens in the market to change the situation drastically, it could be assumed that a similar sales pattern to that in Figure 7.18 will emerge in 19X5 and a rough freehand forecast could be made on this alone. However, an examination of the graph will raise certain questions, the answers to which may influence the forecast.

Table 7.19 *A four-year tabular history of the sales of product A in £000s*

Month	19X1	19X2	19X3	19X4
January	120	140	80	50
February	140	170	200	190
March	200	180	170	180
April	280	240	220	200
May	230	280	260	300
June	320	340	360	370
July	380	370	410	410
August	420	460	490	510
September	310	380	420	540
October	270	300	390	560
November	380	420	500	550
December	460	540	620	720

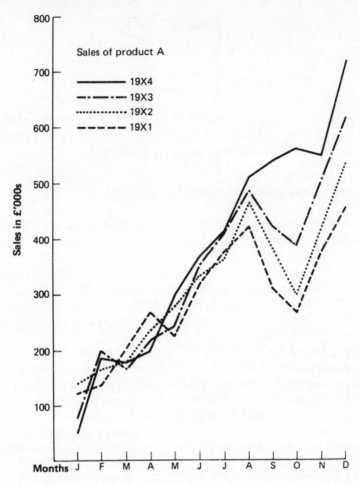

Figure 7.18 *A four-year graphical history of the sales of product A*

For example, why is there a tendency over the last two years for the January values to decline but to be preceded by increased December sales figures? What happened to the 'usual' seasonal decline in sales in September and October 19X4? Is the new pattern for these months likely to become permanent? Investigation of unusual factors reveals important indicators for future sales periods.

In the above example, sets of monthly sales data for four years were superimposed, but a further method of graphically presenting time series data is sequentially, ie monthly, quarterly or yearly data can be presented 'end-on' as in Figure 7.19. Presentation in this way enables trends to be identified and extrapolated through a variety of techniques.

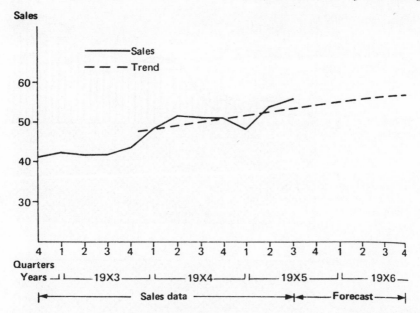

Figure 7.19 *Time series data presented sequentially together with straight line trend projection forecast*

The old cliché that history repeats itself is often very true in consumer/user demand, in the same sense that certain demand patterns for products and/or services tend to recur from time to time. Some markets are more stable than others and if a recurring demand pattern can be identified its use in forecasting is considerable. Even if a particular month's sales one year may be higher or lower than the same month the previous year, it is possible that its overall seasonal pattern can be relied upon.

To attempt to evolve a new forecast using the 'total sales' approach is one method of using time series data. Others take the form of breaking down the time series data into separate component parts. Then each component part is projected to give a forecast and then all these component forecasts are added in the projected forecast period to give a new 'total' forecast. In this way greater accuracy is often achieved because the influence of the separate individual component parts is allowed for.

One such method of analysis is shown in Figure 7.20 which 'decomposes' a time series into deseasonalized sales, trend and seasonal variations. Later, in the analysis of time series by the moving average method (page 240), a further component group is identified; it is that of 'random variations' or the erratic component. These values are relatively small parts of the sales total that cannot be attributed to any of the components mentioned above.

211

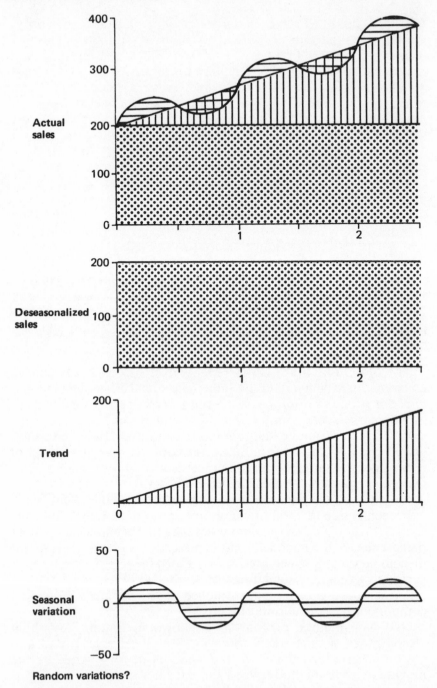

Figure 7.20 *The 'decomposition' of sales data into the component parts of seasonal variations, trend, deseasonalized sales and random variations*

They are caused through either the erratic effects on 'once only', non-typical situations or by the very small beginnings of changes in trend or seasonal patterns. Because of their randomness, it is impossible to show them as a pattern in Figure 7.20. However, they are often considered in time series analysis to permit more accurate forecasting of the various other components. In fact the degree of randomness within this time series data will often affect the forecaster's accuracy in prediction. As a general rule, accurate time series forecasting is possible where there is a low level of randomness and a good, stable, systematic pattern in the other components. The opposite is true where there exists a high degree of randomness (see Figure 7.21).

There is a further component part of sales data that is often identified; it is that of the cyclical pattern. This is sometimes referred to as the medium-term business cycle. There are many types of medium-term business cycles; these are demand and related patterns that appear to operate in cycles over a two- to five-year time span.

One often used for forecasting purposes is the inventory medium-term cycle; the general level of stocks in an industry

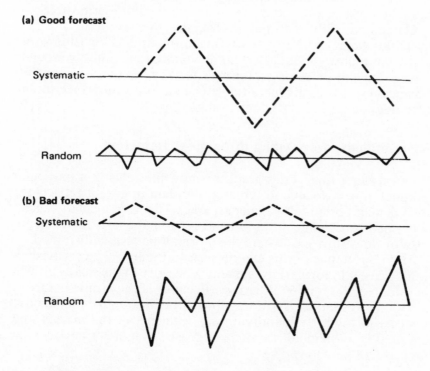

Figure 7.21 *The impact of the level of randomness on forecasts*

builds up in one period and then tends to fall in another. For example, the usage of steel indicates a two- to three-year medium-term cycle. This cycle is found by recording *actual* stocks on a regular basis. Stock figures are obtained by relating tonnage shipments from the steel mills or imports, a plus factor, to the tonnage consumption by steel users, a minus factor. This latter data is obtained from published data on activity in steel-consuming industries. This method is often refined by adding a further factor regarding *normal* inventory and relates to the ideal tonnage of steel that 'consumers' would like to have in stock. This tonnage is roughly a supply of steel sufficient for three months' output of manufactured units, and is determined by demand for the manufactured end product. Normal stocks, therefore, have no relationship to steel physically on hand, but are hypothetical; fluctuating with changes in the attitude of business men and in business conditions.

One machine tool company has found that the medium-term business cycle has revolved once every four to five years since the early 1970s in their particular part of the market. This company uses medium-term business cycle data not only for forecasting purposes, but also for the effective launching of new or improved products, which, after allowing for seasonal influences, are launched just before the up-swing of the medium-term cycle.

Compared with seasonal cycles, the medium-term business cycle fluctuates more irregularly in timing and swing (this varies also from industry to industry) but in some cases relatively accurate forecasting can be achieved through it. Whether the medium-term business cycle is easily identifiable or not, some allowance should be made for it in general forecasting.

More effective forecasting through segmentation

When using a time series graph to show the sales of a particular product, it is advisable to research the data in case it reflects the total demand of a multi-segment market. This is particularly necessary when unaccountable movements occur in the sales curve (an up-turn or down-turn), or where the 'normal' pattern is disrupted.

The importance of this can be seen in Figure 7.22. Obviously it will be easier to forecast in segment A because of the steady growth of sales over a number of periods. Because of the erratic nature of the total sales curve, it will be more difficult to make an effective forecast in total. By identifying the segments of the market and developing individual segment forecasts, a more accurate total forecast is likely to evolve.

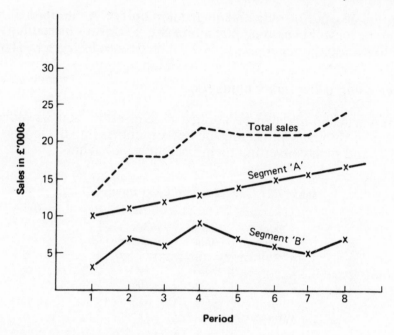

Figure 7.22 *A total sales curve analyzed in terms of individual market segments to permit more effective product forecasts*

Forecasting by percentage change

One simple method of projecting actual sales data into future sales periods is by the percentage change method, that is if the nature of data permits this. By taking known sales data over a number of past periods and determining the percentage increase or decrease over the previous data item, it may be possible to discern a progressive pattern. A simple example is shown in Table 7.20.

Table 7.20 *Sales data and percentage increase/decrease*

Sales period	Sales data	Percentage increase/decrease
1	40.0	—
2	42.0	+5%
3	44.5	+6%
4	47.5	+7%
5	51.3	+8%

In the absence of radical change taking place in the market, it would be logical to assume that a forecast of sales for period No 6 would be approximately 56, ie 51.3 + 9 per cent of 51.3 = 55.917.

Forecasting using index numbers

A similar technique can be applied by converting actual values into index numbers, projecting the index numbers into the forecast period and then converting them back to actual values.

Table 7.21 *Sales data and index numbers*

Sales period	Sales data	Index number
1	5020	100
2	5321	106
3	5773	115
4 (forecast)	—	125

The Index number of 100 is attributed to the sales period No 1. The sales values of periods 2 and 3 are related to this base of 100 giving index numbers of 106 and 115. If the three values (100, 106, 115) are projected forward a forecast index number of 125 is obtained. If this value is related to 5020 = 100 the forecast value of 6275 is obtained.

Simple trend projection allowing for seasonal factors

One of the simplest ways of effectively projecting monthly/quarterly sales data which contains a seasonal element is to deseasonalize the past sales data, project forward the deseasonalized sales trend line into the forecast period and then reseasonalize the projected values. This method is based on the fact that it is often easier to project the straighter line of deseasonalized sales data than the actual sales values containing a seasonal element which makes its pattern more erratic.

The method of calculating an appropriate seasonal factor for each month is to find the monthly average for the last year by totalling all monthly sales data and dividing by 12. The seasonal factor for each month is then calculated, using last year's data, as follows:

$$\frac{\text{sales data for a particular month}}{\text{monthly average for the year}}\% = \frac{\text{January 60 units}}{\text{average 50 units}}\% = 120\%$$

This monthly seasonal factor is then used to deseasonalize last year's monthly sales data and after the deseasonalized data has been projected forward into the forecast period, the forecasted values on this line are reseasonalized by multiplying them by the monthly seasonal factor.

A way of calculating a quarterly seasonal factor is shown in Table 7.14; it is applied to a projected line of best fit in Table 7.14. Quarterly sales data can be deseasonalized, extrapolated and reseasonalized easily by this method.

Another method is to calculate cumulative quarterly seasonal patterns. This is done by converting monthly sales into quarterly totals for each year and then considering these totals as a percentage of the total for the year (see Table 7.22).

Table 7.22 *Calculations for quarterly seasonal sales patterns*

		19X2		19X3		19X4	
Quarters	Months	Sales	%	Sales	%	Sales	%
1	Jan Feb Mar	790	16	750	14	720	13
2	Apr May June	1160	23	1140	22	1170	20
3	July Aug Sept	1510	30	1620	30	1760	30
4	Oct Nov Dec	1560	31	1810	34	2130	37
		5020	100	5320	100	5780	100

The percentages are then plotted on one of four graphs; one for each quarter as in Figure 7.23. They are then projected to the point of the forecast year, 19X5, and the projected percentage values read off. Therefore if the total sales forecast for 19X5 were 6358, the predicted trend of the quarterly seasonal pattern would be:

19X5 Quarter 1 predicted percentage 12% ie	763
19X5 Quarter 2 predicted percentage 18% ie	1144
19X5 Quarter 3 predicted percentage 30% ie	1908
19X5 Quarter 4 predicted percentage 40% ie	2543
	6358

217

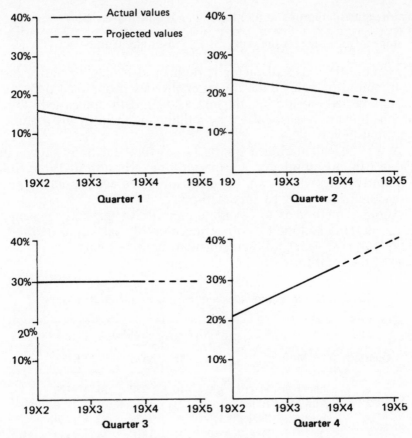

Figure 7.23 *Cumulative quarterly seasonal graphs — actual and projected values*

Forecasting market share and competitor activity

Many sales forecasting techniques are based on the analysis and projection of trends, based on actual volume (units) and/or value (cash). A further method is to plot past market shares and project the trend; this method brings to light certain influential forecasting factors and underlying trends not revealed by other methods.

Market share should be viewed as a multi-dimensional concept, based on the variety of ways in which markets can be measured.

Therefore, the first stage is to identify relevant segments of markets, and then identify the company's share of each.

For example, the market for a consumer goods product can be measured and segmented by total volume, by product type, by total market including alternatives, total cash value, consumer profile, (ie age, sex, socio-economic group, occupation, urban/rural dwellers, etc), type of retail outlet, geographic area, size of product unit, etc.

A consumer durable market can be measured in terms of total volume, model type, sterling value, use by men and/or women, total market to include substitutes, consumer profile, buyers versus users (the gift market), type of retail outlet, socio-economic groupings, geographic areas, etc.

An industrial product market can be measured by total volume, total market to include substitutes, total value, by industry profile (based on Standard Industrial Classification), by user type, geographic area, etc.

In each market segment above, a company's market share can be calculated, analyzed and projected forward as a forecast. If the same procedure is carried out for a number of segments, the speed and influence of various underlying forecasting factors can be identified and the forecast can be weighted accordingly. Also, as the 'residual' market share must be competitors' share, this is an ideal way of monitoring activities and projecting competitive trends.

An example is given in Figure 7.24 where the market for an anti-depressant pharmaceutical product has been measured and segmented in eight different ways. Each of these market segments may be developing at different speeds, and by identifying the company's market share in each segment in recent history a projected forecast may be based on each. It will also be possible to weight certain market segments if it is thought that they have a greater influence on overall sales. Also, the speed of the company's growth/decline in a particular segmented market can be identified and allowed for not only in forecasting but in other aspects of market strategy.

For example, in Figure 7.24 a 20 per cent of turnover share (cash) compared with a 32 per cent share of the volume (prescription share) could suggest that the product was under-priced. Also a 16 per cent total doctor share compared with a 38 per cent patients' share could indicate that only a relatively small percentage of doctors have been 'converted', but that, once convinced, they become heavy prescribers, or that the medical condition needing this form of treatment is concentrated in certain geographic areas. Whatever the case, it has implications for marketing sales strategy.

If market shares of various market segments can be obtained over recent periods and graphed, a diagram such as Figure 7.25 will be obtained. The market is segmented by value (cash) and by volume (units) and the market shares are shown for all products in the particular product class. The important thing to recognize is that, no matter how large or small the market is in terms of value/volume,

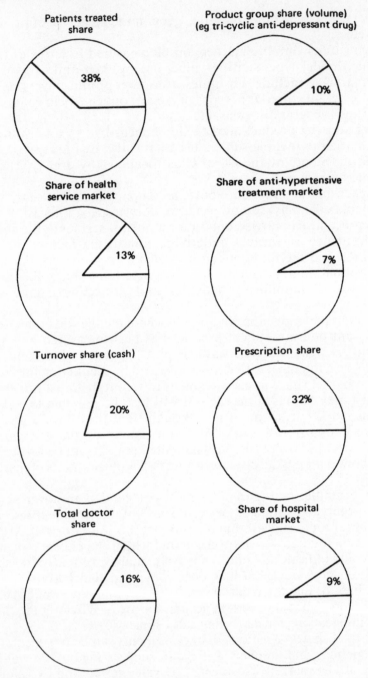

Figure 7.24 *Eight segments of a market for a pharmaceutical product*

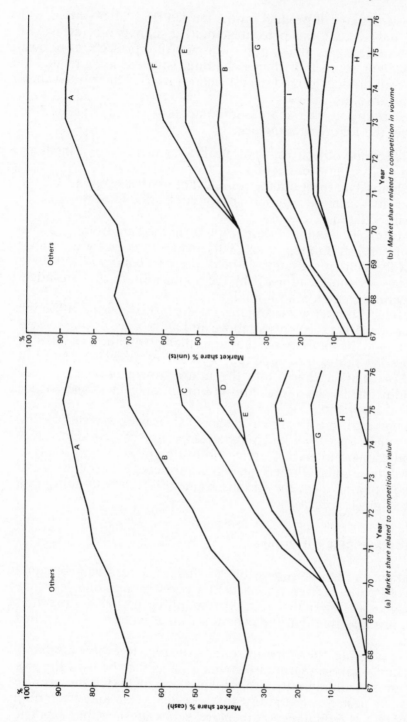

Figure 7.25 *Market share related to competition in value and volume*

the total amount of product on the market from all suppliers will equal 100 per cent; this percentage market share can be measured on the vertical axis at any point in time. After projections of own company or competitor shares, the forecast needs to be related to an overall product group forecast when converted back into value/volume absolute values.

Forecasting market share and competitor activity can best be done in the following sequence:

1. Determine objectives, what market segments to use, methods of analysis and projection.
2. Obtain data for a number of relevant market segments for the last five years sales periods, or for any period less than this, for which data is available.
3. Arrange in tabular and/or graph form the data from (2) above and project into the future. This gives a forecast for a number of the market segments defined in a particular way but these may need to be adjusted by the application of human judgement, experience, and intelligence.
4. Collect company sales figures for the last five years within the same market segments as above and relate sales by market segment to the total sales at that time, thereby obtaining a series of market shares. For each market segment project the trend of these market shares into the future. Again these may need adjusting by the application of human judgement, experience and intelligence.
5. Convert all predicted market share values back to actual values, eg units, tons, £s etc and make a comparison of these values. Any adjustment to market strategy following market share analysis will need to be allowed for. When variances between them can be explained, use the various segment forecasts to build up a composite forecast.

Percentage take-off graphs

In some markets it is possible to discern a recurring seasonal demand pattern. Even if a particular period's sales one year may be higher or lower than the corresponding period the previous year, it is possible that the overall seasonal pattern can be relied upon.

It is possible, therefore, in some industries to evolve a reliable percentage take-off graph to enable a forecast to be used for production scheduling purposes. This is done by taking the average sales per period over the last three to four years and converting them into a cumulative percentage series as in Table 7.2. The

Table 7.23 *The analysis of data to permit the development of a percentage take-off graph*

Bi-weekly period	Average sales per period over last 3 years £000s	Cumulative total	Cumulative percentage (rounded)
1	15	15	1.5%
2	20	35	3.5%
3	20	55	6.0%
4	20	75	8.0%
5	30	105	10.0%
6	50	155	16.0%
7	75	230	24.0%
8	70	300	31.0%
9	60	360	37.5%
10	50	410	42.5%
11	40	450	48.0%
12	35	485	50.5%
13	20	505	52.5%
14	10	515	53.5%
15	10	525	54.5%
16	15	540	56.0%
17	25	565	59.0%
18	40	605	63.0%
19	60	665	69.0%
20	75	740	77.0%
21	70	810	84.0%
22	65	875	91.0%
23	40	915	95.0%
24	25	940	98.0%
25	15	955	99.5%
26	10	965	100.0%

cumulative percentage is the expression of the cumulative total as a percentage of the total average sales for the period, ie 15 is approximately 1.5 per cent of 965.

From the data in Table 7.2, two graphs can be drawn. One to show the seasonal pattern, Figure 7.26, and the other from which can be read the percentage of total sales that can be expected to be sold by a particular time period, Figure 7.27. This latter percentage can then be applied to the *current* total forecast for the year.

If the sales shown are ex-factory sales, then production controllers can read from the graph, eg 40 per cent of the *current* year's forecast must be produced by the 19th week of the year (ie 9½ bi-weekly periods). If the sales data represents retail sales then an appropriate lead time must be added to allow the product to pass through the channels of distribution. The percentage take-off graph is often used in forecasting production scheduling in men's clothing and footwear, but can be used in any situation where the seasonal pattern varies little from year to year.

Further, if a reliable total forecast for a particular year can be obtained then the take-off graph will indicate the percentage of this figure that could be expected to be sold at various sales periods (bi-weekly periods in Figure 7.27).

Sometimes forecasters are required by management to forecast the sales for the next financial year well ahead of the commencement of that year. For example, where a forecast is required for a financial year commencing 1st January, the forecaster is asked to produce it six months earlier, perhaps in the previous August. The percentage take-off graph enables the forecaster to project sales data to the end of the current year so that with a 'total' sales figure prediction for the current year the forecaster can make a better forecast for the next financial year.

If at the end of the first 12 weeks of the current year, ie six bi-weekly periods on the horizontal axis (Figure 7.27), it is indicated on the vertical axis that 20 per cent should be sold by the end of that period, then, as there are 5×20 per cent = 100 per cent, the actual sales achieved for the first 12 weeks in volume/value is multiplied by 5 and this will provide the forecaster with a total forecast for the current year. Thus if the actual sales for the first 12 weeks is £10,000 then the total for the current year, using data in Figure 7.27, could be expected to be £50,000 ($5 \times$ £10,000).

Moving Annual Totals and Moving Quarterly Totals

An organization may record sales in value or volume terms either daily, weekly, monthly or quarterly. Sales thus recorded can show considerable variations and can mask trends. A longer interval tends to show a reduction in variation because time has a 'smoothing' effect. The benefit of the smoothing effect of longer periods can be obtained by identifying a suitable period (day, week, month, quarter, year) and using this on a continuous basis.

A moving total is obtained by adding the value for the most

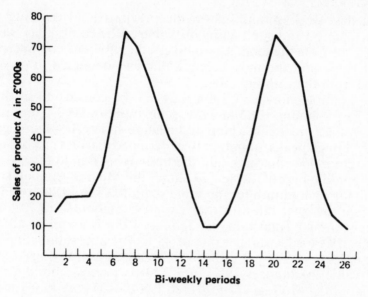

Figure 7.26 *A time series graph of sales of product A*

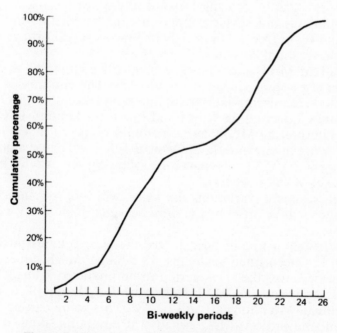

Figure 7.27 *Percentage take-off graph for sales of product A*

225

recent day, week, month, etc to the previous total covering the selected period and subtracting the value of the earliest day, week, month, etc, from the total. Alternatively, the difference between the oldest value and the most recent value can be added to or subtracted from the running total.

The example shown in Table 7.24 can be considered in three parts. The columns 19X3 to 19X6, sales input in £000's, represent monthly sales producing a graphical relationship as shown in Figure 7.28. Although peaks, troughs and certain peculiarities can be seen, the diagram does not highlight the underlying trend of sales.

The middle part of Table 7.24 shows the Moving Annual Total (MAT) for each month for the same years 19X3 to 19X6. It will be seen that the total sales for the year 19X3 amounted to 707. The Moving Annual Total value for January 19X4 is found by adding January 19X4 sales input value of 48 to 707 and subtracting the January 19X3 sales input value of 28, giving a new Moving Annual Total value for January 19X4 of 727. This process continues for February 19X4 MAT, ie 727 + 70 (Feb 19X4) — 53 (Feb 19X3) giving 744.

As the process suggests, it is a Moving Annual Total because it moves by incorporating a new month and ejecting the oldest value. In effect the MAT is a value which always contains 12 months sales history. Also by moving forward adding in the latest value and dropping the oldest value, it does not matter whether the year covers January to December or July to June — it will always contain all the seasonal variations in sales.

When all the MAT values have been calculated they can then be plotted on a graph as shown in Figure 7.29. The continuous line shows that an increasing sales trend line from December 19X3 has changed into a decreasing sales trend line from January 19X5.

When interpreting MAT charts it should be noted that a large upwards swing in one month, eg October 19X4, will cause a downward swing of the MAT sales curve the following year when a more normal level of sales occurs.

Normal seasonal variations in sales will not be indicated because they will be offset by the same seasonal high or low of the previous year.

In Figure 7.29 a line of best fit (see the least squares method, page 168) has been fitted to the last 13 months' MAT values and then projected over the sales period to be predicted. Thus where the last sales input and MAT values are for March 19X6, a 12 months ahead MAT forecast will be 888. This value can be read straight off the projected line because at any point along it will contain 12 months' sales history.

Table 7.24 *Showing sales, Moving Annual and Quarterly Totals*

	Sales Input in £000's				Moving Annual Totals in £000's				Moving Quarterly Totals in £000's			
	19X3	19X4	19X5	19X6	19X3	19X4	19X5	19X6	19X3	19X4	19X5	19X6
January	28	48	60	60	—	727	1078	964	—	140	225	202
February	53	70	60	72	—	744	1068	976	—	154	214	201
March	78	129	100	97	—	795	1039	973	159	247	220	229
April	30	92	91	—	—	857	1038	—	161	291	251	—
May	54	90	91	—	—	893	1039	—	162	311	282	—
June	55	101	76	—	—	939	1014	—	139	283	258	—
July	95	96	95	—	—	940	1013	—	204	287	262	—
August	71	80	76	—	—	949	1009	—	221	277	247	—
September	85	79	98	—	—	993	987	—	251	255	269	—
October	66	116	75	—	—	993	987	—	222	275	249	—
November	56	71	73	—	—	1008	989	—	207	266	246	—
December	36	94	69	—	707	1066	964	—	158	281	217	—

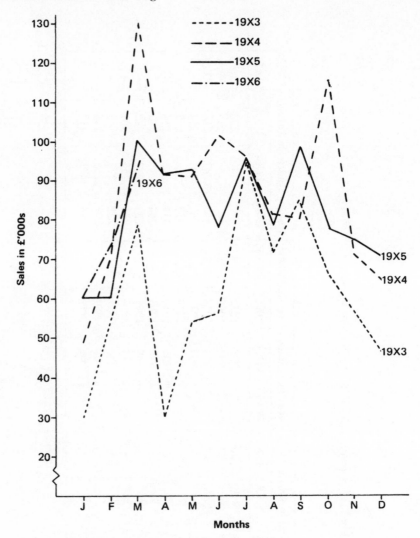

Figure 7.28 *Monthly sales superimposed annually*

The Moving Quarterly Totals are calculated in a similar way and are shown on the right hand side of Table 7.24. Being a Moving Quarterly Total the time interval is three months instead of the 12 months for MATs. Because MQT totals cover a shorter period they reflect seasonal changes in sales more readily, and consequently MQT lines will not smooth the sales variations to the same extent as MATs.

The calculations are simply that a total for three months is taken. January, February, March 19X3 values are 28 + 53 + 78

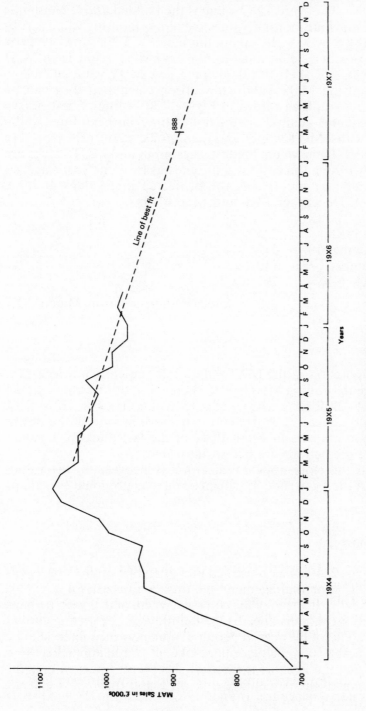

Figure 7.29 *Moving Annual Totals*

229

which gives the MQT value of 159 shown in that section against March 19X3. The April 19X3 value is then added and because this then contains four months' values the oldest monthly value is subtracted, ie 159 + 30 − 28, giving the new MQT for April 19X3 as 161. This process is continued for the next MQT value, ie 161 + 54 (May 19X3) − 53 (Feb 19X3), giving a new MQT value of 162.

When all the MQT values have been calculated they can be plotted on a graph as shown in Figure 7.30. A line of best fit (see the least squares method), ie the dotted line, has been fitted to the last 13 months' MQT values and then projected over the period to be predicted. Thus, where the last sales input and MQT values are for March 19X6 a forecast for four quarters (ie a one year forecast) can be made by identifying the projected line values at June, September, December 19x6 and March 19x7.

June 19X6	223
September 19X6	215
December 19X6	210
March 19X7	207
	855 = forecast for year ending Match 19X7

Conclusion

The extrapolation of the MAT values line indicates a forecast for the 12 months ending March 19X7 as 888. But this would mean an average of 222 for the MQT projected values (ie 4 × 222 = 888). This would appear to be difficult to achieve in view of the downwards trend and the fact that three of the last four MQT values before the predictions are below that value.

It would, therefore, appear that a forecast between the two values of 888 (MAT forecast) and 855 might be more appropriate — perhaps 870.

The Z chart

Earlier (page 224) it was suggested that often one of the forecaster's problems is that management requires a forecast for the next financial year well ahead of the commencement of that year, perhaps as much as six months ahead. One technique for projecting current sales to the end of the year to permit a more informed forecast to be made for next year is the percentage take-off graph; another is the Z chart. In fact the Z chart method of short-term forecasting is the combination of the percentage take-off graph (page 222) and the Moving Annual Total (page 224).

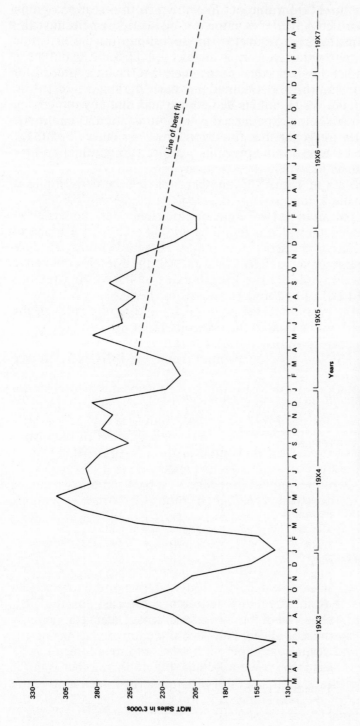

Figure 7.30 *Moving Quarterly Totals*

231

The name arises from the fact that the pattern on such a graph forms a rough letter Z. For example, in a situation where the sales volume figures for one product or product group for the first nine months of a particular year are available, it is possible, using the Z chart, to predict the total sales for the year, ie to make a forecast for the next three months. It is assumed that basic trading conditions do not alter, or alter on an anticipated course and that any underlying trends at present being experienced will continue. In addition to the monthly sales totals for the nine months of the current year, the monthly sales figures for the previous year are also required and are shown in Table 7.25.

From the data in Table 7.25, another table can be derived and is shown as Table 7.26.

The first column in Table 7.26 relates to actual sales; the second to the cumulative total which is found by adding each month's sales to the total of preceding sales. Thus, January 520 plus February 380 produces the February cumulative total of 900; the March cumulative total is found by adding the March sales of 480 to the previous cumulative total of 900 and is, therefore, 1,380.

The Moving Annual Total is found by adding the sales in the current month to the total of the previous 12 months and then subtracting the corresponding month for last year.

For example, the Moving Annual Total for 19X1 is 7,310 (see

Table 7.25 *Monthly sales for the first nine months of a particular year together with the monthly sales for the previous year*

Month	Year	
	19X1 (£'s)	19X2 (£'s)
January	940	520
February	580	380
March	690	480
April	680	490
May	710	370
June	660	390
July	630	350
August	470	440
September	480	360
October	590	
November	450	
December	430	
Total sales 19X1	7310	

Table 7.26 *Processed monthly sales data, producing a cumulative total and Moving Annual Total*

Month 19X2	Actual sales (£s)	Cumulative total (£s)	Moving Annual Total (£s)
January	520	520	6890
February	380	900	6690
March	480	1380	6480
April	490	1870	6290
May	370	2240	5950
June	390	2630	5680
July	350	2980	5400
August	440	3420	5370
September	360	3780	5250

Table 7.25). Add to this the January 19X2 item 520 which totals 7,830, subtract the corresponding month last year, ie the January 19X1 item of 940 and the result is the January 19X2 Moving Annual Total, 6,890.

The Moving Annual Total is a particularly useful device in forecasting because it includes all the seasonal fluctuations in the last 12 months period irrespective of the month from which it is calculated. The year could start in June and end the next July and contain all the seasonal patterns.

The three groups of data, actual sales, cumulative totals and the Moving Annual Totals shown in Table 7.26 are then plotted on a graph as shown in Figure 7.31.

In Figure 7.31 the cumulative data line and the Moving Annual Total line are projected from their September positions (points A and B), along a line that continues their present trend to the end of the year where they meet. The 12 months' accumulation of sales figures is bound to meet the Moving Annual Total as they represent different ways of obtaining the same total. In Figure 7.31 these lines meet at £4,800, indicating the total sales for the year and forming a simple and approximate method of short-term forecasting.

Often the cumulative data line and the Moving Annual Total line are so straight that projection can be effected by using a ruler. However, occasionally it is necessary to superimpose a line of best fit to enable a realistic projection to be made.

Further, there are occasions when the two projected lines do not converge at the 12 months point, either joining before or after that point. This can happen because the data available in, for example, September for the Moving Annual Total contains three months from the previous year and nine months from the current year. The three months' data of last year may cause the MAT line to be higher or lower than the cumulative data would indicate because this latter data contains only the nine months relating to the current year. Where the two lines do not converge at the twelfth month point the method is to open or close the projected lines equally until they meet exactly at the twelfth month point thereby indicating a forecast value.

It could be argued that the Z chart is only of use when the MAT line and the cumulative data is over six months into a year. This is based on the need to have an adequate number of data items (perhaps six months) to fit a reliable line of best fit and project it to the end of the year. It would be difficult to obtain a reliable line of best fit on one, two or three pieces of data.

However, to ensure that this technique can be used all the year round the concept of the 'rolling' Z chart has been brought into use. In Figure 7.31 the Z chart commenced in January with nine months' data to September which was then projected to December. A month later it would be possible to carry out another three-month projection by starting a new Z chart in February with data to October and projecting it to the end of January in the next year. As each month's sales data became available, a new Z chart would be started one month later, thus giving the forecaster a continuous short-term forecast.

The Z chart is suggested later (see page 339) as a means of monitoring forecasts and comparing the forecasted Z chart value with the previously budgeted figure.

Moving averages

A simple method of forecasting is the use and projection of the moving average. This considers past sales data in tabular and/or graphical form and determines a trend which can be projected into the future.

The moving average method tends not to give a completely straight trend line but smoothes out any wide fluctuations in a sales data curve. For example, a three period moving average could be calculated from monthly sales data as shown in Table 7.27.

The moving total (column 3 in Table 7.27) was explained in calculations for the Z chart (see page 230), and the moving average (column 4 in Table 7.27) is calculated by dividing the moving total by the number of items it includes, in this case three periods (24 + 26 + 27 = 77 ÷ 3 = 25.6). Trend differences (column 5 in Table 7.27)

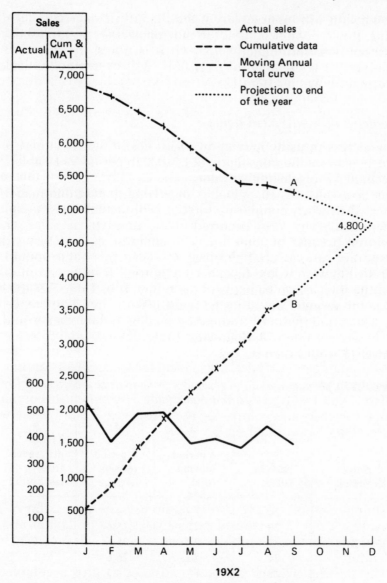

Figure 7.31 *A Z chart of monthly sales for 19X2*

are obtained by considering the increase or decrease of the current moving average with the previous moving average.

In Table 7.27 the forecast for period 13 can be obtained by taking the latest moving average and adding twice the value of the latest trend difference, ie

$$32 + (2 \times 2.7) = 37.4$$

Subtraction will be necessary if the trend difference is a negative value. It will be noticed that the moving average and trend difference columns terminate at item 11. It is necessary, therefore, to multiply the latest trend difference by 2 to overcome the lack of information against item 12.

Problems of non-typical items

A weakness in using moving averages lies in the effect of a non-typical item, eg the sales figure of £26,000 in period 9 of Table 7.27. Mechanical forecasting will not make an allowance for this relatively low value. Often, valuable underlying market information is revealed if, when comparing forecast with actual sales, it can be determined why this occurred. If a non-typical sales value occurred because of some unusual situation, eg a factory strike, temporary raw material shortage, etc, then this value should be adjusted to what would have been a 'normal' level to permit more realistic forecasts to be made in the future. If in Table 7.28 the low value for period 9 was adjusted to £30,000, the trend difference for the last period (period 12) would be smaller and the data would be as shown in Table 7.28. Following Table 7.28, the sales forecast for period 13 would then become

Table 7.27 *Calculation of a three period moving average and trend difference from sales data*

1 Sales period	2 Sales in £000s	3 3 period moving total	4 3 period moving average	5 Trend difference from last period
1	24	—	—	—
2	26	77	25.6	—
3	27	77	25.6	0
4	24	80	26.6	+1.0
5	29	85	28.3	+1.7
6	32	91	30.3	+2
7	30	93	31.0	+0.7
8	31	87	29.0	−2
9	26	87	29.0	0
10	30	88	29.3	+0.3
11	32	96	32.0	+2.7
12	34	—	—	—
13	*	*	*	*

*Forecast required for this period

$$32 + (2 \times 1.4) = 34.8$$

Sometimes non-typical, non-recurring items inflate the moving average, and downward adjustments to values can be made to allow for this. A further disadvantage of the moving average method is found when the market situation changes radically and suddenly, eg sales increase by 50 per cent. It will take a number of periods (depending on the base number used in the calculation) before the average comes within an acceptable range of actual sales figures again. It follows, therefore, that this method of forecasting is more effective with gradually increasing or gradually decreasing data.

If forecasts are consistently low or high, allowance should be made by adding or subtracting an appropriate percentage.

Moving average projection

If the moving average trend line is superimposed on the basic sales data, a trend can be discerned and projected into the future as in Figure 7.32. Notice the inclusion of the forecast for period 13 — one adjusted to allow for the appearance of a non-typical item.

Broad trend projections as indicated in Figure 7.32 are useful for medium- and long-term forecasting. A short-term forecast for the next sales period is best calculated by the tabular method (shown in Tables 7.27 and 7.28), or by seasonally adjusting a straight-line projection, described earlier (see page 179).

Table 7.28 *Re-calculation of the last part of Table 7.27 following the adjustment necessary due to a non-typical item*

Sales period	Sales in £000s	3 period moving total	3 period moving average	Trend difference from last period
7	30	93	31.0	+0.7
8	31	91	30.3	−0.7
9	30 Adj	91	30.3	0
10	30	92	30.6	+0.3
11	32	96	32.0	+1.4
12	34	—	—	—
13	—	—	—	—

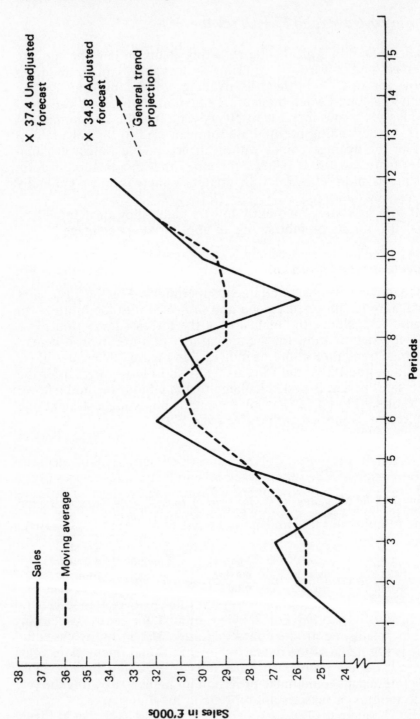

Figure 7.32 *A three period moving average and projection*

Moving averages and cyclical trends

In the data shown in Table 7.27, a cyclical pattern appears to be emerging. In period 4 the upward pattern of the previous periods is reversed and sales dropped 11 per cent from period 3. In period 9 the upward pattern of the previous periods has also reversed and sales dropped 13 per cent from period 8. This type of cyclical reverse would, based on past data, be due to appear again around period 14, and a detailed examination of the underlying factors (seasonal or medium-term) would be necessary to determine the probability of this happening again.

While in the preceding example the moving average is calculated on a three period base, it could be calculated on any number of periods — months, quarters, years, etc, depending upon the data and the requirements of the forecast.

As a general rule a reasonably straight moving average line indicates a recurring cyclical pattern, ie values above the trend line compensate for similar total values below the line. In Figure 7.32 the fact that the moving average trend line is rather erratic indicates a very weak cyclical pattern on a three period basis.

However, if the same data were used to calculate a five period moving average it would produce Table 7.29 and Figure 7.33.

In Figure 7.33 the relative smoothness of the five period moving average line shows that a cyclical pattern exists, possibly coinciding with seasonal fluctuations or the medium-term business cycle found in many industries. It would be of greater use in forecasting if the straight line projection was adjusted to reflect the cyclical pattern.

In fact, this is one way of determining the length of the medium-term business cycle in a market: take industry sales figures over a 10 year period and experiment with moving averages of differing time periods (3, 5, 7, etc) until a reasonably straight moving average line is found and this time period tends to represent the industry's medium-term business cycle.

Seasonal fluctuations and the moving average

In most industries, while an annual sales total is a good general indicator, it is often not detailed enough for many forecasting requirements, eg production scheduling, and in many cases full use is not made of the data available. Seasonal fluctuations often present quite a problem in sales forecasting and, where possible, the forecaster should make provision for them by dividing the year into months or seasons appropriate to his industry.

If the pattern of sales for a particular year was as shown in Figure

Table 7.29 *Calculation of a five period moving average*

Sales period	Sales in £000s	Five period moving total	Five period moving average
1	24	—	—
2	26	—	—
3	27	130	26.0
4	24	138	27.6
5	29	142	28.4
6	32	146	29.2
7	30	148	29.6
8	31	149	29.8
9	26	149	29.8
10	30	153	30.6
11	32	—	—
12	34	—	—
13	—	—	—

7.34, then seasons made up of the values for December, January and February followed by March, April, May, etc would highlight the seasonal pattern more than the calendar quarters of January, February and March followed by April, May and June.

Compare:

Calendar quarters	**Seasonal quarters**
J F M 12	D J F 10
A M J 18	M A M 20
J A S 12	J J A 10
O N D 18	S O N 20

Trend, seasonal and random variation (decomposition) analysis through moving averages

Further, having allowed for a seasonal variation, the forecaster should be able to distinguish more easily between those variations attributable to the seasonal pattern, and those attributable to other random influences. The presence of other random factors would warrant investigation to determine whether they were merely isolated cases or were likely to recur. The moving average method of fitting a trend line to seasonal data and discovering seasonal and random variations could be shown by developing an analysis of the type shown in Table 7.30. This is known as a decomposition technique (see also page 211 and Figure 7.20).

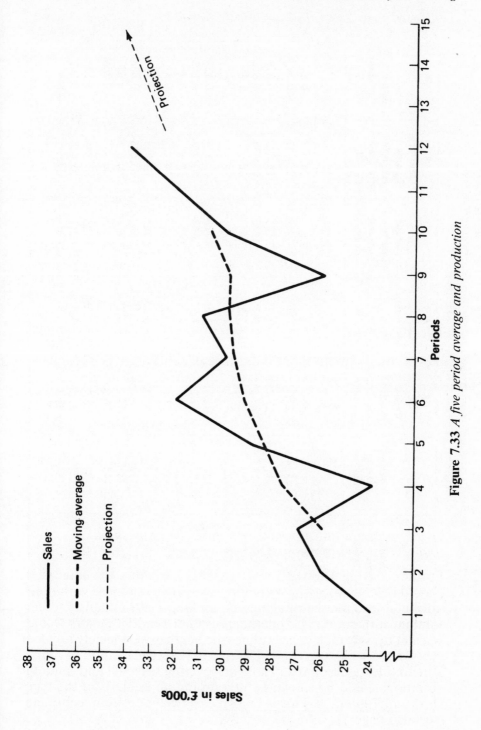

Figure 7.33 *A five period average and production*

Table 7.30 *The development of a 4 period moving average trend, seasonal weighting, seasonally adjusted sales figures and the identification of random variations from basic monthly sales figures*

1	2	3	4	5	6	7	8	9
Year	Quarter	Sales in £000s	4 period moving total	Trend 4 period moving average	Sales deviation from trend (3 − 5)	Average quarterly seasonal deviation	Quarterly figures corrected for season (3 − 7)	Random variation (8 − 5)
19X1	1	30	—	—	—	—	—	—
	2	29	—	—	—	—	—	—
	3	25	112	28	−3	−3.6	28.6	0.6
	4	28	111	27.75	0.25	1	27	−0.76
19X2	1	29	111	27.75	1.25	2.125	26.875	−0.875
	2	29	113	28.25	0.75	1.562	27.438	−0.812
	3	27	117	29.25	−2.25	−3.6	30.6	1.35
	4	32	122	30.5	1.5	1	31	0.5
19X3	1	34	127	31.75	2.25	2.125	31.875	0.125
	2	34	129	32.25	1.75	1.562	32.438	0.188
	3	29	132	33	−4	−3.6	32.6	−0.4
	4	35	134	33.5	1.5	1	34	0.5
19X4	1	36	137	34.25	1.75	2.125	33.875	−0.375
	2	37	139	34.75	2.25	1.562	35.438	0.688
	3	31	141	35.25	−4.25	−3.6	34.6	−0.65
	4	37	145	36.25	0.75	1	36	−0.25
19X5	1	40	147	36.75	3.25	2.125	37.875	1.125
	2	39	150	37.5	1.5	1.562	37.438	−0.062
	3	34	154	38.5	−4.5	−3.6	37.6	−0.9
	4	41	—	—	—	—	—	—

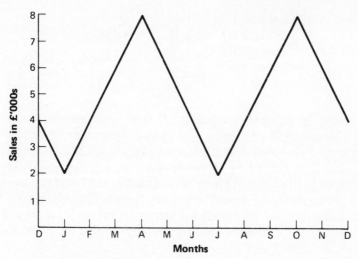

Figure 7.34 *A seasonal pattern of sales obtained from plotting monthly sales data*

In Table 7.30 the data in columns 1, 2 and 3 refers to the sale of a product per quarter over a period of five years; the same type of analysis could be applied to monthly statistics. The trend has been calculated (column 5) on a four period basis by the moving total and moving average method, eg

$$19X1, 30 + 29 + 25 + 28 = 112 \text{ (MT)} \div 4 = 28 \text{ (MA)}$$

Because of the absence of a middle item in a group of four the moving total and moving average have been placed against the third item in each case, ie 112 (MT) and 28 (MA) against the third quarter of 19X1. The advantage of a four period MT and MA is that all seasons of a year are included in each calculation no matter which quarter starts the year.

The purpose of columns 6 to 9 in Table 7.30 is to analyze the sales figure for each quarter, dividing it into its component parts: (a) normal trend, (b) the mean seasonal variation, and (c) random variations.

Data in column 6 is found by subtracting the individual trend items in column 5 from the actual sales items in column 3. The data in column 7 is calculated by taking all the deviations-from-trend items (column 6) according to quarters, adding them, and then dividing by the appropriate number of items. Thus, from the data in column 6 the average quarterly deviation can be calculated for all first quarters in this way:

$$19X2 \text{ quarter } 1 \quad 1.25$$
$$19X3 \text{ quarter } 1 \quad 2.25$$
$$19X4 \text{ quarter } 1 \quad 1.75$$
$$19X5 \text{ quarter } 1 \quad \underline{3.25}$$
$$8.50 \div 4 = 2.125$$

Therefore, in column 7 against all first quarters the value of 2.125 is shown. This process is repeated for the other quarters.

In column 8 in Table 7.30 the actual sales figures (column 3) are then seasonally adjusted by subtracting the average quarterly deviation (column 7) from them. Then by subtracting the trend (column 5) from the seasonally corrected quarterly figures (in column 8), the residue indicates the extent of the other influences present. The sales figure of a particular quarter can be analyzed as in Table 7.31.

Table 7.31 *Component parts of a sales figure*

	19X5 quarter 2
(a) The normal trend	37.5
(b) The average quarterly seasonal variation	1.562
(c) Other random variations	−0.062
Original sales figure	39.0

The analysis in Table 7.31 enables attention to be focused on the random variations after the trend and the seasonal effects have been eliminated. The forecaster must then ask to what causes these random variations can be attributed, ie why should the sales figure for the first quarter of 19X5 be £1,125 above the seasonally adjusted trend? Often the variations from the trend are converted to percentages to allow proportional assessment.

On investigation it may be found that random variations have been caused by the beginning of a new trend, eg increased product usage, a new application, appeal to a new market segment, etc; in which case the forecaster can allow for this in the future forecasting activities. Alternatively, the random variations may have been caused by an ad hoc factor that is unlikely or cannot be guaranteed to happen again, ie a once-only special order, a strike at a competitor's factory, etc. In such a case the unusual sales item can be withdrawn from the total sales volume figure for the period, otherwise it will affect future moving averages and other trend calculations adversely.

The sales data and the trend can be shown on a graph and the general slope of the latter projected into the future (see Figure 7.35). The general trend obtained can be used for medium- and long-term trend prediction.

Table 7.30 represents an analysis of the quarterly sales data, but a sales forecast for the next period, Q1 19X6, could be made based on the method described earlier when calculating the three period moving average (see Table 7.27). The method would be to take the latest moving average value available in Table 7.30, ie 38.5, and add twice the difference between it and the previous moving average, ie 37.5.

Therefore,

$$38.5 + (2 \times 1) = 40.5$$

plus the average quarterly seasonal deviation (see column 7, Table 7.30) for all quarter 1 values. The forecast for quarter 1 of 19X6 would be

$$40.5 + 2.125 = 42.625$$

or £42,000 rounded.

One method of projection forecasting would be to plot on separate graphs the trend, seasonal pattern and deseasonalized sales. In each case these would be projected forward and finally all the component parts added together at a particular point in the future to form a total forecast. Alternatively, a forecast for the next year (four quarters) based on the current trend indicated in Figure 7.35, could be obtained by taking the projected trend values for each quarter and adding or subtracting the appropriate average quarterly seasonal deviation, as in Table 7.32. The seasonally adjusted forecast is shown graphically in Figure 7.35.

Table 7.32 *A seasonally adjusted forecast based on Figure 7.35*

Year	Projected trend value obtained from graph	Average quarterly seasonal deviation	Forecast
19X6			
Quarter 1	39.6	2.125	41.725
Quarter 2	40.4	1.562	41.962
Quarter 3	41.0	−3.6	37.4
Quarter 4	41.6	1.0	42.6

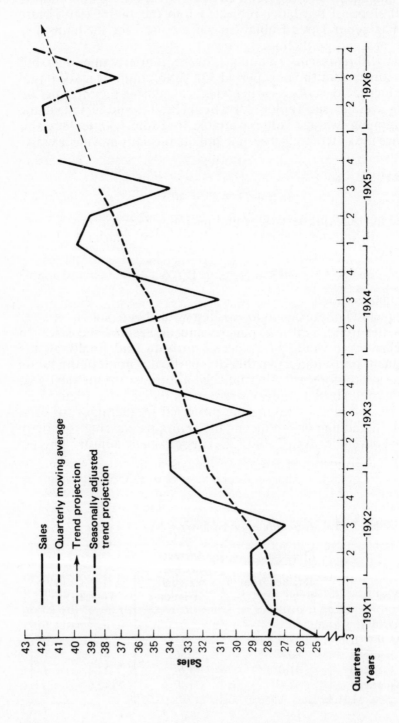

Figure 7.35 *Sales data and quarterly moving average and projection*

Other decomposition methods

In the last example each quarterly sales figure was 'decomposed' into its component parts of trend, mean seasonal average, deseasonalized sales and random variations or residual error.

The so-called *classical decomposition method* of forecasting not only analyzes sales values in this way but also makes a forecast by predicting each of the components separately and then combining them to make a total forecast for the next time period(s).

A more sophisticated decomposition method is known as *Census II*; it provides statistical credibility for the results and uses empirically proven methods of estimation. The Census II procedure has been described as primarily consisting of

> 'several smoothing operations carried out by applying moving averages of varying weightings and orders to the data converted into percentage ratio to trend index numbers. When an initial estimate of the seasonal-irregular component has been obtained, irregular fluctuations are removed by using two-standard deviation control limits[1] and replacing extreme values by averages of surrounding values. In the same ways, values at the beginning and end of the series, which are lost through the moving average procedure, are replaced. The data is then centred for each year and, by smoothing the columns of individual months (or quarters), estimates of preliminary seasonal factors are obtained, again by replacing end-values by an averaging procedure. These preliminary estimates are then used to remove some of the seasonality from the original observations and the smoothed residual is applied to obtain a second or intermediate estimate of the seasonal component. This, in turn, is then smoothed, irregularities are removed and such values, together with end observations, are replaced. The series is centred and by once more smoothing the columns of individual months, estimates of the final seasonal factors are obtained. This series can then be used to finally adjust the original observations for seasonality and by further suitable smoothing and replacing, final estimates of the irregular, cyclical and trend components can be identified.'[2]

Another decomposition technique can be used as a causal model on top of a time series. It decomposes a set of data (both dependent and independent variables) into each of its component parts (mentioned above) and then provides a forecast for each of the variables using a number of smoothing methods. At the same time it provides a measure of accuracy of each of the forecasts, thus helping the forecaster to choose the most appropriate method.

[1] See page 174
[2] G Briscoe & M Hirst *Long Range Planning* Sept 1973, p 79

Ideally, the independent variable should be a leading indicator of the lagging dependent one so that a turning point can be predicted.

Weighted moving averages

One of the problems in using moving averages is that this method gives equal weight to all items, whereas the circumstances that helped to form the sales volume in the most recent period will influence actual sales to a greater extent than those operating a number of periods ago; this is particularly relevant in yearly moving averages.

One method used in forecasting is that of giving more weight to more recent periods. Consider the last four periods of Table 7.27 (page 236) recalculated on a four period moving average basis and shown in Table 7.33.

In fact, the same moving average could be obtained by calculating:

$$\frac{1}{4} \times 26 = 6.5$$
$$\frac{1}{4} \times 30 = 7.5$$
$$\frac{1}{4} \times 32 = 8.0$$
$$\frac{1}{4} \times 34 = 8.5$$

| 1 | 30.5 |

Additional weight could therefore be given to more recent periods by increasing the fraction, ie

$$\frac{1}{10} \times 26 = 2.6$$

$$\frac{2}{10} \times 30 = 6.0$$

$$\frac{3}{10} \times 32 = 9.6$$

$$\frac{4}{10} \times 34 = 13.6$$

| 1 | 31.8 | = weighted moving average |

The effect of this weighting on forecasts can be seen by comparing forecasts based on unweighted and weighted moving averages developed in Table 7.34.

Table 7.33 *Calculation of a four period moving average*

Quarter	Sales in £000s	4 period moving total	4 period moving average
9	26		
10	30		
11	32		
12	34	122 ÷ 4 =	30.5

Table 7.34 *A comparison of unweighted and weighted moving averages*

Period	Sales £000s	4 period unweighted moving average	Difference between current and last moving average	4 period weighted moving average	Difference between current and last moving average
8	31	–	–	–	–
9	26	–	–	–	–
10	30	29.75	–	30.1	–
11	32	30.5	0.75	31.8	1.7
12	34	–	–	–	–
13	–	–	–	–	–

Forecast for period 13 using unweighted moving average
$$= 30.5 + (2 \times 0.75) = 32$$
Forecast for period 13 using weighted moving average
$$= 31.8 + (2 \times 1.7) = 34.2$$

In this case, by giving more weight to more recent periods, the weighted moving average produced a higher forecast. Depending on the values of recent periods it would be possible to obtain a weighted forecast that was lower.

Exponential smoothing

When calculating weighted moving averages in the previous example more weight was given to more recent periods. In fact, the weighting declined by a constant quantity value, ie by the value of 1/10th on each item, 4/10th, 3/10th, 2/10th, 1/10th. Another method is to reduce the weighting by a constant percentage or ratio, eg perhaps by halving the weighting ½, ¼, 1/8th, 1/16th, 1/32nd, 1/64th.

This produces a geometric progression and, when graphed, smoothes the raw sales data into an exponential curve; the method is therefore referred to as *exponential smoothing or weighting*.

It is a simple but highly reliable weighted moving average technique. Its main advantages are that relatively few past observations are required, it is easy to use and is highly reliable in the short term. Its usefulness to the forecaster is that it highlights the effects of current trends and seasonal patterns and diminishes the effect that past forecasts which have failed (perhaps because of sharp non-typical fluctuations) will have on the current forecast. Also, it gives greater weight to more recent periods and tends to give more accurate forecasts.

Using the same data as in the earlier weighted moving average example (Table 7.34) an exponentially weighted moving average could be calculated as shown in Table 7.35.

The reducing exponential weights could go on for ever with everdecreasing fractions, but in practice when the value becomes relatively insignificant (eg where it produced 0.937 in Table 7.35) it is wise to terminate the series. A useful device is to repeat the same fraction, ie 1/32nd against periods 7 and 8. If this is not done the sum of the fractions will not equal 1, and, therefore, the exponentially weighted moving average will be fractionally low.

Table 7.35 *The make-up of an exponentially weighted moving average*

Period 7	$\frac{1}{32} \times 30 =$	0.937
Period 8	$\frac{1}{32} \times 31 =$	0.968
Period 9	$\frac{1}{16} \times 26 =$	1.625
Period 10	$\frac{1}{8} \times 30 =$	3.75
Period 11	$\frac{1}{4} \times 32 =$	8.0
Period 12	$\frac{1}{2} \times 34 =$	17.0
	1	32.280

Table 7.36 *A method of obtaining an exponentially weighted moving average to form the basis of making a sales forecast*

Period	Sales	Exponentially weighted moving average
6	32	
7	30	
8	31	
9	26	30.624
10	30	32.280
11	32	
12	34	
13	—	

When the exponentially weighted moving average has been calculated for the last two periods, a forecast can be made by the same method used with the unweighted and weighted moving averages.

The difference between two exponentially weighted moving averages is 1.656. The forecast for period 13 is therefore 32.280 + (3 × 1.656) = 37.248.

The main disadvantage with this method is that a greater number of items are used to form the average: six in this case (because of the fractions required to make the value of 1) compared with four in the weighted moving average (Table 7.34). Because of this, there are no moving averages against periods 11 and 12, and therefore the difference between the last two moving averages had to be multiplied by three to produce a forecast for period 13.

A second method of exponential smoothing for forecasting

A more useful approach to forecasting through exponential smoothing is to determine the constant ratio factor by examining past data and then use it to forecast the next period.

For example, where y = the prediction to be made for the next period, p = sales in past periods ($p_1, p_2 p_3$ etc) and A = the constant ratio factor.

$$\text{Let } \hat{y} = p_1 + p_2(A) + p_3(A^2) + p_4(A^3)$$

In the last example (Table 7.36) consider how the sales in period 12, ie £34,000, would be arrived at by using this formula.

$$34 = 32 + 30(A) + 26(A^2) + 31(A^3)$$

The factor (A) is found by completing the formula mathematically or by working through various values to find one that completes

251

the formula. This latter method can be tedious initially but in the ensuing periods the factor will vary only slightly when updated. Inserting the factor

$$34 = 32 + 30(0.0634) + 26(0.0634^2) + 31(0.0634^3)$$
$$= (32 + 1.902 + 0.104 + 0.008)$$

Using the same formula and the above factor to predict sales for period 13

$$\hat{y} = 34 + 32(0.0634) + 30(0.0634^2) + 26(0.0634^3) =$$
$$34 + 2.029 + 0.120 + 0.006 = 36.155$$

or, rounded to the nearest £100, £36,100 which is the forecast for period 13.

Alternatively, factor A (the constant ratio factor) can be found by completing the formula mathematically as follows using the same basic formula and the same data as used above:

Period	Sales
8	31
9	26
10	30
11	32
12	34

What is the best estimate for period 13 using the formula:

$$\hat{y} = p_1 + p_2(A) + p_3(A^2) + p_4(A^3)$$
$$34 = 32 + 30(A) + 26(A^2) + 31(A^3)$$

Using the formula

$$ax^2 + bx + x = 0, \text{ ie } 26(A^2) + 30(A) - 2 = 0$$

To solve the equation using formula

$$x = \frac{-b \pm \sqrt{(b^2 - 4ac)}}{2a}$$

insert appropriate figures:

$$A = \frac{-30 \pm \sqrt{[30^2 - (4 \times 26 \times (-2))]}}{(2 \times 26)}$$

$$= \frac{-30 \pm \sqrt{(900 + 208)}}{52}$$

$$= \frac{-30 \pm \sqrt{(1108)}}{52} = \frac{-30 + 33.29}{52}$$

$$= \frac{3.29}{52} = 0.06327$$

To forecast the sales ($\hat{y}$) for period 13

$$\hat{y} = 34 + 32(A) + 30(A^2) + 26(A^3) + 31(A^4)$$

= 34	34.0000
+32 (0.06327)	2.0204
+30 (0.06327²)	0.1200
+26 (0.06327³)	0.0066
+31 (0.06327⁴)	0.0005
	36.1511

Best estimate of sales for period 13 = £36,151.

Exponential smoothing forecast using deseasonalized data

Another approach to exponential smoothing is one that modifies the value of the previous forecast according to the value of the resulting sales performance. As actual sales data becomes available for a particular sales period, the forecast for that past period is updated by a part of the difference between the two values. The resulting value then becomes the forecast for the next period. The formula is:

$$\hat{y} = F_{-1} + A(S_{-1} - F_{-1})$$

Where y = forecast for next period
A = the alpha factor or smoothing constant
F_{-1} = forecast for last period
S_{-2} = actual sales for last period

Table 7.37 illustrates a hypothetical forecasting flow for the next six sales periods. The sale of the product experiences period-to-period variations but the 0.6 smoothing constant adjusts the forecast according to the most recent forecasting 'error'. The size of the smoothing constant can be initially set by experience of variations in the market or by the previously described method of exponential

Table 7.37 *A forecasting flow for the next six sales periods*

Sales period	Volume forecast (000s)	Actual sales (000s)	% Variance forecast related to sales
1	118	124	−4.8
2	118 + 0.6(124 − 118) = 122	126	−3.1
3	122 + 0.6(126 − 122) = 124	122	+1.6
4	124 + 0.6(122 − 124) = 123	125	−1.6
5	124 + 0.6(125 − 124) = 124	127	−2.36
6	126 + 0.6(127 − 124) = 126	124	+1.6
7	126 + 0.6(124 − 126) = 124		

smoothing or even arbitrarily. Any value between 0 and 1 may be used, but the larger the value of the constant, the greater will be the influence of the most recent period. The smoothing constant can be adjusted should basic conditions in the market change.

In the above table the value of 118 at the commencement of the series could either represent a 'guesstimate' of the sales of a new product to be launched into the market or could be obtained by another forecasting method to start the series. This is important as there must be a forecast and an actual sales performance figure to determine the error. It is upon the adjustment of the error that the method works.

Thus, in period 2 the previous forecast is taken (118) and 0.6 of the error between the forecast and actual is added, giving a forecast of 122 for period 3.

In period 4, as the forecast is higher than the sales achieved, the error is negative (122–124); 0.6 of this negative error is, therefore, subtracted from the previous forecast value of 124.

The method is more effective with a stable time series and, should seasonality be a major factor, sales will need to be deseasonalized before being subjected to this method. After being exponentially smoothed and projected, the ensuing values can be reseasonalized (see page 179) to give a seasonally adjusted sales forecast.

The main advantage of this method of forecasting is that it needs little data (forecast and actual) to calculate a forecast; contrast this with the amount of data needed to calculate a 13 period moving average. Also it is based upon the most recently known sales period, whereas the middle point of a 13 period moving average which forms the trend is six months back.

Table 7.38 *Part of the quarterly sales data taken from Table 7.30*

Year	Quarters	Sales (£000s)
19X4	4	37
19X5	1	40
	2	39
	3	34
	4	41

Seasonally weighted exponential smoothing

The exponential smoothing method can be adapted for use with seasonal data (monthly, quarterly, etc).

If the data for the last five quarters from Table 7.30 are used the exponential smoothing factor can be determined in this case by again using the formula

$$\hat{y} = p_1 + p_2(a) + p_3(a^2) + p_4(a^3)$$
$$41 = 34 + 39(0.153) + 40(0.153^2) + 37(0.153^3)$$

The factor in this case has been found by working through various values to find the one that fits the formula. In the above case the prediction actually equals 41.033 but this was the nearest obtainable and has been rounded for convenience.

The forecast for quarter 1 of 19X6 can now be calculated using the same formula and constant ratio factor:

$$\hat{y} = 41 + 34(0.153) + 39(0.153^2) + 40(0.153^3)$$
$$= 41 + 5.202 + 0.9226 + 0.1433$$
$$= 47.2679 \text{ or rounded to £47,250}$$

However, using the exponential smoothing technique in this way does not allow for seasonal difference with individual quarterly predictions, although values for all four seasons are present in the four quarters moving average. Therefore, certain data in the current example can be extracted, rearranged, and developed to show a moving average, a trend, a forecast and seasonally adjusted forecast, thereby making the fullest use of available data — this is shown in Table 7.39. As the sales data becomes available each month, the constant ratio factor used above, 0.153, can be applied or recalculated and a continuous sales forecast can be evolved.

In Table 7.39 the year, quarters and actual sales are shown in

Table 7.39 *The calculation of a seasonally weighted exponential moving average and forecast*

1	2	3	4	5	6	7	8
Quarters	Actual sales in £000s	Average sales based upon trend value = 36.75	Actual difference	Difference trend	Straight forecast for the next quarter	Mean quarterly seasonal deviation (col 8 in previous table)	Seasonally adjusted forecast for the next quarter
19X5 1	40	37.24	+ 0.49	+ 0.49	39.94	1.562	41.502
2	39	37.50	+ 0.26	+ 0.45	39.98	– 3.6	36.38
3	34	36.96	– 0.54	+ 0.35	38.98	1.0	39.89
4	41	37.57	+ 0.61	+ 0.38	39.67	2.125	41.795

columns 1 and 2. In column 3 the previous average sales value, 36.75 (see trend value quarter 1, 19X5 in Table 7.30), is multiplied by 0.847, that is 1 minus the constant (A) 0.153, and then added to the current quarter's sales (in column 2) multiplied by the constant; for example, in quarter 1,

$$36.75 \times 0.847 + (40 \times 0.153)$$

which indicates the new average sales value of 37.24.

The actual difference shown in column 4 of Table 7.39 is found by subtracting the previous month's average sales from the current month's average sales. For example, in quarter 2,

$$37.50 - 37.24 = 0.26$$

The difference trend (column 5) is found by taking its values in the previous month and multiplying it by 1 minus the constant, ie 0.847, to which is added the actual difference (column 4) for the current month multiplied by the constant 0.153. For example, for quarter 4,

$$0.35 \times 0.847 + (0.61 \times 0.153) = 0.38$$

In column 6 the current difference trend is multiplied by 1 minus the constant divided by the constant and added to the average sales figure in column 3. For example, for quarter 1,

$$0.49 \times \frac{0.847}{0.153} + 37.24 = 39.94$$

In column 7 the mean quarterly seasonal deviations are extracted from Table 7.30 column 8 and listed, and in columns 8 of this table these weightings are added to or subtracted from the values shown in column 6. Using this method, the forecast for quarter 1 of 19X6 is, therefore, 41, 795, or £41,800 approximately.

Exponential smoothing — more sophisticated techniques

It will be seen from the above examples that exponential smoothing is very similar to the moving average approach but does not use a constant set of weights for the 'n' most recent observations. In fact, an exponentially decreasing set of weights is used so that the more recent values receive more weight than older values.

Exponential smoothing in its 'pure' form (as originally suggested

257

by C C Holt) should only be used by itself for stationary, non-seasonal time series. The methods on pages 251 and 253 are examples.

Many time series are in practice both seasonal and non-stationary. But such time series can be converted into non-seasonal and stationary series by appropriate deseasonalizing. The series can be then extrapolated exponentially and the trend and seasonal pattern then added to the projected values; such a method was suggested on page 216. However, methods have been developed which integrate these stages and which take into account the seasonal pattern; one such method is one suggested by Brown (see example on page 255).

The Holt-Winters exponential smoothing method handles time series and allows for both trend and seasonal variations, both of which are updated by exponential smoothing.

Auto-Regressive Integrated Moving Average (ARIMA) techniques are the most sophisticated of the single time-series approaches to fore-casting. Basically they follow the same philosophy as the methods mentioned previously but use a different procedure for determining how many of the past observations should be included in preparing the forecast and in determining the appropriate weight values to be applied to those observations.

A series of techniques that fall into the **ARIMA** category are *adaptive filtering techniques* which can be used for any type of data whether seasonal, cyclical or trend. They are similar to other smoothing techniques in the sense that they weight past observations in such a way that the error between actual and forecast value is minimal. They are called adaptive filtering because, in the process of minimizing the error, they 'filter' the 'disturbances' out of the data.

The most commonly used **ARIMA** method is the procedure developed by Box and Jenkins. Like adaptive filtering this method assigns varying weights to past observations until an optimal set of weights is discovered. In fact they differ only in the way the weight values and the terms to be included are determined. The *Box Jenkins method* is more sophisticated than adaptive filtering methods because it can handle more than two variables and because it makes use of the statistical properties of estimation to test the appropriateness/quality of the model being used and its significance. It is based on the assumption that successive observations of economic/industry/market series are correlated. Further, it tries to discover and make use of such autocorrelations to obtain accurate predictions about the future.

Table 7.40 *A comparison of advertising expenditure and sales over a 12-month period*

	Advertising expenditure last year £	Percentage of last year's advertising %	Sales last year £	Percentage of last year's sales %
January	3,100	7.3	50,000	5.8
February	3,400	7.9	62,000	7.4
March	3,800	8.8	68,000	8.0
April	4,200	9.8	76,000	8.9
May	3,600	8.4	84,000	9.9
June	3,150	7.3	72,000	8.5
July	2,600	6.0	63,000	7.4
August	3,050	7.1	52,000	6.1
September	3,850	8.9	61,000	7.2
October	4,350	10.1	77,000	9.1
November	4,900	11.4	87,000	10.2
December	3,000	7.0	98,000	11.5
	43,000	100.0	850,000	100.0

Forecasting sales by the assessment of advertising

An analysis of advertising expenditure related to sales is often a good indicator of future sales. But it would be wrong to assume that to increase or decrease advertising expenditure will automatically increase or decrease sales. Normally, sales are not only a function of advertising but also of other factors such as price, performance and function of product, seasonality of demand, effectiveness of the sales force, competitive effects and distribution. Also increased expenditure on, or increased quantity of, advertising does not necessarily mean improved quality. But it is important to recognize that advertising affects sales by influencing consumer/user knowledge, opinions, reactions or attitudes towards a product or service.

Comparisons of advertising expenditure and sales

As long as the limitations are recognized, the amount spent on advertising could be used to indicate future sales based on past expenditure and results. An elementary way of doing this is shown in Table 7.40.

From Table 7.40, indications of the likely effects of changes in advertising expenditure could be examined. In Table 7.40 there appears to be a lead/lag relationship of advertising expenditure to sales: increases in advertising appear to have an effect on sales in the following month. Also, seasonal patterns have been allowed for in advertising expenditure.

A graph of the advertising expenditure and sales percentages can also indicate that a company is missing marketing opportunities if the two plot lines do not run together in similar patterns. Advertising may be appearing too early or too late to do the best possible marketing job.

Sales leads as a basis for forecasting

In some cases companies can directly determine future sales. This situation is found where companies use advertising to get sales leads, ie where the advertisement includes a form to be completed and forwarded to the company. This may request literature or a demonstration of the product or a visit by an engineer to discuss particular problems. For example, this method is used to sell vending machines to factories and central heating installations to householders.

The company gears its advertising to the number of sales it wishes to achieve. From past experience the company determines the number of replies it will receive from various newspapers, magazines or trade journals. As in central heating installation marketing, ratios can be established between the number of replies to initial visits by engineers, to quotations submitted, to orders finally received. Thus, by increasing advertising in the correct advertising medium, predicted sales are not only achieved but can also be measured.

Share of advertising expenditure versus share of the market

Another approach that is particularly useful during the launch of a new product is to analyze data that compares the attained market share with the average share of advertising during the introductory period.

Table 7.41 shows that with six household products the level of advertising expenditure had a marked effect upon the share of market attained.

By analyzing past market share and advertising expenditures as in Table 7.41, sales forecasting can be made more effective.

Table 7.41 *The effect of share of advertising expenditure on share of the market*

Product	Attained share of sales	Average share of advertising during the introductory period
A	39	47
B	19	33
C	13	32
D	12	30
E	6	13
F	4	8

The percentage increase/decrease method

A further advertising/sales technique is that of comparing the annual percentage increase or decrease in market share with the annual percentage increase or decrease in a company's share of all advertising expenditure (see Table 7.42).

It has been said that the market share of a product will tend to increase/decrease in direct proportion to the difference between its market share and its share of total advertising in the market.

Naive correlations between advertising expenditure and sales are not reliable in effective sales forecasting because of the possible effects of other variables of the marketing mix and the market place. But the device of historical analogy (history repeating itself) causes forecasters to look at past data to consider the effects of changes in advertising expenditure upon sales or market share.

Model building and forecasting

Models have become popular marketing management devices in some organizations, but every operating rule in marketing could be defined broadly as a model. For example, where company reaction or response to a change in a particular variable is laid down. This could apply where courses of action are pre-determined to deal with changes in consumer response to advertising, or in a competitor's strategy or in the effectiveness of certain channels of distribution. In model building the marketer evolves rules and/or equations which express the relationship of certain variable and non-variable factors in the marketing system and uses them to predict the effect of the changes on the system. Models can be used to

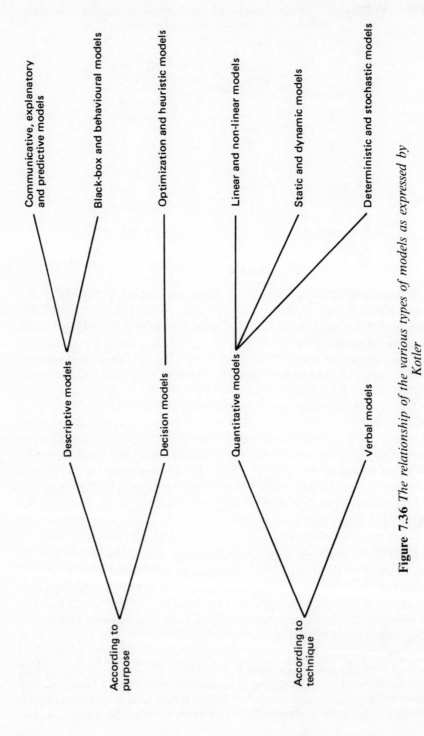

Figure 7.36 *The relationship of the various types of models as expressed by Kotler*

Table 7.42 *Relating increase/decrease of share of all advertising expenditure with increase/decrease in market share*

Product	Annual increase/decrease in market share	Annual increase/decrease in share of all advertising expenditure
A	+ 4%	+ 13½%
B	+ ¾%	+ 5½%
C	+ 2½%	+ 2½%
D	− 1¼%	− 3¾%
E	− 4½%	− 8½%

explain, select, optimize and predict markets and marketing sub-systems.

The variety of model types has been classified by P Kotler[1] and is shown in Figure 7.36

Some of the types of models shown in Figure 7.36 are more relevant to forecasting needs than others. Also, a number of the elementary forms of model building have already been explained in earlier sections and can be used to explain the basic principles of each group.

'Black box' models[2] were examined qualitatively in the section dealing with sociological and consumer behavioural change, by showing that certain patterns of group or individual behaviour were inputs into the marketing system and the outcome was a pattern of sales, eg the trend towards increased leisure and its effect on demand for recreation and leisure products (page 125 *et seq*)

Behavioural models seek to explain what happens between the input and the output of the 'black box', eg the qualitative and descriptive examination of individual behaviour on page 130.

The input/output method described on page 134 is a model of the national economy reflecting interrelationships with the various

---

[1] P. Kotler p 222 *Marketing Management* Prentice Hall, New Jersey, USA, 1967.
[2] The concept of the 'black box' was examined by P Kotler in the *Journal of Marketing*, Vol 29 (October 1965, p 37). 'The buyer is subject to many influences which trace a complex course through his psyche and lead eventually to overt purchasing responses . . . The buyer's psyche is a "black box" whose workings can be only partially deduced. The marketing strategist's challenge can be only partially deduced. The marketing strategist's challenge to the behavioural scientist is to construct a more specific model of the mechanism in the "black box".'

component industries. It examines the inputs into each industry and the resulting outputs, but does not seek to explain how the result was arrived at within the 'black box'.

The methods of least squares (page 168 *et seq*) and exponential smoothing (page 249 *et seq*) could also be described as quantitative 'black box' models. They are based on equations

$$\text{and } \begin{aligned} \hat{y} &= a + bx \\ \hat{y} &= p^1 + p^2\,(A) + p^3\,(A^2) \end{aligned}$$

respectively, that are set up to describe a particular system or situation and the relationships of the inputs and outputs without analyzing why the variables changed or why the outcome has happened.

The equation $\hat{y} = a + bx$ used in the least squares method (page 175) illustrates the input/ouput mechanism. Consider a situation where sales data and advertising expenditure for three years were as in Table 7.431.

Table 7.43 *Sales volume and advertising expenditure over a three-year period*

Year	Sales £000s	Advertising expenditure £000s
19X1	86	2.0
19X2	122	4.0
19X3	113	3.5

The equation $\hat{y} = a + bx$ becomes
$$\text{sales} = 50 + 18x$$

This means that for every extra £1,000 of advertising expenditure an increase of £18,000 in sales would be expected and that with no advertising at all, sales of £50,000 could be expected. A simple, though perhaps naive, 'black box' model.

Decision models

Decision models usually incorporate factors that permit analysis and assessment of the various courses of action and/or suggest optimum strategies to management. Within the overall decision making theory area, one of the most useful aspects for forecasting is that of the expected value concept. Examples of expected value in two of its forms as used in forecasting are shown on pages 340 *et seq* and 308 *et seq*.

Effective use of the expected value concept for forecasting depends on the ability of the forecaster and/or company executives to identify the various business environmental conditions that affect sales and the situations likely to prevail in changing situations. It also depends on their ability to provide realistic probability factors and potential outcome values (eg profits at various levels of activity) for each.

Closely linked with the expected value concept is Bayesian decision theory, which combines objective and subjective probabilities with revised data and information derived from such sources as the field sales force, research, economic and political fact situations. An example of an application of part of Bayesian decision theory is shown on page 305 *et seq*.

Linear models

An example of a linear model has already been shown to illustrate its role as a different type of model of the 'black box' category: it is the equation $\hat{y} = a + bx$ or as it was re-stated, sales $= 50 + 18x$ (see previous page). Such an equation establishes a linear or straight-line trend suggesting that continued increments of £1,000 spent on advertising would on each occasion increase sales by £18,000 *ad infinitum*. In practice, returns on advertising would begin to level out after a particular point and eventually decline. Regression analysis and the least squares method (pages 152 *et seq* and 168 *et seq*) are also examples of linear models.

Models based on learned behaviour

Purchasing/consumption in many cases is a form of learned behaviour. This is particularly true of consumer goods and services but also occurs in industrial markets. Preferences are developed and purchasing habits develop and consumer/users tend to repeat their past purchasing/consumption activities/decisions. Consumer/users do not objectively evaluate and compare competing/alternative product/service 'deals' every time they make a purchasing decision. There is often a measurable degree of 'brand loyalty' that exists at varying levels of intensity until some 'cue' (eg a change in price, quality, availability, etc) causes consumer/users to re-consider and possibly change their brand or product loyalty.

Market share models

Obviously the fewer the number of companies competing in a market the easier it will be to develop a market share model, but even when a number are competing it is possible to consider the companies with major market shares and group all others together. The sales of a particular company are often dependent upon its actual/relative/perceived market position with regard to its competitors. Because of brand/product loyalties there is a tendency for competitors to share a market with each other at a relatively constant rate. Although changes in market shares take place, the percentage market share held in one sales period is a good indicator of the starting point for market shares in the next period.

As a prerequisite for market share forecasting it is normal for the market to be segmented; both segmentation (page 214 *et seq*) and forecasting using market share and competitor activity (page 218 *et seq*) were considered earlier.

Brand-switching models

Another quantitative model useful in forecasting is the brand-switching model. In many areas of marketing, effective forecasting will depend on the ability of the forecaster to seek explanations for and/or measure the tendency of consumers to be loyal to a brand, or to switch to another. The importance of brand-switching models to forecasting in certain areas of marketing is obvious, as it is concerned with the measurement of repeat purchases and the switching-in and switching-out rate for each brand. As Kotler says:[1]

'The attitude of marketing executives toward brand-switching is quite simple: the switching-out rate must be slowed down, and the switching-in rate must be increased. The factors affecting brand choice must be analysed, and this knowledge applied where possible in order to alter existing brand-switching rates.'

These activities will affect sales and, therefore, forecasts. The forecaster will be able to determine product sales patterns over a period of time, whether the switching rates are constant or are changing in a predictable direction.

It is usual to construct brand-switching models concurrently with models concerning price/supply situations, and models relating to competitive response. Which competitors will have or

[1] Philip Kotler, *Marketing Management*, Prentice Hall, New Jersey, USA.

already have the resources to react, and what will be the nature and timing of counter activities and their effect on sales?

The primary model for brand-switching analysis is the Markov process which is concerned with the consumer's preference for a particular brand. But the consumer's preference may change from time to time, and he may switch brands. In a total market, brand-switching by groups can be aggregated and expressed as a probability.

Consider an elementary application of the Markov process to illustrate the principle involved: a situation with three brands, A, B and C, which have 20 per cent, 30 per cent and 50 per cent shares of the market respectively. A 'transition matrix' can be evolved that will express the probabilities of the various types of brand-switching that can occur. These probabilities could be derived from panels of expert opinion, or from past market behaviour (historical analogy) or from a survey of buyer's intentions, etc. Such a transition matrix based on the above data is shown in Table 7.44.

After the formation of Table 7.44, the next step is to apply the probabilities to the existing brand shares. This is shown in Table 7.45.

The calculation of the new brand share values for A in Table 7.45 is based on the expectation that it will retain 0.5 of its existing 20 per cent share of the market, ie 10 per cent, plus a brand-switch of 0.4 of B's existing market share of 30 per cent, ie 12 per cent, plus a brand switch of 0.3 of C's market share of 50 per cent of the current market, ie 15 per cent: a total of 37 per cent of the anticipated market in the next period.

In turn, the probabilities can be applied to the new brand shares. This process can be repeated a number of times to produce a forecast pattern of demand for the three brands for any number of future periods.

This method assumes that the probabilities remain constant or will change at a predictable rate. At some later point they may have to be adjusted if new information becomes available.

Preference analysis

This is a progression from the Markov and other brand-switching models which have a number of disadvantages as well as a number of advantages for direct forecasting applications. The main disadvantages of many brand-switching models are that they do not take account of once-only brand purchases or the buying of several brands at the same time and that they are unable to cope with variations in pack size and price. However, methods for measuring

Table 7.44 *Probability that consumers will switch brands*

	A	B	C
A	stay 0.5	change 0.3	change 0.2
B	change 0.4	stay 0.4	change 0.2
C	change 0.3	change 0.3	stay 0.4

Table 7.45 *The application of probabilities to the existing brand shares to determine the post-switch market shares*

				New brand shares anticipated
A	0.5 of 20% = 10%	0.4 of 30% = + 12%	0.3 of 50% = + 15%	= 37%
B	0.4 of 30% = 12%	0.3 of 20% = + 6%	0.3 of 50% = + 15%	= 33%
C	0.4 of 50% = 20%	0.2 of 20% = + 4%	0.2 of 30% = + 6%	= 30%

market response to promotional activity can be built into some more advanced brand-switching models.

Preference analysis is designed to show the short-term effects of advertising, sales promotion and product change on all the brands being offered in the market.

The information input for the preference analysis model is obtained weekly from a regionally and socially representative sample of 5,000 households reporting their household purchases by brand, price, shop and special offer. From this data, brand loyalty, brand switching and the effects of sales promotion can be estimated. The interpretation of the data is important. What may appear to be loyalty to a brand may, in fact, be loyalty to a particular retail outlet that stocks only one brand, or to changes in stocking patterns by retailers, rather than a change in consumer preference.

Preference analysis allows for sub-preferences within households perhaps due to the presence of more than one purchaser, or because the purchaser is relatively indifferent to the choice of brand available or because different products in the same product field are complementary or are substitutes.

Product life cycle models

Product life cycles were considered in depth in Chapter 1 and as such the characteristics of each stage of the life cycle and the appropriate marketing strategy responses have already been considered. However, the fact that the rate of change in sales revenue/units differs throughout the life of the product/service may have a significant effect on forecasts, especially those covering the medium and long terms. Depending on the product/service type being considered the length of life cycles will differ, but in modelling terms can be considered either as historic fact to be projected forward by trend analysis or in terms of a predictive model based on historical analogy, ie that history will repeat itself.

Other models

Other models linked with learned behaviour can relate to the effect of advertising and promotional activities and changes in them (see page 259). There is an obvious link between the sales forecast and the ability of advertising and sales promotion to influence sales. In this area, media planning models have developed and, through the technique of linear programming, consider a variety of viable combinations of how much time and/or space to buy in general and in specific media and at what frequency of interval, to achieve a particular market objective.

Various marketing-mix models have been evolved by companies. These attempt to measure the effect of different combinations of the various sub-functions of marketing (marketing research, advertising, direct selling, distribution, etc) and marketing strategies, on sales.

Simulation models

Models have been constructed to simulate the market and marketing situations facing a company; particular variables are then changed and a prediction made of how the other variables will react. Simulation can be defined as a general method of studying the behaviour of a real system or phenomenon; the method usually involves the following features:

1. devising a model, or set of mathematical and logical relations, which represents the essential features of the system;
2. carrying out step-by-step computations with these relations which imitate the manner in which the real system might perform in real time.

Because of the increasing complexity of a number of the models mentioned, particularly those involving simulation and the need to cut calculation time, the development and use of computers has led to an increased awareness of the use of models in forecasting.

Examples of market simulation models are 'market correlation with economic indicators' (page 153 *et seq*), correlation and company sales (page 155 *et seq*), and multiple correlation (page 165 *et seq*). However, all these methods operate with a small number of variable factors, whereas it is possible, using a computer, to increase the number of variables and analyze the system created by their interrelationships, using them as a series of interacting factors. As certain key variables are changed, the effect upon the other factors can be assessed. These methods are often referred to as market/business throughput systems and are developed as mathematical models.

A further development of this is the concept of a simulation model forecasting the immediate period ahead and then continuing to move on through the ensuing periods; the model is moved on artificially through time.

Which method to use?

In a later chapter ('Monitoring and Controlling the Forecast') one of the controls suggested is to 'audit the machinery of forecasting' (ie the methods used). In this way, by comparing actual sales with forecasts, the most effective methods of forecasting for a particular company can be identified.

Often the forecaster wants to know which methods to use before the forecast is made and therefore before an 'audit' can be carried out. One method is to take data for the last five sales periods and apply various techniques to the first four pieces of data and then compare the resultant forecasts with the sales that were actually achieved in the fifth period. Those methods which give the closest forecasts to the actual sales figures can then be used to make some real forecasts for the next period, ie period six.

8

The Use of Computers in Forecasting

'Beware of making 5 year predictions, unless you are thinking of leaving the company after 4 years'

Stan Winston, Ogilvy & Mather Direct

Introduction

This chapter examines the various aspects of computers and computing, that are of direct relevance to market and sales forecasting and the work of the forecaster. It examines computer types and their role in forecasting, relevant peripheral equipment, the various categories of software and gives an example of what two forecasting related packages can offer and an information source for all other software packages that are currently available. These packages cover all the techniques mentioned in the previous chapter and many others.

The drive for productivity has always been one of the main justifications for the use of information technology in general and of computing in particular. The first computer systems were used to speed up mundane clerical tasks like stock control, calculation of company payrolls and the issuing of sales delivery notes and invoices. The extended use of main-frame and mini-computers increased the number of business applications but the computing activity tended to remain in the hands of the computer specialist.

In the 1980s and 90s, the wider availability, the declining price and increased power of personal computers helped to boost personal productivity generally, and in particular, enabled the individual forecaster to carry out a wider range of complex tasks, formerly too complicated and/or too time consuming to be carried out routinely. The computer (especially the micro-computer) has become a fundamental forecasting tool and has opened up new horizons for more effective forecasting.

The drive towards information technology and computer innovation continues at an ever increasing rate and a chapter of this kind can only reflect the current state of 'the art', knowing that further exciting developments in the art and science of computing, computer capability, capacity and applications will appear almost monthly.

Figure 8.1 shows an overview of computers relevant to forecasting and their peripheral equipment, ie hardware.

Computer Hardware

The functional units of a computer.

Computers consist of a number of functional parts, each carrying out one or more tasks; these include reception and input of systems and data, their storage, retrieval, processing, output and transmission. Each functional part performs a specific task and they are connected to other parts through well defined 'interfaces' and organized and managed by installed systems.

An overview of the main computer types shown in Figure 8.1 is as follows:

Super-computers These are very powerful high-performance computers, designed to make extremely rapid calculations on complex problems, involving large quantities of information. Until now, their cost restricted their use to relatively few locations; yet despite their relative rarity they have had a major impact on science and technology. They are involved in numerous pure science studies, in certain economic and industrial applications, and in other specialized areas, eg meteorological forecasts and atmospheric and oceanic modelling, etc.

The supercomputer's main market forecasting potential is in the econometric modelling of whole economies, where they can cope with, and rapidly calculate, the impact and interrelationships between the mass of economic and other data that contributes to the 'economy'. For example, important forecasts of demand and supply can be made.

They are comprised of a number of central processors and a 'front-end' processor which controls the flow of data between the central processors and the peripheral devices in the system, disk drives, a separate communications processor (to control the flow of data to and from the terminals and the data communications links), a backing store control unit that controls the passage of data to and from the various backing store units, key-board and printers and/or plotters.

Transputers This is, in effect, an entire computer on a single chip. It is designed to be used as a component for building computers that execute many steps of a program at the same time, ie in parallel, unlike conventional computers which carry out programs

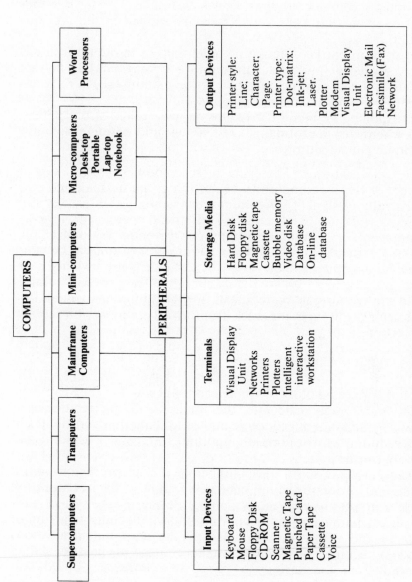

Figure 8.1 *The principal items of forecasting computer hardware*

273

sequentially, ie one step/stage after another. Their parallel processing approach means that networks of transputers can be used to
speed up the execution of programs, leading to cost-effective, high-
performance computer systems. They have been used in the development of supercomputers, which were mentioned in the previous
section.

Their main market forecasting potential lies in the transputer's
ability to accept multiple inputs into economic and/or market
models at the same time, thereby effecting simultaneous relationships of demand factors and demand outcomes.

Transputers are being used across a wide range of of applications where cost, performance, size, weight and power dissipation
are prime considerations.

Main-frame computers These are large computers, comprising a
number of free standing units. Main-frames are normally housed
in specially designed, air-conditioned rooms. Main-frames are
very powerful (in capacity and capability) and operate and support
a number of applications running concurrently. In forecasting,
they are particularly useful when the amount of data to be processed is vast, when a large variety of parameters are involved and
the forecasting methods are highly complex. They are particularly
useful, in a forecasting context, for building and operating
econometric and market models from which a variety of forecasts
can be obtained.

Mini-computers These are smaller than main-frames, with several
functional devices mounted in a rack in a single unit. Mini-computers cannot support and operate as many applications running
concurrently as main-frames.

Micro-computers are based on a 'single-chip' microprocessor. They
are small and relatively cheap, and are contained in a few units.
The micro-computer is comprised of a VDU (Visual Display Unit
or monitor), processor, hard disk, floppy disk drives, keyboard,
mouse, and printer. As computer technology and the computing
needs of users in terms of convenience, mobility, instant accessibility
to data, etc, have developed, so have versions of the micro-computer.
This is reflected in the availability of types of micros, such as the
desk-top, portables, lap-top, notebook, and dedicated word-
processors.

Associated peripheral computer hardware

'Peripherals' fall into four main categories; input devices, terminals, storage media, and output devices. Those relevant to forecasting are listed in Figure 8.1.

Hardware information sources for computer users

There are a number of hardware information sources including magazines, catalogues, sales brochures and specialist directories. In the latter category, the author would refer the reader to *The Computer Users Year Book,* published by VNU Business Publications, VNU House, 32–34, Broadwick Street, London, W1A 2HG, for more information on computers and peripherals. This year book is, in fact, divided into four parts: Volume 1, computer equipment; Volume 2, computer services; Volume 3, computer and network sites; Volume 4, suppliers guide; all giving highly detailed information in each of the specialized computer subject areas mentioned. The suppliers guide (Volume 4) is particularly useful, as it comes with a free computer disk for faster supplier/product search.

The company has also developed a CD-ROM of manufacturers and suppliers of computer equipment with detailed specifications of all major kits. Users of this CD-ROM benefit from information drawn from the complete library of VNU Books.

Computer Software

Computer programs can be categorized as systems software, utility software and applications software.

Systems software (also known as 'the operating system') is a collection of programs containing instructions and facilities for setting up, operating and managing the particular computer system as a whole.

The most widely used operating system used on Personal Computers (PCs) is MS-DOS; on IBM PCs, it is PC-DOS. For practical purposes, both systems are the same and comprise a number of programs, which are on the floppy disk used to start-up the computer, or may already be on the computer's hard disk. (DOS stands for Disk Operating System; MS for Microsoft, the originators of MS-DOS).

There are other operating systems, some of which are applicable to micro-computers but mainly they relate to and are associated with main-frame and/or mini-computers; their use being deter-

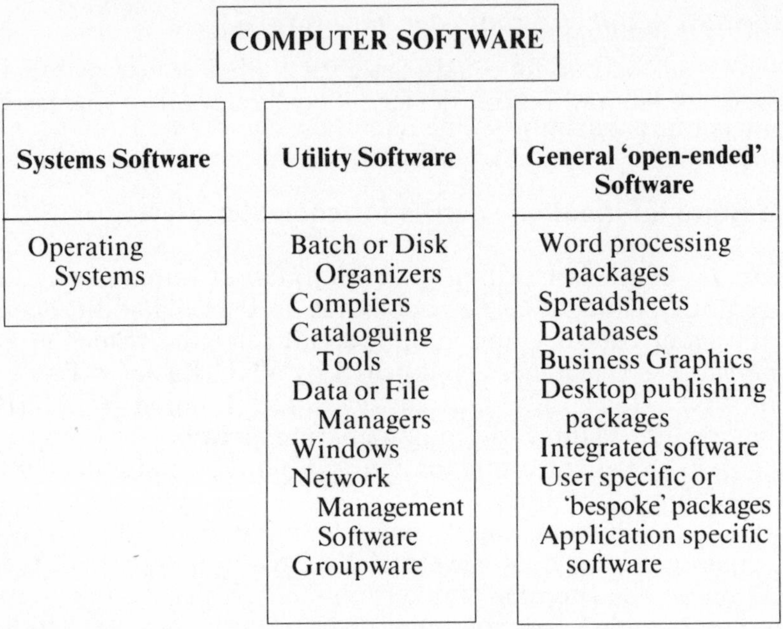

COMPUTER SOFTWARE		
Systems Software	**Utility Software**	**General 'open-ended' Software**
Operating Systems	Batch or Disk Organizers Compliers Cataloguing Tools Data or File Managers Windows Network Management Software Groupware	Word processing packages Spreadsheets Databases Business Graphics Desktop publishing packages Integrated software User specific or 'bespoke' packages Application specific software

Figure 8.2 *The principal items of computer software relevant to forecasting*

mined/dictated by the complexity and scope of work being carried out on these larger machines. There are 'utilities' available that enable these other systems to be translated and used with MS-DOS and vice versa.

Utility software is a facilitating type of software whose activity lies between the other two categories. 'Utilities' enable the operating system to work more effectively and ensure that applications are 'interpreted' and run more efficiently. They include batch or disk organizers, compilers (these translate and/or interpret commands into computer 'machine language'), cataloguing tools, printer control and routines for keeping track of data, such as data or file managers. The latter helps the user organize files and directories in the same way as organizing a filing cabinet.

A highly specialized aspect of utility software is the use of *Windows* which permits the immediate access of a number of different applications packages, and allows the user to do more than one task at a time.

This has led to the development of the Microsoft Windows graphical user interface' package, which organizes the user's application software packages loaded into the computer and provides a simple, easily understood access system. With Microsoft

Windows technology, it is possible to work on one file and simultaneously see and merge information from another. Furthermore, it enables the user to merge information from multiple files and print a comprehensive new document; this, and other features, are achieved through selection on easy-to-read menus and with the aid of logical pictorial commands, icons (symbols), selected with and obtained by a few clicks of the 'mouse'.

Microsoft also market *Windows for Workgroups,* an extension of *Windows* which lets groups of users link their PCs and work together rather than in isolation. This package has three main features, electronic mail, scheduling, and file sharing; it is the latter function that is most relevant for forecasters sharing data files with other specialists (eg data from the Accountancy Department).

A further specialized area of 'utilities' is that of *Network Management software.* If improved communications (eg electronic mail) or the sharing and/or accessing of data (eg to form the basis of forecasting) is necessary, then an extra, multi-level software infrastructure is also needed. Network management software, communications software and appropriate 'front-end' software (eg graphical user interfaces) must be installed before the network can be fully exploited.

If networks of personal computers are to be used effectively by groups of people, the applications software must be able to cope with the interactions between users. This is why *Groupware* has been developed. It is an extra, multi-level of software infrastructure, which aims to create genuine interaction between people at different workstations, in different functional parts of an organization, and thereby allows access and/or use of data in the development of, among other things, more informed business forecasts. *Groupware* is a simple evolutionary next stage on from Electronic Mail, where instead of simply sending messages, it permits the sharing of information across the network.

A number of Groupware packages have been, and are being developed; these include *Lotus Notes, Staffware, Beyond Mail* and *Microsoft Mail 3.0.*

It is only through Operating Software (System) and Utility software that the third group, *Applications software*, can run.

Applications software can be conveniently considered in the following four categories:

General 'open-ended' software packages These perform a variety of functions and activities, with a wide range of business applications in assembling, processing, analyzing, interrogating, projecting, and presenting information. They include the following groups that are directly or indirectly relevant to forecasting or presenting forecasts.

Word processing packages These are useful for the efficient creation, editing, re-arrangement, correction (many contain dictionaries for checking spelling and a thesaurus) of forecast reports and the merging of documents. They are also useful for the technique of scenario writing (see 'Subjective Methods' in later chapter) and presenting judgemental /subjective forecasts.

Spreadsheets There are useful for laying out data in tabular form, making rapid calculations and identifying characteristics of data (eg instant calculations of averages, standard deviations, etc), identifying statistical relationships, analyzing and projecting data, making forecasts, building forecasting models (all the objective techniques shown in the previous chapter can be operated on spreadsheets) and instantly up-dating data/calculations.

Spreadsheets can be used for creating marketing plans based on market and sales forecasts. In Table 8.1, the five years marketing plan (modelled on a Lotus 123 spreadsheet) is based on a sales forecast (see top line of data) that shows, not only revenues and expenditures, but can also be used for identifying income and expenditure break-even points related to particular forecasts, for generating a variety of marketing/business ratios and for interrogating data/tables (often referred to as its 'what if...' role) for determining the effects of potential over and under achievement of forecasts. This is the case in Table 8.1, where absolute data or equations are entered into each cell on the spreadsheet, so that the changes in data in one part of the plan will 'update' all the rest of the ensuing data, results and ratios.

Databases are useful for creating, updating and manipulating related and unrelated records of data, obtaining general statistics about the data, and retrieving and reproducing it as a whole, or as relevant structured parts, to meet specific characteristics or conditions and to enable statistical analysis to take place.

Business Graphics Some of the above mentioned spreadsheet and database packages have in-built graphics facilities so that the data or statistics they generate can be viewed, produced and presented graphically. Also, there are a number of specialized business graphics packages into which data from spreadsheets and databases can be imported. Both types produce a variety of graphs such as vertical and horizontal bar charts (some two and three dimensional), line graphs, area charts, pie charts (whole or segmented), combination charts and tables. Some of the graphs can be projected, thus producing forecasts or data can be read from them which, in turn, produces a forecast (see 'percentage take-graphs method' in Chapter 7).

Table 8.1 *Financial statement of new product launch*

| | YEARS | | | | |
	1	2	3	4	5
SALES ('000'S. UNITS £'000'S	1,000	1,250	1,500	1,500	1,500
NET SALES VALUE per unit 1.5	1,500	1,875	2,250	2,250	2,250
VARIABLE COST per unit 0.9	900	1,125	1,350	1,350	1,350
CONTRIBUTION per unit 0.6	600	750	900	900	900
LESS:					
a) Promotional	150	100	110	110	110
b) Media	250	200	50	50	50
CONTRIBUTION	200	450	740	740	740
LESS FIXED COST:					
a) PRODUCTION	50	50	50	50	50
b) MARKETING	15	2	2	2	2
NET PROFIT	135	398	688	688	688

ADDITIONAL CAPITAL EMPLOYED

Plant and Machinery	200	200	200	200	200
Stocks	96	120	144	144	144
Debtors	58	72	86	86	86
Total	354	392	430	430	430
1. Profit % of Capital Employed	38.1	101.5	160.0	160.0	160.0
2. Profit % of Sales	9.0	21.2	30.6	30.6	30.6
3. Contribution % of Sales	13.3	24.0	32.9	32.9	32.9
4. Promotion % Sales	10.0	5.3	4.9	4.9	4.9
5. Media % Sales	16.7	10.7	2.2	2.2	2.2
6. Fixed Cost % Sales	4.3	2.8	2.3	2.3	2.3
7. Sales: Capital Employed	4.2	4.8	5.2	5.2	5.2

A number of graphics packages have a library or gallery of symbols, images and borders that can be selected and used to make the general presentation of forecast reports more visually alive, dynamic and interesting, especially by highlighting key features.

Desktop Publishing packages can be used to create interesting and forecast reports that look 'professionally printed'. There is a very close link between desktop publishing and wordprocessing packages; fundamentally, desktop publishing packages are concerned with layouts, print fonts, graphics and then text, whereas wordprocessing packages give priority to text but nowadays incorporate some aspects of graphics and use various fonts. The choice of fonts offered by a wordprocessing package is often determined by the scope and type of printer being used.

Integrated Software A number of general application software packages are said to be 'integrated' because they incorporate several applications in one software program. They combine the various functions of spreadsheets, wordprocessing and mailmerge, graphics, database and report generation. Their main feature is that data entered in the database for example, becomes available to the spreadsheet. In the best packages, additional information put into any functional area of the program will automatically update data held in all other functions.

User specific or bespoke software packages are commissioned to suit the needs of the individual user. For example, a company may require a 'tailor-made' forecasting program, based upon 13 four weekly periods rather than on 12 calendar months, with the facility of 'reforecasting' three times during any year.

During the 1980s, the idea of getting software developed precisely to a particular organization's needs became less popular as users switched to the growing number of standard packages being offered. The practical reasons were obvious. Packages sold in volume cost a fraction of a bespoke, specially designed development. They can be installed in a fraction of the time needed for a bespoke program. Further, they often bring self-analysis and discipline to many companies because the organization's processes have to be adapted to the package rather than the other way around.

However, the basic idea of adaptable packaged software, which can be used repeatedly in a variety of different situations, is now contributing to the revival of bespoke systems. Systems integration, using some existing software 'kernels', has become a very common form of bespoke development, with appropriate 'kernels' from existing software being bought in from another software company.

Application specific software packages These are systems/programs that are dedicated to, and perform, a specific business function. For example stock control, purchase ledger, payroll, advertising media planning, marketing planning and, of course, market and sales forecasting. In this latter group, the forecasting aspect is either a part of, or an additional module to a wider statistical package (eg *Minitab, SPSS, Javelin, StatPac Gold*) or is an integral aspect of an application specific program, eg part of a marketing planning package (eg *PREDICT!*), or is a package primarily dedicated to business forecasting (eg *SmartForecasts*).

Over a long period of time, the author has used the latter two programs (*PREDICT!* and *SmartForecasts*) on higher education programmes with specific market and sales forecasting inputs (MBA, MA(Marketing), BA (Hons) degree in Business Studies), and on short courses. Although acknowledging that other programs of this nature exist, it would be helpful to use these two user-friendly programs as examples of the type of specific forecasting software programs that are available, their scope and the various functions they perform to help the market and sales forecaster.

First PREDICT! (based on extracts from program literature): *PREDICT!* is a spreadsheet-based modelling and simulation tool which helps the forecaster to analyze uncertainty and risk. *PREDICT!* combines the power of a sophisticated modelling tool with the flexibility, familiarity and ease of use of a spreadsheet. For the first time, with the aid of *PREDICT!*, the forecaster will be able to answer questions like:

- What market share can we be 90 per cent certain of achieving on this new product launch?
- Which inventory policy gives us the greatest confidence of achieving a given cost level?
- How confident are we that this project will exceed our profitability criteria?
- What is the chance that this activity will end up on the critical path?
- What is the chance of a loss in this business area?
- What per cent participation in this project gives us maximum return with minimum risk?

The major benefits of *PREDICT!* to the decision maker are:

- better decisions, based on more realistic models — ones which cope with uncertainty;
- quantified risks, plus pictures (literally) of risks against rewards;
- automatic 'what-ifs', with each 'what-if' properly weighted for how likely it is to occur;

- friendly and flexible modelling environment, offering a powerful spreadsheet tool in its own right.

PREDICT! is designed for decision-makers in the widest sense of the word — it can be used by anyone modelling uncertain situations (made to measure for market and sales forecasting needs!).

PREDICT! recognizes the shortcomings of traditional modelling packages and overcomes them by using probability and statistical techniques. Each spreadsheet cell in a *PREDICT!* model can describe uncertain behaviour using probability distributions. You can use these distributions to incorporate 'gut-feel' estimates into your model — for example, a simple ball-park estimate is a distribution; alternatively, you can use the distributions, to describe the wealth of raw data.

Eight standard probability distributions are available and you can also define your own distributions. Once you have described a situation's uncertainties using distributions, *PREDICT!* automatically simulates the model, using the Monte Carlo method, performing a potentially infinite number of 'what-ifs', each one weighted for how likely it is to arise. The result is a set of distributions for important variables in the model which in turn describe their uncertainty. In other words *PREDICT!* generates uncertainty 'maps' for important decision variables, which reflect the uncertainties in the underlying variables.

Once the required store of results has been built up, you may examine these output distributions using *PREDICT!*'s interpretive facilities. These let you highlight important characteristics of a distribution. Specifically, they let you answer questions like:

- What profit/loss can we be 90 per cent confident of achieving?
- What is the chance of a loss arising in the second year of the project?
- What level of sales can we be 70 per cent certain of achieving?
- How reliable is this system?

You can draw graphs to see the variability of distributions you are interested in, or read off the chance of obtaining outcomes around a chosen value, or find a value you can be x per cent confident of achieving, and so on. You can then interrelate and compare them with other distributions in the model.

You can obtain more precise information about a distribution by carrying out statistical analysis: standard deviation, percentile, mean/median/mode, chi-square statistic and maximum/minimum are some of the many functions you can perform.

You can glean other important information from the model by

performing sensitivity analysis to discover which items in the model your resultant variables are sensitive to.

PREDICT! has a wide range of applications, including capital investment appraisal, credit analysis, queuing simulation, inventory planning and control, critical path analysis, etc. Especially relevant are its applications in the areas of sales forecasts and market share estimation.

For sales forecasting, it covers:

- *Uncertainties* Volume and timing of sales, warranties and sales returns, possible competitor action and resulting impact, performance of each sales channel, margins, exchange rates, commissions.
- *Results* Chance of achieving various sales targets, sales volumes/ values you can be x per cent confident of achieving.

For Market Share Estimation it covers:

- *Uncertainties* Marketing survey results, buyer switching probabilities, possible competitor action and results, impact of pricing, marketing response rates, possible castastrophic events, growth rates, demographic changes.
- *Result* Chance of achieving various market shares and by when, level of market share you can be x per cent confident of achieving.

Secondly 'SmartForecasts' (extracts from program literature): *SmartForecasts* adds a unique dimension to your portfolio of business productivity and analytical tools. It helps business executives and professionals make better forecasts and, therefore, better business decisions. *SmartForecasts* also provides features for graphical and statistical data analysis and data management.

In almost every business and industry, decision-makers need reliable forecasts of critical variables, such as:

- sales
- revenues
- inventory
- market share
- budget expenditures
- product demand
- personnel requirements
- industry trends

The many kinds of people who make these forecasts can benefit from a tool like *SmartForecasts*. Some are sophisticated analysts such as business economists and statisticians, whose specialized training and job titles identify them as professional forecasters.

Many others regard forecasting as an important part of their overall work: general managers and functional specialists in fields like finance, strategic planning, inventory control, logistics, product and sales management or market research. Others seldom think of themselves as forecasters but often have to make forecasts on an intuitive, 'back-of-the-envelope' basis.

SmartForecasts has something to offer everyone. To professional forecasters, it offers a flexible, low-cost alternative to cumbersome and expensive mainframe or time-sharing models. To general managers and functional specialists, it offers independence from data processing backlogs and the chance to let know-how shape forecasts. To back-of-the-envelope forecasters, it offers sound and helpful techniques, packaged so that people who are not statistical experts can get useful results in a hurry.

SmartForecasts is the first forecasting software to successfully combine statistical and judgemental forecasting. You can start by forecasting from your historical data using any of several statistical techniques. Then you can adjust the statistical forecast to take account of your special knowledge and insight. This synthesis of professional judgement and statistical analysis is important for making reliable business forecasts.

Some of the special features that distinguish *SmartForecasts* include:

- Popular Time-Series Forecasting techniques, including single, double and Winters' exponential smoothing and simple and linear moving average.
- Multivariate Regression, specially tailored for forecasting applications, using up to 20 independent variables.
- Advanced Box-Jenkins (ARIMA) Forecasting technique, including an iterative process of model identification, estimation and diagnosis, leading to a mathematical model which serves as a basis for user forecasts.
- 'Eyeball' Forecasting, permitting users to make and adjust forecasts directly on the computer screen, using interactive graphics, trend line projections and 'what if' projections.
- Management Overrides of statistical forecasts, incorporating users' professional judgement for increased accuracy and credibility.
- Automatic Forecasting, for users who want SmartForecasts to select and use an appropriate forecasting method automatically.
- Simultaneous Multiseries Forecasting of up to 60 well-related variables and their total, as in product line forecasting.
- The ability to quickly repeat and apply a particular time-series forecasting method to a large number of individual data series.

- Fully integrated colour graphics and on-screen annotation of all graphs.
- Graphical and numerical reports of forecasting uncertainty.
- Speed and flexibility for extensive analysis of alternatives.

The *SmartForecasts* package is not only useful for forecasting, but also for rapid statistical and graphical analysis of data. With the program's data analysis commands, the forecaster can quickly discover the key features of available data and select appropriate forecasting techniques.

Some of *SmartForecasts* special data analysis capabilities let you:

- Summarize data with descriptive statistics (mean, median, maximum 75th percentile value, 25th percentile value minimum range, standard deviation, coefficient of variation and total count).
- Plot the distribution of data values with 'histograms'.
- Plot one variable against another in scatter diagrams or 'X-Y plots' that expose relationships useful for prediction.
- Plot up to six data series against time on the same 'timeplot' or 'linegraph'.
- Detect seasonal patterns in a data series using a display known as an 'autocorrelation plot'.
- Decompose data with a seasonal pattern and produce seasonally adjusted data for further analysis.
- Identify leading indicators using a display known as a 'crosscorrelation plot'.
- Annotate graphs to highlight interesting features and add comments and labels.
- Make permanent copies of your graphs by printing them on a dot matrix or laser printer or saving them as PCX graphics files.

A key step in the forecasting process is the creation and maintenance of data files. *SmartForecasts* has many features that make it easy to manage data, including:

- A simple way to exchange *Lotus* worksheets and other data files with other software, such as *Lotus 1-2-3, Symphony* and *Excel.*
- A quick way to issue standard DOS file commands to maintain data files.
- Rapid data entry from the keyboard or from a DOS data file.
- Full data editing capabilities with 'Lotus-like' cursor key controls.
- Data table with room for 60 variables and 260 cases per variable (15,600 total data points per data file).
- Movable data window that can display any three variables,

even when they are not next to each other in the data table.
- Automatic sequential labelling of time-series data.
- Compatibilty with both time-series and cross-sectional data (eg data by month for one corporation or one year's data for many corporations).
- Easy insertion and deletion of variables and cases for updating data files.
- An OOPS command that undoes mistaken changes to the data table, as when you accidentally delete the wrong variable.
- Self-contained SmartForecasts Worksheet for rapid storage and retrieval of work in progress,
- Powerful data transformations combining arithmetic, log, square root, lead/lag, percentage change and other commonly-used functions.

Both *PREDICT!* and *SmartForecasts* packages improve the speed, scope and effectiveness of market and sales forecasts.

Software information sources for Software Users

There are a number of software information sources including magazines, catalogues, sales brochures and specialist directories. In the latter category, the author would refer the reader to *The Software Users Year Book*, published by VNU Business Publications, VNU House, 32--34 Broadwick Street, London, W1A 2HG, for more information on the availability of various types of Software packages. This *Year Book* is, in fact, divided into four parts: Volume 1, software suppliers and services; Volume 2, systems software; Volume 3, industry specific software; Volume 4, general applications software; each volume giving highly detailed information in each of the specialized software areas covered. The *Software Users Year Book* contains details of over 11,500 software packages; this list is updated annually.

For example, there are a number of forecasting related software packages in the last two volumes that are either forecasting specific or contain specialist forecasting aspects or in which forecasting models can be readily developed.

A CD-ROM version of this *Year Book* is also published; this saves time in software search. Simple text retrieval software makes this CD-ROM version of the *Software Users Year Book* extremely fast and speeds up software search considerably.

Conclusion

The development of mainframe, mini and micro-computers has

presented the forecaster/marketing executive with more effective methods of processing data and has also provided a problem-solving tool. This is particularly so in forecasting, where computers can be used to handle highly complex problems that would otherwise be impossible or too costly to solve in terms of money or time. But they can also be used to handle many of the traditional/routine types of statistical forecasting techniques. Using computers, many types of statistical forecasts can be more rapidly obtained, in greater detail, with a wider variety of 'breakdown'/analysis/classifi- cations, than previously.

One of the main uses of computers in forecasting, is to maintain past and present records of sales/purchasing patterns. It can analyze demand history and 'breakdown' past patterns of sales into trend, seasonal, cyclical and random variation values.

Computers can be used to search for relevant key market-related factors, external to the company, that have a degree of correlation with, and therefore give an indication of, the potential level of sales. The computer's capability/capacity to handle a large number of variables often makes it the best way, and sometimes the only way, of using multiple correlation techniques.

It is possible to build models and simulate many market situations on a computer and, by changing the size of one or more variables (eg price, cost, product range, etc), to assess and quantify the effect this will have on potential sales volume and/or profit in a particular market segment.

Computers can be used to assess and improve the 'machinery' of forecasting, by examining basic patterns of demand, and applying and testing various techniques (eg those shown in Chapter 7) and their variations. This will identify the most suitable combinations of forecasting techniques, especially with regard to their most recent performance in relation to sales totals actually achieved. One method is to obtain the last five years data and, using the first four years figures, apply a number of techniques to obtain a fore- cast. The technique to use is the one that produces a forecast nearest to the actual sales achieved in the fifth year.

Some forecasting-specific packages (eg *SmartForecasts*) have a degree of 'artifical Intelligence' in their make-up, so that before forecasting they identify the statistical technique most appropriate to the pattern of the data.

Storage and retrieval of appropriate forecasting data can be obtained from data disks, company data banks, and commercial data banks. Also the actual forecasting calculation, together with its probability and graphs, can be stored and instantly retrieved and comparisons made with other forecasts and actual sales. It must be appreciated, however, that the computer is merely a forecasting tool developing a series of quantified relationships between sales and a variety of variables, and that the forecast produced by the computer is only as good as the data put in and the effectiveness of the program used. Furthermore, it must also be appreciated that computer forecasts should be validated by being subjected to human judgement and intelligence not only for being desirable but also for viability/feasibility.

A further application of computers is in the auditing of forecasts, ie monitoring the accuracy of the forecast by comparing it regularly with actual sales. Built-in warning systems can be arranged to indicate when actual sales fall outside acceptable probability limits so that corrective action can be taken.

9

Subjective/Judgemental Methods of Forecasting

'Persons pretending to forecast the future shall be considered disorderly.'
New York Crime Code

Subjective methods of forecasting

Subjective methods of forecasting tend to be intuitive techniques that are the application of experience, intelligence and judgement to the forecasting situation; in fact they tend to be based on deduced conclusions. Some methods included in this section are wholly subjective, basically representing an averaging of a variety of opinions, eg a survey of consumer/user intentions. Others, although derived subjectively, can be made more useful by the application of an objective method, eg the addition of probability values to panel forecasting.

Indicator assessment method

The indicator assessment or 'balance the facts' method again makes use of economic indicators. An assessment is made of the general factors which are likely to be operating, and will affect the company, in the next sales period.

Where particular economic data have been found to reflect the economic climate in a particular industry, the appropriate economic indicators are listed in two columns. One column will show all those indicators that are favourable towards an expansion of trade, and the other column those that indicate a contraction of trade. The strength and effect of these indicators is assessed and a final conclusion formed and written up. To illustrate this technique, take a hypothetical case where a forecaster is endeavouring to determine the extent of future business activity in the economy related to a particular company's markets (see Figure 9.1). Actual figures and graphs for each indicator have been omitted but these would be necessary for a clear assessment.

Unfavourable factors

1. *Employment*. Allowing for high seasonal peaks, unemployment has increased especially in certain capital goods industries.

2. *Government spending*. This has been curtailed in the last four months due to signs of inflation in the economy.

3. *Industrial production* has levelled out again in the last part of the year.

4. *Home building starts* are again levelling out.

Favourable factors

1. *Machine tool orders*. Following a decline in the early part of the year, there has been a steady increase in orders from July onwards.

2. *Factory building approvals*. There has been a slow but steady upward trend throughout the year.

3. *Bank advances* are rising strongly.

4. *Terms of trade*. These were steady in the early part of the past year but turned in our favour from August onwards.

ASSESSMENT

Business activity in the coming year will tend to level out. Although government spending has been temporarily curtailed, it can be expected to increase again and introduce a boost to the economy if the present decline in employment continues. The machine tool orders and factory building starts indicate confidence in the present situation by business men generally. This is encouraged by the fact that bank advances are rising strongly, and this will have a good effect upon the ability of consumers to purchase durable products.

Favourable terms of trade indicate that import prices have become cheaper relative to export prices and this should help to increase consumer spending power without increasing the present inflationary tendencies when terms of trade advantages are reflected in retail prices.

The conclusion is, therefore, that, although business activity will tend to level out, total national disposable income will continue to rise, but not at the same rate of growth as last year.

Figure 9.1 *An assessment of appropriate economic indicators*

A variation of this method is to identify various appropriate indicators and send recent past data and current data to three or four interested company executives asking them to 'sort' the items into currently 'favourable' or 'unfavourable' columns. A further refinement is to ask the executives to rank the favourable and unfavourable factors in order of their importance to the company/product range.

Sometimes one executive may place an indicator in the opposite column to the others. In such a case the economy/market is being assessed taking different influences into account; it is important for the forecaster to investigate these differences.

The indicator assessment or 'balance the facts' method can be used either to give some indication of anticipated business activity, or to gauge the effect of various economic indicators upon the sales of a product or range of products. It is a balancing technique, where the statistical/data approach is counter-balanced by experience and judgement.

Subjective factor assessment

Earlier it was suggested that no matter whether an objective/mechanical method of forecasting was simple or highly sophisticated, its prediction should always be subjected to human judgement, intelligence, reasoning and logic; is the projected forecast feasible within what is known of the total situation?

The forecaster and/or the expert being consulted is being asked for an opinion as to the credibility of the forecast and if and how he would adjust it. The effectiveness of this approach will depend upon the breadth of the expert's knowledge and experience, his ability to identify relevant factors and their trends, his ability to quantify and measure the factors' impact on the forecast. Many good experience-based forecasts are made by 'experts' not apparently wholly aware of the stages through which they should proceed if their ultimate forecast is to be more than an unrelated guess. It may help therefore to get them to formalize their approach by asking them to complete such a form as in Figure 9.2; the factors included would be necessarily different for each company.

Experts are asked to identify influencing/impact factors under each heading, to rank them in order of importance, to grade according to anticipated impact and then to indicate whether they consider it to be favourable or unfavourable. By assigning rank and weight to factors a quantitative dimension is given to a qualitative (judgemental) opinion. The expert can now be asked to modify a 'mechanical' forecast in the light of the weight of his opinion; it also permits quantitative comparison to be made between periods.

The Delphi method

This method eliminates the committee activity seen in some types of subjective forecasting in favour of a programme of questionnaires designed on a sequential basis. It attempts to make more effective use of informed intuitive judgement. It is based on personal expectations of individuals and therefore may take into account forecasting and influencing factors not considered by other people or included in the calculation of statistical forecasts.

Influence/impact factors	Rank in order of importance	Considerable (5)	Some (4)	Average (3)	Little (2)	None (1)		Favourable	Adverse	Neither
				IMPACT						
1) International factors a) b) c) d)										
2) Economic factors a) b) c) d)										
3) Industry factors a) b) c) d)										
4) Market factors a) b) c) d)										
5) Company factors a) b) c) d)										
6) Consumer/user a) b) c) d)										
7) Competition factors a) b) c) d)										
8) Environmental a) b) c) d)										
9) Psychological factors a) b)										

etc

Figure 9.2 *Subjective factor assessment form*

A panel of experts is selected and the first questionnaire which asks a series of questions on the likelihood of some particular event/situation/phenomenon happening is put to them. It attempts to establish median values of the particular variable. This is summarized and, together with extreme values, is passed back to the members of the panel. The members are then asked to reconsider their previous answers and modify them if they think appropriate; those who made extreme estimates are asked to explain why such estimates were made. The procedure continues in this manner until a consensus is reached.

The questionnaires usually contain a means of indicating whether individual members of a panel consider themselves ill-equipped to respond to a question in a particular area. Some examples of Delphi type questions are as follows:

A. In what year do you forecast with 100% probability the first specific legislation on population control?
Year...
Expertness — Yes No
Control —

B. In what year do you forecast that vegetable sources will provide 25% of the human protein consumption now obtainable from animal sources?
with 20% probability Year...
with 80% probability Year...
Expertness — Yes No
Comments —

C. By what percentage do you forecast the present telephone network based on cable being superseded by a network based on radio waves by 2000, with 50% probability?
...%
Expertness — Yes No
Comments —

D. What % probability do you give to the forecast that the issue of motor vehicle licences will be selective by a defined system of priorities in the year 2000?
Probability...%
Expertness — Yes No
Comments —

E. What percentage of private motor cars do you forecast will be propelled by the following in the years stated, each at 50% probability?

	Year	
	2000 %	2010 %
Internal combustion		
Steam		
Gas turbine		
Electric		
Other		

Expertness — Yes   No
Comments   —

Survey of consumer/user purchasing intentions

A simple and direct method of forecasting sales is to ask customers and potential customers what they are planning to purchase. In consumer goods markets, where sheer numbers make it impossible to interview everyone, an appropriate representative sample must be approached if the eventual forecast is to be meaningful. It may involve a sample survey at two levels: the consumer's intention to buy a particular product or brand, and the wholesaler/retailer's intention to stock and promote it.

With industrial products the number of customers and /or potential customers may be relatively few, and sampling may not be necessary. The main problem will be to persuade customers to make such a prediction or to give enough reliable information regarding future production, plans, future expenditure, manufacturing capacity, new product development policy, existing stocks, etc, so that a forecast can be made.

Various aspects of surveys were considered earlier in the sections dealing with the collection of data and original field research. Survey results should not be used alone for forecasting but in conjunction with other methods. Executives of customer companies may think that in forecasting for a supplier they cannot be held responsible as in their own organization, and an arbitrary guess rather than a considered estimate may result. Further, it will be difficult to gauge changes in policy matters within a customer company (eg the possibility of a change in the size of stock holding), or genuine market reaction (eg the effect of their or your competitors' activities), or the effect of changes in price and/or discount policy. Despite these problems, a good estimate by a 'buyer' will provide forecasting information regarding how 'buyers' feel *at the moment.* Over a period of time a pattern of reliability will be established regarding various 'buyers'.

The forecaster may modify the survey results by his own interpretation of anticipated future events in the economy, market or company.

Panels of executive opinion

Whereas the previous method concerned a prediction of the market from the customer's point of view, this technique obtains a forecast, short-, medium- or long-term, based on the facts and the considered opinion of key executives within the company's own organization. Executive forecasts are evaluated, combined and averaged, and through discussion a single forecast emerges. Executives should appreciate the need for forward planning and will realize that this is based ultimately on the number of items that can be sold. If executives can be encouraged to obtain forecasting data and opinions from within their own functional areas and make a considered forecast of these, this method is in effect the distilled forecasting thinking of the company. Company policy will be known and the panel fed with basic economic and market information and assumptions.

The various marketing executives (marketing research, new product development, advertising and sales promotion, sales, and distribution) are obvious members for such a panel. But so are production, purchasing, finance and personnel executives, not only because the best mental resources within a company are being brought to bear on the forecasting problem, but also because their forecasts will be influenced by their own specialized areas of operation and the distilled forecast of their particular business environment. Executives have an interest in the continued existence of the company and often have very definite views of the future under existing policies and how these could be improved.

One use of a panel of executive opinion is that of assessing and adjusting other forecasts based on mathematical and mechanical projection. Specialized human judgement and intelligence are used to check the credibility of objective techniques.

Panels of executive opinion can also be used in the final stages of the development of a forecast. Where forecasts have been obtained from various sources, there is a need to assess and evaluate each one before adopting an actual forecast. A panel of executive opinion is one way of achieving this.

'Prudent manager' forecasting

A variation of the previous method is where a small panel of specialists from all parts of a company is set up. They are asked to assume the role of members of the purchasing decision making unit in a customer company. They are asked to evaluate the supplying company's total sales proposition and to forecast the sales of various products. They are asked to do this from a customer's point of view, prudently assessing the facts that are available, and to produce purchasing requirements that customers would be likely to want in the conditions prevailing in a market.

Composite forecasts of the sales force

The term 'grass-roots' has been used to describe the relationship of the salesperson, area or regional managers and sales managers to the customer. The close proximity of the sales force to the roots of demand (the customer) is the justification for its use in many cases to carry out research and forecasting functions.

This type of forecast can be used as a prediction technique in its own right, particularly if statistical data from other sources limits the amount of forecasting that can be done by other methods. It can also be used as a practical check on more mechanical methods of forecasting.

Ideally, the salesperson should be given some basic tuition in elementary forecasting. Also he may be given historic data on past sales over an appropriate period of time or may be expected to derive this information from his own records. The ensuing forecasts are totalled to give an overall sales forecast for the company. Special forecasting forms to be completed by the salesperson can be arranged in such a way as to produce not only a total sales forecast but one analyzed in terms of product group and/or sub-group size or value, by area or type of customer or industrial classification. The main justification for this type of forecasting is that it is presumed that salespeople have a detailed knowledge of their own areas of a market. One of the main disadvantages claimed for this method is that of bias by members of the sales force. One type of salesperson may deliberately undervalue the forecast because he thinks that it may become the basis of his sales target; by setting it lower it becomes easier to achieve. But, although this may be a problem initially, after a small number of sales forecasting periods a salesperson's method of operating soon becomes apparent. It is possible to discover an average percentage, eg salesperson A's sales always tend to be 5 per cent up on his forecast: salesperson B tends to be 12½ per cent down on forecast. There will always be differences due to external forces, but the pattern of bias will be indicated fairly clearly.

Other disadvantages claimed are that forecasts by salespeople are influenced by recent successes or failures rather than by future sales opportunities.

An additional use of obtaining forecasts from the individual salesperson is as a motivational device. Forecasts by salespeople are made and then discussed with sales executives and agreement is reached eventually on the forecast which then becomes the basis of the salesperson's target. The salesperson feels that he has had a part in calculating his target, and he has been consulted. This in turn often makes him more enthusiastic in his attempts to achieve the target, and he will, therefore, be more likely to reach and pass the agreed sales value than if the target figure had been arbitrarily imposed from above.

A refinement of the above technique is where, in addition to the individual salesperson making forecasts, area, regional and national sales managers can be asked to produce forecasts for their own appropriate areas of responsibility. At each level these can be totalled and a sales forecast obtained. Further, comparisons can be made between the sum total of a salesperson's forecasts in each area with the area manager's forecast and the variance between the two figures analyzed, eg why is the salesmen's composite forecast 15 per cent above the area manager's forecast? What factor has the area manager taken into account that has not been considered by the sales force or vice versa?

In addition to bias, it is said that this method is a costly way of obtaining information, is unreliable because of lack of forecasting training for salespeople and uses valuable selling time. On the other hand, the salesperson can produce the necessary data fairly easily in many marketing situations, appreciates technical considerations in industrial marketing situations, is already known to the customer, has the customer's confidence, and also tends to discover market intelligence additional to the forecasting data.

Surveys of expert opinion

This approach can range from buying in forecasts from consultants to running a panel made up of experts from within the company (marketing researchers, salespeople, etc) and specialists from outside, ie economists, marketing experts, specialist psychologists, typical customers, etc. Further, the method can be of the kind where each panel member makes a forecast and never meets the other members, or where they meet as a committee and, through discussion, arrive at a composite forecast. In the former case the variations in the different forecasts can be analyzed and an eventual forecast obtained (sometimes by the simple device of averaging); but in the latter case the role of forecasting has been delegated to the committee.

The main danger of such composite forecasts is that they may contain a number of judgements or arbitrary forecasts, and their validity may be dubious. It is difficult for the forecaster to know whether such forecasts are soundly based, and, therefore, difficult later to determine and analyze why the forecast varies from actual sales. Further, with the individual parts of composite forecasts it is impossible to distinguish between what is optimistically desirable and what is realistically possible.

In spite of these difficulties the survey of expert opinion is a useful forecasting tool, because the individual component part forecasts suggest the range of possibilities and, by averaging them, a 'middle of the road' forecast can be obtained.

Uncertainty and probability in subjective forecasting

One of the biggest problems in top management decision making today is how to cope with the uncertainty in information regarding the organization's external environment.

Many capital budgeting policies and their input forecasting procedures require only one-number forecasts/estimates, thus neglecting the problem of uncertainty completely. For example, two experts may forecast 1750 units, but one may be 95 per cent certain of his forecast and the other only 50 per cent certain.

Misinterpretations and ambiguities occur simply because judgements about uncertainty are difficult to transmit to others, and also because forecasts/estimates from subordinates can be biased and because the capacity for risk-taking differs among individuals.

Suppose an expert forecasts/estimates that there is a 'good' chance that sales will exceed 200,000 or a 'fair' chance that sales could be as high as 300,000. Or there is a 'reasonable' chance that Competitor X will introduce a new product next year that will adversely affect sales. What do these statements mean? Does 'fair' mean that the chances are two out of 10, or four out of 10? Does 'reasonable' mean five out of 10 or perhaps seven out of 10?

A number of companies require 'optimistic', 'pessimistic' and 'best estimate' forecasts from various experts. These supposedly widely understood terms open up the possibility of very different interpretations and to some extent may even encourage 'political' manipulation because of their ambiguity.

For example, even the range from the optimistic to the pessimistic level could vary widely between two 'information specialists' even though they both guess the actual uncertainty to be about the same.

Much staff and analytical effort goes into estimating the 'single-number' forecast, whether it is the sales to an individual company or the overall sales of a particular product or product type. The manager either has to accept the expert's forecast/estimate about the future or make a compensating judgement. However, if compensation is made at a number of levels or points, the true position will become blurred, as the uncertainty underlying the eventual forecast is not visible.

In some companies information experts are more concerned with attaining their own personal rewards than they are with choosing estimates that reflect their best estimates of future sales. In practice some companies tend to reward information experts when sales performance exceeds their original forecast, penalize them when performance falls below forecast, and do neither when they are 'spot-on'. In such circumstances the expert has little to gain by reporting an impersonal, objective forecast, and much to gain by estimating conservatively or even by under-forecasting and over-achieving.

Making uncertainty visible

There are several ways of presenting uncertainty in a visible and precise manner.

(a) Probability judgements. Probabilities are given by the forecaster to various levels of sales as in Table 9.1. This table shows, for instance, that the chances are only one out of four (or 0.25) that sales will be less than 500; or conversely, the chances are three out of four (0.75) that sales will be greater than 500. Similarly, the chances are 50/50 that sales will exceed 600, and three out of four that they will be less than 700. The chances also are 50/50 that sales will fall within the 500 to 700 range. Identifying the uncertainty in this manner provides a more comprehensive view of a forecast figure.

(b) Visual probability range displays. Figure 9.3 shows the information expert's judgements regarding the underlying uncertainty in a visual manner. The probabilities on the vertical

Table 9.1 *Probability judgements*

Cumulative Probability	Maximum sales expected
1.00	1200
0.95	900
0.75	700
0.50	600
0.25	500
0.05	300
0.00	0

scale show the chances of actual sales falling within a particular range. For example, the chances are one out of 10 that sales will fall in the 300 to 400 range, and one out of 10 that they will fall in the 400 to 500 range.

(c) Uncertainty index. Often for the purpose of simplifying the subsequent financial evaluation and for implementing planning and control objectives, a 'single-number' forecast eventually has to be decided upon. In Figure 9.4, the uncertainty index shows the probability of sales falling below the forecast. Thus the index indicates that for a forecast of 500 the chances are only one in four that actual sales will be below this level.

Presenting forecasting information in these various ways does not prevent the top-level manager from applying his own judgements to a situation, but, before he does, he has a better idea of what experts and information specialists were actually thinking when they made their forecast/estimate. But even where experts are expected to produce a 'single-number' forecast/estimate, they will tend to produce more effective and objective forecasts/estimates if they 'think probabilistically'.

Probability and forecasting by composite opinion

In the previous section it was suggested that experts who were asked to make subjective forecasts should be required to give not only their best estimate/forecast but also their most optimistic and their most pessimistic. There is an analogy between this and the least squares (line of best fit) method on page 174 *et seq*, where the best estimate could be construed to be the projected trend line and the most pessimistic and the most optimistic forecasts could be

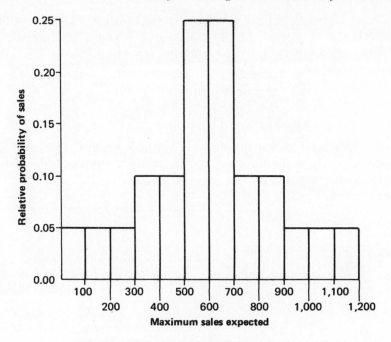

Figure 9.3 *Visual probability range display*

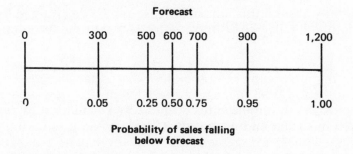

Figure 9.4 *An uncertainty index*

likened to the control lines set two standard deviations above and below the trend line.

In fact the range between the most pessimistic and the most optimistic forecasts can be used to 'adjust' the best estimate forecast and also calculate the probability of its being within certain limits. This can be done when asking one expert or when asking a panel of experts to forecast subjectively (although part of the forecast may be based upon facts/experience). This will add a quantitative 'sharpening up' of a qualitative (judgemental) forecast.

For example one 'expert' (perhaps a product manager, salesperson, etc) is asked for his highest (most optimistic), best estimate (expected) and lowest (most pessimistic) forecasts of a particular product's sales in a specified time period. He gives the following information:

> *Lowest:* 99 units
> *Best estimate:* 110 units
> *Highest:* 112 units

First a weighted average method is applied; weighted because if a value is really what he expects (his best estimate), it should be given more weight than the two 'outsiders' (highest and lowest).

$$\text{weighted average} = \frac{\text{lowest} + (4 \times \text{expected}) + \text{highest}}{N}$$

The weighting of 4 has been given to the 'expected' but the size of this weight depends purely on the subjective judgement of the forecaster. In this case the divisor is 6 because 4 (expected) + highest + lowest are six items. Therefore:

$$\text{weighted average} = \frac{99 + 440 + 112}{6} = 108 \text{ adjusted forecast}$$

Probability around this adjusted figure can be determined by first calculating the 'degree of uncertainty' (D) with the formula:

$$D = \frac{(H-L)^2}{6^2} = \frac{(112-99)^2}{36} = 4.69$$

The standard deviation can be found by calculating the square root of the 'degree of uncertainty' (*D*), ie.

$$\sqrt{(4.69)} = 2 \text{ (approximately)} = \text{standard deviations}$$

To obtain 99 per cent certainty 2.5 standard deviations are needed (to be exact, 2.5 standard deviations give 98.7 per cent certainty, see page 194); therefore the probability will be:

$$2.5 \times \text{standard deviation} = 2.5 \times 2 = 5$$

Therefore, using the adjusted forecast of 108, there is:

a) 99 per cent chance of sales being not less than $108 - 5 = 103$
b) 99 per cent chance of sales being not more than $108 + 5 = 113$

Suppose this method is now applied to some of the panel situations described earlier in this chapter, our expert above being one of four experts consulted. Each expert is asked for his best estimate forecast and his highest and lowest, assuming no change in present policy. Each forecast should be given without consultation and should be supported by the individual's reasoning.

	Lowest	Best estimate	Highest
Panel expert 1	99	110	112
Panel expert 2	90	95	104
Panel expert 3	97	100	102
Panel expert 4	80	90	95

Calculate for each set of figures:

a) weighted average $= \dfrac{\text{lowest} + (4 \times \text{expected}) + \text{highest}}{6}$

b) degree of uncertainty $= D = \dfrac{(H - L)^2}{6^2}$

	Weighted average	Degree of uncertainty
Panel expert 1	108	4.69
Panel expert 2	96	5.5
Panel expert 3	100	0.6
Panel expert 4	89	6.25

Calculate the average mean figure:

$$\frac{108 + 96 + 100 + 89}{4} = 98$$

$$\text{average } D = \frac{4.69 + 5.5 + 0.6 + 6.25}{4} = 4.26$$

$$\text{standard deviation} = \sqrt{(4.26)} = 2.06$$

$$2.5 \times \text{standard deviation} = 2.5 \times 2.06 = 5 \text{ approx}$$

Circulate the results as follows:

Average forecast 98;
with 99 per cent chance of sales being not less than $98 - 5 = 93$
with 99 per cent chance of sales being not more than $98 + 5 = 103$

Ask experts to give reasons for high/low forecasts, request revised forecasts, repeat exercise and establish agreed forecast and levels of certainty.

Probability and expected values

A further forecasting application of probability is with the concept of expected values. In some subjective/probability forecasting methods it is possible to incorporate factors that permit analysis and assessment of the various courses of action or choice open to management. For example, a company considering two alternative product projects, A and B, and wanting to forecast the profit outcome, could, by using a model based on market share, net outcome and the probability of achieving particular market shares, calculate the expected values of the two alternatives and forecast which would be the best alternative to take. An example is given in Table 9.2.

In Table 9.2 for simplicity only three levels of market share have been considered; a wider range of market share calculations is possible in a practical marketing situation.

If the market shares indicated were achieved, it has been calculated that the profits that would be achieved (net financial outcome) would be as shown for project/markets A and B. If the best current judgement of the likelihood of these market shares being obtained is then expressed as a subjective probability (columns 3 and 5), the expected values are found by multiplying the net financial outcome (column 2) by the appropriate pobability.

In the example shown in Table 9.2, the forecast 'best' project/market would be A as the expected value for it is £6,500 as against £4,100 for B.

Table 9.2 *Showing the expected value of two alternative product projects*

1 Market share %	2 Net financial outcome	3 Probability project A	4 Expected value of A	5 Probability project B	6 Expected value of B
0 to 30	− £10,000	0.3	− £3,000	0.2	− £2,000
31 to 60	+ £3,000	0.5	+ £1,500	0.7	+ £2,100
61 and over	+ £40,000	0.2	+ £8,000	0.1	+ £4,000
		1.0	+ £6,500	1.0	+ £4,100

A forecasting application of Bayesian decision theory

Closely linked with the expected value concept is Bayesian decision theory, which combines objective and subjective probabilities with revised probabilities. Revised probabilities are influenced by relevant updated data and information derived from such sources as the field sales force, research, economic and political fact situations.

The key element in using Bayesian decision theory is the development of decision trees. A decision tree is a network of lines showing the outcome of each considered decision alternative, the expected values and the associated probabilities. A decision tree is constructed from left to right by sequentially sub-dividing the major decision alternatives into their component parts. An application of part of Bayesian decision theory appropriate to sales forecasting is shown in Figure 9.5.

In Figure 9.5 the company had originally intended to re-launch an existing product with an additional size, a new pack and an updated promotional/product image. However, following market rumours (confirmed by marketing research) that a competitor was intending to launch an improved version of the product, the company has a decision to make from three alternatives:

(a) launch a new generic product, or
(b) launch an improved version of existing product, or
(c) continue with plan to re-launch the existing product.

For each of these alternative courses of action, the company obtained an optimistic and a best estimate and a pessimistic forecast; it also obtained the probabilities associated with each. It was decided to consider the optimistic and best estimates forecast as viable for any course of action.

The expected profit on each forecast is shown to the right of Figure 9.5. The expected value should now be calculated for each forecast and then totalled for each alternative course of action.

Action	Probability of forecast	Expected profit	Expected value
A. Launch new generic product			
Launch	0.3	£400,000	£120,000
Launch	0.5	£190,000	£95,000
Abandon	0.2	−£20,000	−£4,000
Total EV for this alternative			£211,000

B. Launch improved product

Launch	0.3	£300,000	£90,000
Launch	0.4	£200,000	£80,000
Abandon	0.3	−£75,000	−£22,000
Total EV for this alternative			£148,000

C. Re-launch existing product

Launch	0.2	£330,000	£66,000
Launch	0.5	£160,000	£80,000
Abandon	0.3	−£30,000	−£9,000
Total EV for this alternative			£137,000

It would appear that to launch the new generic product is the best alternative (A) and even to launch an improved version of the existing product is better than to re-launch the existing product itself.

Such analysis is only a guide for the forecaster/executive decision maker and there are obviously other factors that would have to be taken into account, eg cash flow implications, financial position of company, the opportunity cost of not following other alternatives and even whether it would be worth spending more money on marketing research to obtain more or better information. Market forces and/or management style may also play a part as to the choice of alternative that has the least likelihood of failure or that poses the greatest risk of failure.

Probability forecasting with large contracts or 'lumpy' items

Many forecasting techniques require continuous data (weekly, monthly, quarterly sales) to enable trend, seasonal and cyclical patterns to be identified and projected. But some sales situations relate to noncontinuous data; single, large, multiple item contracts (eg a pharmaceutical manufacturing company bidding for a foreign government contract for antibiotics) or a potential order for a single high value item (eg a large scale earth moving machine). In such cases it is not possible to 'trend' historic data and although regression analysis and correlation using economic indicators may be able to forecast the total market value/volume it will not help the individual company in determining whether its individual bid or group of bids will succeed. Some forecasters are confronted with a situation where the company, having made a number of bids, requires a forecast of sales for this part of its potential sales revenue. It may

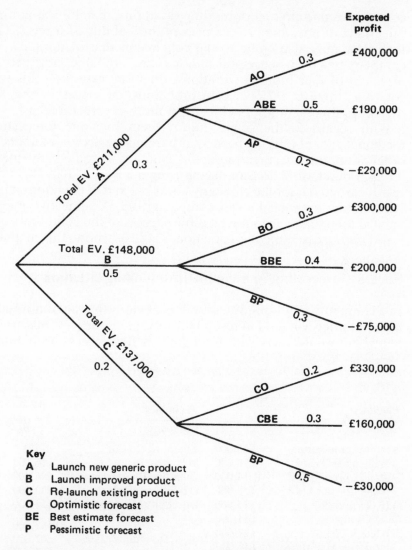

Figure 9.5 *A decision tree relating to alternative choices of action with probabilities of achieving forecasts and expected profits against forecast*

be possible for the forecaster to divide the forecast into two stages; one when the bid is first made, ie possible sales, and secondly when negotiations and discussions have taken or are taking place and some of the contenders for the business have dropped out or have been 'eliminated' by the purchasing company, ie these contracts could be described as 'probables'. By analyzing past success/ failure rates the forecaster could come to the conclusion that in the past the company has been successful in obtaining the 'possible'

307

contracts in one out of four bidding situations; therefore, assuming this will continue, there is a 25 per cent probability of success. The forecaster may also come to the conclusion that in the past the company has been successful in obtaining 'probable' contracts in three out of four bidding situations; therefore assuming this will continue, there is a 75 per cent probability of success. Table 9.3 illustrates this method of achieving a multi-contract forecast.

With regard to the single 'lumpy' item bid, one forecasting method is that of ranking particular purchasing decision factors in order of importance, then rating the company's product advantage for each purchasing decision factor using the base of 100. This process is carried out for the company's own bid and, if the information is available, for each known competing bid. A subjective judgement is then made as to the possible success of the company's bid based on the assembled information. Table 9.4 shows this method.

Success forecasting in a competitive bidding situation

In a competitive bidding situation it is obvious that an abnormally high bid price will tend to result in a very good sales revenue/profit return but would carry with it a relatively low success probability.

Table 9.3 *Possible/probable contract forecasting*

Possibles		Probables	
Company	*Bid*	*Company*	*Bid*
Acme Manufacturing	£15,000	T James & Co Ltd	£17,000
A Williams & Co Ltd	£19,000	M Hobbs & Sons Ltd	£16,000
Sutton Publishing Ltd	£14,000	Guardian Pharmaceuticals	£46,000
Quostaphortune Ltd	£58,000	G B Enterprises Inc	£32,000
GJB Corporation	£25,000	Durability Manufacturing	£58,000
Otley Group	£31,000		£169,000
T White & Co Ltd	£23,000	Discount @ 25%	£42,000
Queenie Bee Manufacturing	£48,000		
Coldharbour Production	£33,000		£127,000
	£266,000		
Discount @ 75%	£199,500		
	£66,500		

Total contract forecast based on past probabilities, £66,500 + £127,000 = £193,500.

Table 9.4 *Factors influencing purchasing decisions*

Factor	Rank in order of importance in this bid	Product advantage (using base of 100)
Price Performance Design Delivery Product image Company image Technical service After sales service Spares availability etc		

Alternatively, if the bid price quoted is particularly low (with comparable quality and/or performance), it may almost certainly ensure that the bid will be accepted by the purchasing company but at an unacceptable level of sales revenue/profit return for the supplying company. These two extreme situations will both lead to low or no sales revenue/profit return but at some price point on the spectrum between them is a postion which optimizes the level of sales revenue/profit and the success probability.

The main objective of any bidding analysis therefore is to identify a contract bid price which maximizes the sales revenue/profit pay-off. At the same time there is a need to determine the probability of success and to calculate the potential marginal loss (or penalty) which will be incurred if the contract is not awarded to a particular bidding company.

The first stage is to estimate the chance of being awarded a contract over a range of bid prices and to calculate the profit percentage and what this means in terms of money; from this can be calculated the net worth of bidding at a particular price which optimizes the situation for the supplier.

The net worth is calculated by multiplying the various levels of profit by the probability of being awarded the contract at a particular bid price. Thus at a bid price of £6,000 the net worth is £600 × 70 per cent = £420. It will be seen in the situation depicted in Table 9.5 that the highest net worth value is £1,260 and therefore the contract bid price which optimizes sales revenue/profit return and the probability of success is £14,000.

In many sales/marketing situations, price is not the only purchasing factor; the question of the customer-perceived market position of a

Table 9.5 *The calculation of net worth values of contracts over a range of bid prices*

Subjective certainty of getting contract	Bid price	Profit percentage at bid price	Actual profit	Net worth (probability ×profit)
90%	£2,000	0	0	0
80%	£4,000	5%	£200	£160
70%	£6,000	10%	£600	£420
60%	£8,000	15%	£1,200	£720
50%	£10,000	20%	£2,000	£1,000
40%	£12,000	25%	£3,000	£1,200
30%	£14,000	30%	£4,200	£1,260
20%	£16,000	35%	£5,600	£1,120
10%	£18,000	40%	£7,200	£720
0%	£20,000	45%	£9,000	0

supplying company's product/service, the company/product/service image, past relationships and experiences, etc, all have an influence on the final decision whether or not to award a contract. Many of these factors are qualitative and add up to a bias for or against a supplier. Because of the multi-aspect nature of this bias, the degree of impact can only be arrived at subjectively. Its application is carried through by considering what the chance would be for the contract to be awarded if there was an exact match in the bid price between a company and its competitors. If it was considered that the company/customer relations were very favourable, it might be estimated that the company could expect a 60 per cent/70 per cent chance of being given the contract in the event of an exact match of bid price with a competitor.

Where there are wide differences in product specifications wide differences in bid prices will emerge, although the purchasing company may have very specific objectives for product performance. There is therefore an element of 'appropriateness' of the company's 'total deal' (product, service, etc), which must be estimated, perhaps as in the method described on page 309. The concept of a total deal rather than simply aspects of a product is important as it could relate to the advantages of before and after sales service, availability of spares, credit and/or financing facilities, etc.

However, there are usually several factors to be considered in price differential situations. Where there is little product difference and price differentials are nominal, an estimate of 'favourable/ adverse relations' bias mentioned above will normally be enough

Table 9.6 *Cumulative probability for a company over a range of bid prices compared with a major competitor*

Bid prices	Company cumulative probability relating to bid prices	Competitor cumulative probability relating to bid prices
£4,000	1.0	
£6,000	0.8	1.0
£8,000	0.6	0.8
£10,000	0.5	0.6
£12,000	0.4	0.4
£14,000	0.2	0.2
£16,000	0.1	0
£18,000	0	

to cover this. But where major bid price differences are expected between a company and its competitors, then several questions need to be asked and judgements made. For example, how much higher (in percentage terms) would the company's bid price have to be for this to outweigh any bias in favour of the company? Conversely, how much lower (in percentage terms) would the company's bid price have to be, compared with competitors to be certain to be awarded the contract? For example, it could be estimated that there is an 80 per cent chance of the purchase decision being based on a small/medium/large price differential. Conversely, this implies that there is a 20 per cent chance that a small/medium/large price differential will not be the deciding purchasing decision factor.

Further, it should be possible for a company to estimate, on a 'spread' of expected bid prices, the relationship of the company's prices to those of a competitor, and consequently the 'certainty' of getting a contract at a particular price and the 'certainty' of not getting it at another.

Thus in Table 9.6 it is estimated that the company has a 50/50 chance of being awarded the contract at £10,000 and (not taking into account whether the potential customer is for or against the company) a 60/40 chance that it would be awarded to a competitor bidding the same price. The table also implies that at £4,000 the company would be certain to get the contract and at £16,000 it has only a 10 per cent chance and at £18,000 the company will definitely not get the contract.

This is based on the concept of cumulative probability. For example, in the situation in Table 9.6 there is certainty that there will be no bids below £4,000 or above £18,000; so all the probabilities will be contained within the limits set by these two values. Further, all the probability values within this range must total 1.0, ie 100 per cent. Just as there is a 50/50 chance of the company getting the contract at £10,000, there is a 60 per cent certainty but still a 40 per cent uncertainty of getting the contract at £8,000.

Further, if there were just two competitors there is a 0.5 chance (ie 50/50 chance) of one of them quoting above or below the middle value bid price, ie £10,000. The chance of them both quoting above or below the middle value bid price is $0.5 \times 0.5 = 0.25$ chance. As a general indicator it could be said that with more than 4 or 5 competitors it becomes very unlikely that the contract will be awarded above the middle value bid price.

If a company's bid price is consistently higher than those of competitors, an investigation of how fixed/overhead costs are allocated in comparison with competitors should be carried out (if this is possible). It could be that the contracts concerned are carrying an undue fixed/overhead cost in relation to the opportunity cost which, in real terms, they afford the company.

A further consideration in determining the value of the optimum price will be the degree of risk involved. The larger the risk and the greater the marginal loss/penalty incurred if the contract is lost, the more aggressive will be the bidding and value of bids; lower than 'normal' bid prices tending to emerge. Thus, if a company and/or its competitors are more dependent on bid contracts than on 'normal' continuous sales, the more aggressive will be the bidding. Contrast the situation where a company's business is divided into 80 per cent from normal continuous sales and 20 per cent from contracts, with the converse situation of only 20 per cent from 'normal' continuous business and 80 per cent from contracts; more aggressive bidding can be expected in the latter case. A weighting factor therefore needs to be estimated for the company and each of its competitors; how important is the contract to them and how aggressive (price cutting, cutting of profit margins, increased discounts, favourable trade-in prices, etc) are they likely to be in bidding?

Another influencing factor that follows on from the division of the type of business done (contracts or 'normal' continuous sales), is that of the penalty on under-utilized production (or other) capacity if a contract is not received. Thus it may be more desirable to quote a lower price in an effort to increase the certainty of getting a contract than to risk losing it if under-utilized production/plant or other capacity exists. In such a case, as long as the variable costs involved are covered, any revenue in excess of this is at least a contribution to fixed/overhead costs and profit. A weighting value for the risk or penalty factor needs to be built into the bid price considerations.

Conclusion

Success forecasting in a competitive bidding situation is a highly subjective process and assumes the use of the best managerial fore-casting judgement available based upon well informed knowledge of the industry, market, competition, customers, etc. The process can be summarized as follows:

1. Obtain the net worth to the bidding company of obtaining a contract at a certain bid price; this is calculated by identifying a range of prices, and profit at these prices, which is then multiplied by the subjective certainty value of obtaining the contract at these prices.
2. Estimate the 'bias' probability factor (favourable or adverse) which is expected to be effective in the event of an exact match or tie of prices with competitors.
3. Identify the 'appropriateness' of the product/service 'deal' being offered by the company compared with competitors and in the light of the purchasing company's specific needs.
4. Estimate the probabilities of obtaining the contract in the case of small/medium/large price differentials.
5. Calculate the range of cumulative probabilities of the company and its competitors over the range of possible bid prices.
6. Calculate the probabilities of competitors making bid prices at various levels above and below the expected middle value bid price.
7. Consider recalculating the allocation of fixed/overhead costs if the company's bids are consistently high.
8. Calculate the risk factor and/or the marginal loss/penalty incurred if the contract is not obtained, with special considera-tion of:
    (a) the emphasis of the company and competitors' dependence on contract business ie an 'aggressive bid' allowance.
    (b) the amount of under-utilized production (and other) resources that exist in relation to the company and its competitors, ie a further 'aggressive bid' allowance.
9. Carry out a basic calculation to determine over a range of bid prices the ideal 'true net value'; this is:
    (Bid price x probability of getting contract) — (marginal loss/penalty × probability of not getting contract)

Even though this method is based on many subjective/judgement factors it does provide the forecaster/company with a considered forecast of the likelihood of being awarded a particular contract.

Major customer forecasting

Earlier (pages 214 and 218 et seq) it was suggested that greater forecasting accuracy could be achieved and the forecasting role made easier by segmenting markets.

Similarly, more accurate forecasting can usually be achieved by forecasting the separate product-groups that make up total company sales. The well known management 80/20 rule often applies, ie companies tend to obtain 80 per cent of their sales/profits etc from 20 per cent of their products. This applies particularly to companies with a large product range. If time availability of computer capacity is not available to carry out forecasting on, say, 3,000 different products, then priorities must be established. This is done by identifying those products/product groups that are most critical/important to the company's sales/profits contribution, ie the 20 per cent of products that make up the 80 per cent of sales/ profits. The sales of these critical/important products could be forecast individually (or at least in sub-groups) whilst the remaining 80 per cent of the product range which contributes 20 per cent of the sales/profits could be put together in sub-groups and forecasts made for them, perhaps using market indicator factors obtained for the 'critical' products forecasts.

The same rule sometimes applies to customers; where a company obtains 80 per cent of its business from 20 per cent of its customers. For example, one metal components company obtained 62 per cent of its business from four customers. One specialist trade journal obtains 42 per cent of its advertising from three advertisers. Sometimes the same principles can be applied to individual salesmen's territories, where a relatively small number of active accounts provide most of the sales/profits from that territory. Obviously the identification of these major customers and the establishment of precise sales forecasts/objectives for them individually is crucial to the overall forecast for the company.

Because so much sales/profit performance depends upon these major customers, more time is often given to them and more details considered about them than is the case with the large number of customers who make relatively little contribution to the sales/ profits total.

It is normal, for example, for the forecaster/salesperson/sales manager to research a fairly detailed customer profile covering home address, type of business, know-how, resources, experience, sales/market area, reputation, image, whether a subsidiary, industry/national/international connections, estimated number of employees, estimated sales/profits, product lines supplied, their quality, range, suitability, market position, price relativity, cost-effectiveness, etc.

This is usually followed by an analysis of the business done generally by the major customer and the business done specifically with the forecasting company. For example, what is the major customer's management philosophy — is it to rationalize, expand, maintain the status quo, retrench, re-invest, diversify, etc? Is its general business remaining stationary, expanding or declining? What has been its overall purchasing 'spend' over the last few years and particularly last year, and what is its intention for the coming budget period? How much of this purchasing 'spend' comes to the forecasting company and how much in absolute terms as a percentage went to the forecasting company's competitors?

A list of pre-forecasting factors that have to be considered is then compiled before a subjective prediction can be made. These would include the historic trend of recent sales with the major customer, the seasonal/purchasing pattern of sales, the company's strengths and weaknesses regarding this account, an estimate of possible business and probable sales, possibly related to outstanding quotations/bids etc; how much repeat business can be expected and how much business would be possible if given additional sales/marketing/public relations support, what new market business is desirable/feasible, what action/reaction can be expected from traditional and/or new competitors?

At the same time as the major customer profile, analysis, pre-forecasting factors and forecast is carried out, some companies also require their salespeople/sales managers to indicate an action plan with specific objectives, showing their strategies and/or tactics as to how the forecast will be achieved.

10

Sales Forecasting for New Products

'To seek out the best . . . we must resort to other information, which, from the best of men, acting disinterestedly and with the purest motives, is sometimes incorrect.'

Thomas Jefferson

The major difference between forecasting sales of an existing product and a new product is the lack of historical data: there is no past performance pattern to consider. Because of this absence of hard facts, there is a tendency for forecasting methods to be subjective rather than objective and the use of intuition and the crystal ball is readily rationalized. But because of the increased degree of uncertainty and the high level of investment risk, effective new product forecasting is essential.

Some forecasting techniques that have particular relevance to the new products are:

— The historical analogy approach
— The marketing research approach
— The test market approach
— The life cycle approach
— The substitute approach
— The composite forecasts of salesmen and sales executives
— Most subjective/judgemental techniques

The historical analogy approach

Often the sales of a new product will follow the pattern already set by an existing product in the same or similar type of consumer or industrial goods market. Many types of household appliances have followed a similar product life cycle curve, although it is important to define product similarities clearly in terms of potential consumer appeal in particular market segments. The product benefits, logical or psychological, may not appeal to all social or economic consumer groups. Alternatively, an analogy may be found from past history in another country. It will be necessary to allow for the differences in environment that exist in these other countries, eg the standard of living, incomes, national characteristics; but a sales pattern may be identified that will enable the forecaster to make a better than arbitrary guess.

The marketing research approach

This can take two forms: a survey of a sample of potential customers for the new product which is then multiplied to give a picture of total market demand, or a survey of the channels of distribution (wholesalers, distributors, retailers) to obtain their view as to whether their customers will buy the new product and to what extent. The main problem with the first form is that if the new product is fairly revolutionary the potential consumer may not be able totally to comprehend the new concept or be able to identify himself with its use. And with the second form the forecast depicted by the enthusiasm of middle-men because of product profitability may not be matched by consumer enthusiasm for the real benefits the new product may offer. Alternatively, a negative attitude from middle-men because of such factors as stocks of existing products, increased investment required, etc, may produce a lower forecast than the new product warrants. Obviously, this latter method should be used only to supplement or confirm other forecasts. See page 69 *et seq* for marketing research methods applicable to forecasting.

The test market approach

In the absence of historical data for the demand of a new product, it is possible to gauge consumer reaction by test marketing the new product. This can be done on a limited scale, ie to sell the product from one shop or get one industrial customer to use it. Obviously, they would have to be 'typical' outlets, although samples of one are highly dangerous. Alternatively, a test town, test industry or test area would reveal more of the sales potential for the product. At this stage it might be necessary to ensure that the product had adequate general acceptance, in terms of performance, size, colour, taste, price, etc, before proceeding to forecast sales. In the case of consumer products where the effectiveness of advertising and sales promotional media can affect demand considerably, a test area might be more appropriate. In this case an area is chosen (such as television area) and the same amount of promotional expenditure per head of population is used as is envisaged for the national launch of the new product, and the sales reaction is measured. Finally, allowing for regional differences, the test area sales are projected on to a national scale to become a forecast.

The life cycle approach

The forecast is obtained by considering the new product as a further logical stage in the life cycle of some overall customer satisfaction market, the sales of which will continue to grow at an anticipated rate. Thus in the home laundry market the sales growth of detergents continued and extended directly from soap powder, and in industrial machine tool situations numerical control devices have evolved directly out of the demand for manual control machines.

The substitute approach

Where a new product replaces an existing one, a straight continuation and possible extension of demand may be able to be predicted for the new product. For example, in the packaging industry an aerosol container or plastic sachet may be substituted for a bottle. But it is not simply a case of considering the existing demand level being transferred to the demand for the new product, but also the length of the transition period must be estimated. Also, a prediction should be made of the proportion of this it will be possible to capture. Further consideration should be given to the extent of consumer reaction to the new product. For example, if a substitute packaging material has a high convenience factor, the sales of the product it contains may increase.

The composite forecasts of salesmen and sales executives

This method was mentioned earlier as a viable method of general forecasting, but it has also been used effectively in the special situation relating to new products, particularly in industrial markets. In some cases the combination of the salesperson's technical knowledge of the product together with his personal knowledge of customers, their purchasing methods and their own marketing requirements, enables him to give an informed estimate of the future sales potential of the new product, or at least to predict reaction to it, and even to interpret customer reaction to the new product concept when confronted by it.

Combinations of the above techniques are often used to forecast the sales of new products, but such predictions should always be accompanied by the assumptions made about the new product and the market, stating as clearly as possible the risks involved.

11

The Application of Forecasts

'There are no such things as applied sciences, only applications of science.'
L Pasteur

The forecast as a decision-making tool

The completed sales forecast presents the management of a
company with a prediction on which several decisions must be
made, eg whether to go ahead with production to meet the predicted
demand or not. This is a typical management go/no-go decision.
Also, there is the decision of how to apply the forecast to company
functions (production, the sales force, etc) and/or to consider it in
terms of external factors such as the choice between various
alternative channels of distribution.

There will be a market size and/or market share below which it
will not be profitable (in the short, medium or long term depending
on the company objectives) to consider producing or purchasing.
Such a decision is linked with the pattern and climate of competition,
the optimum size of operation and the structure of the actual market
(size and location of customers, etc), in fact with the total environment in which the company hopes to operate profitably. At this
stage the sales forecast could be used to determine which markets
or segments of markets to enter, or whether company resources
could be used more profitably in alternative markets.

Break-even analysis

A major technique in the go/no-go decision-making process is
break-even analysis.

This type of analysis considers the cost-volume-profit relationship of producing and marketing. It produces a break-even percentage value which indicates at which level of activity or production
total cost will equal total revenue.

Break-even analysis shows the position of the forecast in relation to

319

the break-even point and indicates whether it would be profitable for the company should the forecast demand be achieved. It indicates whether or not profits would be made, but whether it is an acceptable level of profit is a management decision.

The break-even point can be calculated as follows. With a particular product a company has an annual fixed cost of £5,000; at 100 per cent capacity/activity its variable costs are £20,000 and its sales revenue £30,000.

$$\text{total cost} = £5000 + \frac{x}{100} \times 20000 = 5000 + 200x$$

$$\text{total sales} = \frac{x}{100} \times £30000 = 300x$$

The break-even point ($x\%$) is where total cost equals total sales, therefore:

$$5000 + 200x = 300x$$
$$5000 = 100x$$

$$= \frac{5000}{100} = 50\%$$

This data is shown graphically in Figure 11.1

If a forecast is considered as a point on the total revenue line in Figure 11.1, then a forecast below 30,000 units, or £15,000 sales revenue, is clearly not profitable. However, the product may still be made if it is in a developing market, or if as a complementary product it is to be used to help sell more profitable products. Any forecast or sales above the 50 per cent break-even point would be profitable, but the degree of profitability may or may not be acceptable. A forecast beyond 60,000 units or £30,000 sales revenue (ie 100 per cent capacity) is not possible to achieve with existing equipment unless some new factor such as shift working is introduced, but it does present a marketing opportunity and it must be considered whether to add another machine or production unit. This will depend on a comparison of the short-term and the medium-term forecasts, ie to determine if the higher level of demand is to continue in the more distant future.

Alternatively, the excess demand indicated by the sales forecast could be met by sub-contracting or obtaining 'private label' goods from other sources. Adding another increment of production will have the effect of increasing committed cost, thereby lifting up the total cost line and cutting profitability at lower volumes. In capital goods industries companies often sell the extra products with an ever lengthening order book.

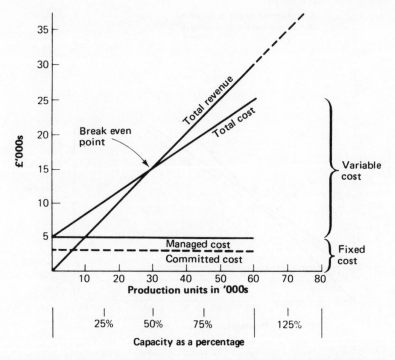

Figure 11.1 *A break-even diagram showing the point in production and sales where a product moves from a position of loss to one of profit*

Committed and managed costs

An unprofitable situation indicated by the sales forecast and break-even analysis may be made profitable in several ways, for example, if sales volume can be enlarged by a less than proportionate increase in the cost of an expenditure variable such as advertising or sales promotion. A more profitable situation may follow from increasing or decreasing the price, although this may in turn affect volume. A reduction in the variable cost per unit and the 'appropriation' of managed cost will increase profitability. Managed costs are those costs that do not vary with situation, they could be avoided if the profit situation required it. For example, the making of films for TV commercials, once completed, becomes a committed cost, but the cost of exhibiting on TV is a managed cost. The managed cost must be budgeted for but could be avoided by cancelling the television time purchased to show the commercials up to eight weeks before the showing date. The effect of 'appropriating' £1,000 of managed costs can be seen on the break-even chart in Figure 11.2.

In Figure 11.2 fixed costs have been reduced by £1,000 to £4,000

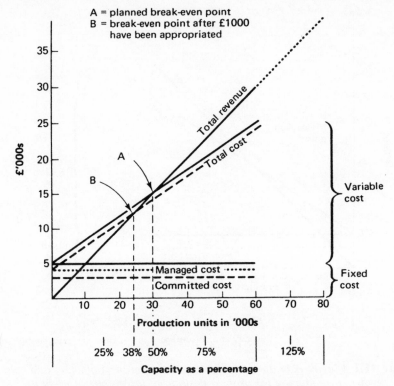

Figure 11.2 *The effect upon total cost and the break-even point of 'appropriating' £1,000 of managed cost*

by appropriating £1,000, thereby increasing profitability by the same amount. But the most significant factor is that the break-even point is now at 38 per cent capacity instead of 50 per cent, and profits can be made after 22,000 units or £11,000 sales revenue. The appropriation of managed cost will sometimes make a forecast level of sales profitable, but if the planned expenditure was justified and then does not take place, the company will lose some benefit in the short, medium or long term.

Product mix and ratio analysis

Other methods in the go/no-go decision-making process of applying a sales forecast include product mix and ratio analysis. In multi-product companies the total sales forecast should be refined by breaking down the forecast in terms of profit, contribution to profit, sales volume, assets used, etc, applied to individual product groups, salesmen's areas, industry groups, and immediate and ultimate customer types.

Table 11.1 *A sales/profits/assets analysis matrix*

Product	Sales	Profits	Assets
A	40%	30%	20%
B	10%	10%	30%
C	20%	25%	10%
D	30%	35%	40%

The forecast is applied to production by the allocation of the various product requirements to production facilities and, in fact, the forecast should form the basis of all production budgets. The total forecast could be achieved by a variety of combinations of product sizes, models, colours, types, etc. Therefore, before applying the forecast to production facilities, the optimum product mix must be considered. From this a decision can be made as to which combination of products, and the variety within each product line, will be most profitable.

Product-range mix analysis was mentioned in Chapter 1 as one of the stages of an operational marketing plan (Figure 1.7). It assumes that an optimum profit can be obtained by selling the various product lines in a certain ratio, perhaps

A B C D
7 : 4 : 3 : 1

If a total forecast has been given, it should be applied to products in this most profitable ratio pattern. Product mix analysis should relate profits to the sales needed to make them, and the assets used. A sales/profits/assets analysis matrix is shown in Table 11.1. Here, if B is a declining product and its resources can be applied to product C, then this transfer should take place if the forecast indicates an appropriate level of demand in the C market.

The use of these two devices at this stage of forecasting enables predicted sales of individual products to be related to the profitability of various combinations of products. The application of the forecast in this way permits the best possible product mix to be chosen in situations of limited company resources.

Application of forecasts to profit centres

Another variation of the application of the forecast is to apply it to the various 'profit centres' throughout a company. The profit centre concept treats the various functional parts of a company (production, purchasing, marketing, and subdivisions such as selling and distribution), as separate centres that should each show a profit from the raw materials it buys after costs of its own operation have been met and the materials 'resold' to production. Application of the forecast to profit centres permits a more effective profit target to be set for each centre.

Application of forecasts to sales territories

The sales forecast should also be applied to sales territories and where this is done it can form the basis of sales targets for salespeople. The sales potential of each area should be calculated to ensure that an appropriate target is set in relation to a company's expected share of a market.

Application of the forecast in industrial markets

In industrial markets user industries can be classified (using Standard Industrial Classification definitions and numbers), the size of these industries determined, and the percentage of business they each generate calculated. The share of business each company in an industry accounts for can be determined by taking the total sales of an industry and allocating them to companies on a basis of percentage of the total of the number of employees or the value of assets used. For example:

Total sales in industry £10m
Total employees in industry 10,000
Therefore every employee = approximately £1,000 of sales turnover

Application of the forecast in consumer goods markets

In consumer goods industries, area potential can be calculated on a basis of the pattern of population spread, related to the type of consumer expected to purchase the product. It may be company marketing strategy to use TV areas as a basis for area planning. Data is published by specialized information sources, the TV companies and others, giving a breakdown of population in terms of age, sex, socio-economic grouping, location, etc. For example, the information shown in Tables 6.3 and 6.4 is published regularly.

From data of the kind in these tables it is possible for the forecaster to determine a pattern by which the forecast should be applied over the country, and/or the priority in developing national coverage region by region. This approach to applying the forecast will not only permit the setting of sales targets for individual members of the sales force, but can also be used to set area goals that can be used later to compare performance with forecast in a region.

But the share of the sales potential that a company can expect in any area must be determined before the sales forecast is finally applied. The sales target set for a salesperson must be realistic as well as desirable. A guide can be obtained from past records; what was the territory potential in past periods and what share of the market did the company achieve? Allowances must then be made for any changes in local external factors (eg a new competitor) and internal factors within the company (eg an increase in advertising expenditure).

Application of the forecast by distribution channels

Another approach to applying the forecast is by means of detailed analysis of the profitability of using various types or sizes of retail outlets, individually or in combination. In many companies the bulk of the contribution to overheads and profit (ie the sales revenue minus direct costs) is produced by relatively few outlets. Often as much as 75/80 per cent of the contribution comes from 20/25 per cent of the number of retail outlets (by size or type). However, because the cost of marketing in general, and selling and distribution in particular, is broadly proportionate to the number of outlets used, a large part of total cost is generating a relatively small part of the contribution. For example, in a particular sales period the situation shown in Table 11.2 could arise.

Table 11.2 *The cost of dealing with outlet types related to contribution-to-over heads and, therefore, to profit*

Outlet type or size	Percentage of total outlets %	Sales (£)	Contribution to overheads and profit (£) (%)	Marketing costs (£)	Profit/ loss (£)
A	40	1,000	500 50	650	−150
B	30	2,000	800 40	500	300
C	20	4,000	1,200 30	400	800
D	10	13,000	2,600 20	350	2,250
	100	20,000	5,100 25.5	1,850	3,200

Table 11.3 *Number of retail businesses, outlets, turnover and employees:*
Great Britain, 1989

	Number of Businesses	No. of Outlets	Turnover[1] £ million	No. of Persons Engaged, '000
All retailers	**242,356**	**350,015**	**123,556**	**2,463**
Single outlet retailers	215,736	215,736	33,551	837
Small multiple retailers	25,726	67,760	14,541	318
Large multiple retailers	894	66,520	75,464	1,307
Food retailers	**67,849**	**90,075**	**43,562**	**845**
Single outlet retailers	61,469	61,469	7,546	222
Small multiple retailers	6,188	16,367	2,912	83
Large multiple retailers	191	12,238	33,104	541
Drink, confectionery and tobacco retailers	**48,744**	**61,641**	**12,061**	**328**
Single outlet retailers	46,382	46,382	7,076	224
Small multiple retailers	2,284	5,486	1,031	27
Large multiple retailers	78	9,773	3,954	77
Clothing, footwear and leather goods retailers	**31,429**	**58,538**	**12,252**	**304**
Single outlet retailers	26,393	26,393	2,898	82
Small multiple retailers	4,783	12,909	2,259	49
Large multiple retailers	253	19,236	7,095	173
Household goods retailers	**48,735**	**69,599**	**20,371**	**319**
Single outlet retailers	41,585	41,585	7,066	134
Small multiple retailers	6,978	18,030	4,126	70
Large multiple retailers	172	9,984	9,180	116
Other non-food retailers	**39,156**	**52,543**	**11,323**	**248**
Single outlet retailers	34,416	34,416	5,499	129
All multiple retailers	4,739	18,126	5,824	119
Mixed retail businesses	**4,149**	**11,542**	**22,704**	**383**
Single outlet retailers	3,429	3,429	3,301	40
Small multiple retailers	661	1,747	1,092	25
Large multiple retailers	58	6,365	18,311	318
Hire and repair businesses	**2,294**	**6,079**	**1,283**	**35**
Single outlet retailers	2,062	2,062	165	7
All multiple retailers	233	4,018	1,118	29

Note: [1] Inclusive of VAT.
Source: Business Monitor SDA25, Business Statistics Office.
Overall Source: *The Retail Pocket Book 1993*, page 36, Published by NTC Publications Ltd, Oxford, in association with A C Nielsen Co Ltd.

In the situation depicted in Table 11.2, the cost of dealing with outlet type A is more than the contribution produced. If the sales through the other outlet types (particularly D) can be increased by £1,000, it may be desirable and, indeed, more profitable, to cease distribution through outlet type A.

In consumer goods industries the pattern of application of forecasts by specialized retail outlets can be determined from data of the kind shown in Tables 11.3, 11.4 and 11.5.

Table 11.4 *Retail sales by type of business: Great Britain, 1985–91*

Current Prices, £ billion

	1985	1986	1987	1988[1]	1989[1]	1990	1991
All retailers	**87.92**	**95.66**	**103.22**	**113.24**	**120.80**	**128.71**	**134.96**
Food retailers	**32.99**	**35.26**	**37.44**	**40.54**	**44.17**	**48.52**	**51.99**
Grocers	25.90	27.97	29.78	32.63	35.99	40.14	43.50
Dairymen	1.84	1.84	2.14	2.43	2.58	2.67	2.71
Butchers	2.75	2.75	2.69	2.67	2.78	2.75	2.69
Fishmongers	0.21	0.25	0.24	0.24	0.25	0.26	0.26
Greengrocers, fruiters	1.29	1.35	1.37	1.37	1.46	1.52	1.52
Bread and flour confectioners	1.00	1.16	1.17	1.18	1.23	1.32	1.35
Clothing and footwear retailers	**8.68**	**9.72**	**10.50**	**11.28**	**11.71**	**12.23**	**12.32**
Men's and boys' wear	1.27	1.37	1.65	1.94	1.98	1.99	1.88
Women's, girls', children's and infants' wear, general clothing; leather and travel goods	5.32	6.12	6.49	6.92	7.29	7.67	7.82
Footwear	2.09	2.25	2.36	2.38	2.46	2.59	2.63
Household goods	**14.72**	**16.63**	**18.54**	**21.05**	**22.08**	**22.66**	**23.84**
Furniture, carpet and textiles	4.90	5.49	6.08	7.06	7.21	7.16	7.40
Electrical, music goods, gas and electricity showrooms	5.01	5.51	6.26	7.17	7.22	7.32	7.57
Hardware, china and fancy goods	1.19	1.35	1.55	1.79	1.93	2.10	2.20
DIY	2.36	2.88	3.23	3.79	4.29	4.67	5.19
TV and other hire and repair	1.25	1.43	1.40	1.34	1.35	1.42	1.52
All other non-food retailers	**15.68**	**16.77**	**18.34**	**20.53**	**22.26**	**23.98**	**24.92**
CTNs	7.16	7.73	8.09	8.88	9.38	10.24	10.96
Off-licences	2.29	2.45	2.63	2.79	2.93	3.11	3.27
Chemists[2]	1.45	0.16	1.78	2.07	2.30	2.43	2.57
Booksellers, stationers, specialist newsagents	1.21	1.27	1.44	1.65	1.85	2.01	2.05
Jewellers	1.25	1.32	1.50	1.72	2.02	2.13	2.02
Toys, hobby, sports goods and cycles	1.05	1.12	1.33	1.52	1.65	1.81	1.79
Other non-food	1.27	1.38	1.57	1.90	2.09	2.20	2.23
Mixed retail businesses	**15.87**	**17.13**	**18.40**	**19.83**	**20.62**	**21.42**	**21.89**
Very large mixed businesses[3]	11.97	13.04	14.12	15.43	16.15	16.87	17.23
Other mixed businesses	0.93	1.01	0.93	0.90	0.98	1.08	1.13
General mail order houses	2.97	3.15	3.39	3.45	3.45	3.48	3.57

Notes: [1] These figures differ from those on pages 36 & 37 due to differences in the methods of compilation of the Retailing Inquiry and the monthly retail sales index (from which these annual figures are drawn)
[2] Excluding receipts under the National Health Service.
[3] With turnovers of £11 million or more in 1988
Source: Based on Business Monitor SOM28, Business Statistics Office.
Overall source: The Retail Pocket Book 1993, page 35, published by NTC Publications Ltd. Oxford, in association with A C Nielsen Co. Ltd.

Table 11.5 *Turnovers and average weekly sales per shop, 1990*

	Grocers	Pharmacies/ drug stores[1]	CTNs	Cash & Carries
Turnover, £ million				
GB	40,827	4,145	5,633	6,510
London	9,605	994	1,277	1,275
Anglia	2,784	210	684[2]	319
Southern	3,924	316	684[2]	402
Wales & Westward	4,227	427	561	693
Midlands	6,044	591	923	1,045
Lancashire	4,916	618	903	942
Yorkshire	4,023	402	805[3]	711
Tyne Tees	1,799	196	805[3]	362
Scotland	3,506	391	480	760
Average weekly sales per shop, £				**(£ 000)**
GB	16,287	6,563	3,086	295
London	25,167	6,059	3,329	409
Anglia	17,736	7,092	3,217[2]	236
Southern	21,081	6,994	3,217[2]	266
Wales & Westward	13,774	6,559	2,651	247
Midlands	13,629	6,646	3,408	279
Lancashire	13,605	6,689	2,801	302
Yorkshire	13,026	6,828	2,853[2]	279
Tyne Tees	13,415	6,928	2,853[2]	367
Scotland	15,420	6,617	3,373	266

Notes: [1] Excluding Boots.
[2] Figures are for Anglia and Souther regions combined.
[3] Figures are for Tyne Tees and Yorkshire regions combined.
Sources: Nielson: Grocery, Health & Beauty, Confectionery and Cash & Carry Services.
Overall Source: The Retail Pocket Book 1993, page published by NTC Publications Ltd, Oxford, in association with AC Nielsen Co Ltd.

Table 11.3 shows the number of retail businesses, outlets, turnover and employees in Great Britain in 1989. Table 11.4 shows the trends of retail sales (and therefore consumer expenditure in particular types of retail outlets), by type of business in Great Britain over the period 1985 — 1991 at current prices. Table 11.5 shows the turnovers and average weekly sales per shop in 1990 in selected types of retail outlets. A forecast in a particular product area based on retail outlets or turnover and/or trend, plus the pattern of a company's past experience in a region/outlet type, could make a useful predictor of sales.

Other useful retail distribution data can be found in survey data publications such as *The Retail Pocket Book, The British Shopper, The Food Pocket Book* and *The Marketing Pocket Book,* all published by NTC Publications Ltd, Oxford UK.

In industrial markets the forecast can also be applied in terms of profitability of dealing direct with industrial users or through industrial wholesalers, factors or distributors.

This method of analysis applied by industrial product companies operating in a variety of industries (eg a range of pumps may have applications in many industries) could mean that unless there was future potential in certain user industries, a supplying company may find it more profitable not to actively market or sell to such industries.

The forecast as a basis for budgeting and control

By applying the forecast in the various areas described above, specific sales targets can be set, and the sales forecast can become the basis of all budgets in the company, ie production, finance, marketing, plant and equipment, raw materials, manpower, etc. In fact, all budgets in a company are based eventually on how many items the company anticipates selling. Further, from the sales forecasting data available, controllable operational plans can be evolved with appropriate strategies and tactics.

Not only is the total sales forecast attributed to various areas, outlets, salesmen, etc, who are responsible for achieving various levels of sales and profit and performance, but conversely it is attributed to production, purchasing and distribution functions to ensure that products and/or services are available in the right quantities and at the right time.

Combined objective/subjective forecast plan

Throughout this book a combined objective/subjective approach has been advocated. In the sections dealing with objective (statistical) methods, the application of human judgement, experience and intelligence to modify 'mechanical' methods has been recommended. In the sections on subjective (intuition, conclusions, 'gut feel') methods, some objective methods (eg weighted averages, probability) have been suggested to 'sharpen up' the subjective approach. In getting the forecaster/product manager/sales manager to calculate a forecast both approaches need to be brought together. Also, such personnel must obviously turn the forecast (after it has been costed and accepted) into an action plan (being responsible for the sales performance) and as such can make the forecast happen or at least influence it. Therefore it will be necessary to take into account any activities such personnel (and others) intend to carry out that will improve the organization's standing in the market place, and therefore influence sales.

One approach is to summarize (perhaps on one sheet of paper) the main components of a forecast/action plan; it would include the following sections.

1. General identification data — product/service group; market covered; year and forecast period(s), date of forecast.
2. Relevant economic data and forecasts — growth or decline trends, money supply, interest rates, government policies.
3. Relevant industry data and forecasts — growth or decline trends, changing methods, new materials and/or applications, substitute industries, etc.
4. Appropriate competitor data — identification of direct and indirect competition, estimated competitor shares, whether these are (slowly or rapidly) increasing, static or declining, key product/service changes.
5. Factors that influence purchasing/using decisions, weighted and ranked in order of importance, eg quality, price, delivery, design, image (product and company), performance, perceived market position, technical services, spares availability (if appropriate) and before and after sales service.
6. Present situation — totals for previous sales periods, value of quotation submitted and active, partly completed contracts, etc.
7. Forecasts
    (a) Strategy — either global forecast broken down into component parts, or the component parts added together to make a total forecast. Identifications of purpose/aims of forecast.
    (b) Objective forecasts using appropriate techniques from those examined earlier, where possible giving maximum/ minimum values as well as best forecast. This should be done for the market as a whole, the product group generally, and for specific products in the context of short-, medium- and long-term forecasts. Forecast market potential, market share, and probable forecast.
    (c) Subjective forecasts using appropriate techniques from those examined earlier, giving most optimistic, pessimistic and best estimate values. Also applying subjective judgement to the mechanical method forecasts in 7(b).
8. Action/activities by company and/or individuals that will affect (favourably/adversely) company standing/competitiveness/ image in the market place. These actions/activities should be described, a date fixed for implementation, their duration and

their expected effect identified and whether this will be an immediate, short-, medium- or long-term effect. Contingency plans if forecasts are not being achieved. Rules for reforecasting or updating.

The format of such a forecast/action plan will vary from company to company and not all the above factors will be appropriate, desirable or feasible in all cases. However, such an approach will ensure that all relevant factors are taken into account in making a forecast, that a range of techniques is used to ensure a balanced approach and that the anticipated effect of proposed action/activities during the forecast period is allowed for in the forecast.

12

Monitoring Controlling Forecasting and the Forecast

'I claim not to have controlled events, but confess plainly that events have controlled me.'

Abraham Lincoln

Scope of control

Effective control requires the measurement of performance against pre-determined objectives and standards, and the interpretation of trends and results. It also implies knowing where, when and how to take corrective action on time. A further aspect of control is recording performance data for use as a guide in planning future operations and to highlight marketing opportunities.

These aspects of control apply to effective forecasting and take the form of comparing, evaluating, interpreting and auditing the performance of the economy, the market, the market segment and the company's sales with the various forecasts. Then remedial action can be taken if necessary to update the forecast or change the methods used.

In fact, in many organizations it is normal to have several updates of a forecast during a sales period, eg one year. Further, 12 or 18 months ahead rolling forecasts are often made at predetermined points during the year. This is done to ensure that company strategy is reacting quickly to market/economic forces, to ensure continuity of forecasting and to confirm that the cash flow position will be as predicted.

It is also important to recognize that a sales revenue performance in any times/sales period is the result of a number of key market-related forces all moving at different speeds or having different degrees of influence at different times. The control activity is to identify the factors that were of a different intensity/magnitude at the time the sales were made compared with what was anticipated in the forecast. Activity in this stage of the forecasting process can be classified into three main areas:

(a) The running audit which makes daily, weekly, monthly or quarterly comparisons of economic data, company sales and/ or market performance against forecast.
(b) The annual audit which makes an assessment and comparison of forecasts over a longer period and in greater detail.
(c) The audit of the 'machinery' of forecasting within the company in terms of the objectives, policies, and the methods used; some forecasting techniques are more effective in certain market circumstances than others.

Within these three areas, forecasting can be made more effective by obtaining more or improved information for techniques at present in use or by developing methods, and by improving existing techniques or replacing ineffective forecasting devices.

Forecasts versus actual sales

There are various approaches to assessing forecasts against actual sales; they include:

1. Comparison between sterling and unit forecasts and sales in absolute terms.
2. Sales related to sterling and unit forecasts as a percentage achieved figure (eg 95 per cent of forecast).
3. Sales related to forecast on a cumulative basis of 'the year to date' and the percentage achieved.
4. Percentage increase/decrease over last year.
5. Measurement of difference in timing or pace of sales as planned in the forecast compared with actual performance.

However, these assessments merely indicate deviations from the anticipated situation, and it further requires a curious and analytical approach to discover why, when and how they occurred, which factors were involved, and the likelihood of the situation occurring again. This is necessary to determine whether the forecast should be amended or whether other action should be taken, ie a change in marketing strategy or a change in forecasting techniques.

The degree of sophistication of assessment depends on marketing needs and/or what is economical for the company.

Variance analysis

The simplest approach is to graph the forecast and sales values. A visual examination will indicate any lead or lag effects and also highlight the magnitude of the differences between the two sets of values.

It will often show where short-term method forecasting has been correct but the outcome has been influenced by medium- and/or long-term factors. This will be indicated on the control graph by the sales performance pattern horizontally matching the forecast pattern but its level being higher or lower, the outcome being a poor forecast (see page 56). It then becomes a matter of priority to identify, take account of, measure and predict the forces causing the difference in the sales performance level.

Another approach is to make a comparison between forecast and sales value in absolute terms to obtain a ± variance. For example:

Sales	210
Forecast	200
± Variance	10 units

It is useful to list the variances month by month (or by other appropriate time periods), and to convert them into percentages. When plotted on a graph a pattern of percentage variance, either by season or product or forecasting method, etc, is often indicated. Investigation will show the reasons for the pattern and either the methods of forecasting can be changed or the anticipated degree of variance allowed for.

Ranking variances

An alternative method of listing is to rank all the variances in their order of magnitude, ie starting with the largest positive variance through to the largest negative variance. If plotted on a graph this data should form a normal distribution curve, which indicates that there should be, over a period of time, just as many positive variances as negative variances, and the same magnitude of forecasting error. If the distribution is shown and there tends to be a greater number of variances in one direction, or the magnitude of errors is greater in one direction, then investigation into long-term bias is necessary.

Ratios

It is possible to calculate the ratio of the period sales to forecast, allowing for seasonal and medium-term cyclical factors, and to obtain an adjusted ratio. Acceptable levels of ratios can be established; they can also be graphed to permit comparison over a period of time.

The sum of forecasting errors

A further monitoring method is to take the sum of the forecasting errors over a period and divide by the mean absolute deviation. As sales emerge and a comparison is made, it is possible to detect where the forecast is not in line with the anticipated actual sales pattern.

The standard error as a monitoring device

At the end of each sales period the difference between the forecast and actual sales is calculated, these differences are squared and the squared values for all items are totalled (Σ). This total is then divided by the number of sales periods, and finally the square root is calculated. The result is the standard error and the calculation can be expressed:

$$\text{standard error} = \sqrt{\left[\frac{\Sigma(\text{actual sales} - \text{forecast value})^2}{\text{number of sales periods}}\right]}$$

where $\Sigma = $ sum over all sales periods

The forecasting method giving the lowest standard error is therefore the most efficient method during the period under consideration. As this method is calculated by using 'differences', it affords a method of comparison of the efficiency of various methods where different units of measure are used, eg pounds sterling, weight, bulk barrels, yards, boxes, etc. An objective of all forecasters is to minimize the standard error with any forecasting method.

Investigation of variances

In comparing actual sales with forecast, the important factor is not only the variance itself, but why it occurred. Analysis will indicate whether an aspect of forecasting was at fault or whether some new sales factor has emerged. The ± variance may have been caused by the beginning of a new trend, eg increased product usage, a new application, an appeal to a new market segment, etc, in which case the forecaster can allow for the new factor in future forecasting activities.

Alternatively, the variance may be caused by an ad hoc factor that is unlikely to occur again or cannot be guaranteed to happen again, eg a once-only special order, a strike at a competitor's factory, etc. In such a case the unusual sales item could be adjusted to a more normal level for the period, otherwise it will affect future forecasting, ie it will unduly weight moving averages and other trend calculations.

Levels of accuracy

Acceptable levels of accuracy of forecast depend largely on the company and market situations. A market that experiences wide fluctuation from one period to the next can obviously expect a greater average error than an industry where sales are relatively stable. Thus, while an 8 per cent error may be acceptable in one market, a 4 per cent error may be considered too high in another. There appears to be a correlation between the degree of accuracy and nearness to the eventual customer. Thus, as a general rule, consumer goods manufacturers are able to produce more accurate forecasts than component goods manufacturers who are several stages removed from the customer. There also appears to be a correlation between the accuracy of the forecast and the amount of money and number of techniques used to obtain it. Thus, in industries where forecasting is not considered too important or where sophisticated methods cannot be afforded, the level of accuracy tends to decrease. This does assume that a high degree of accuracy is necessary. In some industries a less sophisticated system meets the forecasting needs.

Formats for comparative assessment

A useful format for a combination of some of the forecast assessment methods mentioned above is one that permits a running audit and also produces the data to enable an annual audit to be made later.

The format used in Figure 12.1 would permit easy analysis and comparison of data and immediately highlight important variances.

A further simple format is, in each time period and for each product or product group, to lay out

— the cumulative forecast
— the cumulative actual sales
— the cumulative variance
— the cumulative variance as a percentage

Another format is shown in Figure 12.2. This is a forecast control sheet which shows last year's actual sales in each period and the forecasts of 12 sales periods commencing January of the year in question; this was possibly calculated three to six months before the beginning of the forecast year. It follows therefore that, in a dynamic market situation, it may be necessary to re-forecast in

Sales forecast control sheet

Month ending ——

Product, type size or model	This month			Year to date			Sales last year to date	Percentage increase/decrease over last year
	Actual sales	Forecast	% Achieved	Actual sales	Forecast	% Achieved		
Totals								

Figure 12.1 *A format for comparative assessment of sales and forecasts*

Forecast control sheet										Product:			
Month		Jan	Feb	Mar	Apr	May	Jun	Jul	Aug	Sep	Oct	Nov	Dec
Last year actuals	Units												
	Revenue												
Forecast Jan 1	Units												
	Revenue												
March reforecast	Units												
	Revenue												
July reforecast	Units												
	Revenue												
Actuals	Units												
	Revenue												
Actuals	Units												
	Revenue												
JAN	Units												
	Revenue												
FEB	Units												
	Revenue												
MAR	Units												
	Revenue												
APRIL	Units												
	Revenue												
MAY	Units												
	Revenue												
JUNE	Units												
	Revenue												
JULY	Units												
	Revenue												
AUG	Units												
	Revenue												
SEPT	Units												
	Revenue												
OCT	Units												
	Revenue												
NOV	Units												
	Revenue												
DEC	Units												
	Revenue												

Figure 12.2 *Forecast control sheet*

March (ie perhaps six to nine months after the original forecast was made) and again in July (which would be half way through the year), so these re-forecasts are shown. Under these, the actual sales values are inserted as they occur.

A three months rolling analysis of actual sales is then shown; this helps to highlight seasonal patterns, where sales expected in one period are carried over to the next, and also helps in the two re-forecasts.

All these calculations are shown in both volume (units) and in value (revenue) but, if appropriate, could be analyzed also in any other sub-divisions.

The Z chart as an auditing device

Another method for auditing forecasts is the use of the Z chart; this type of chart has already been discussed as a forecasting tool (page 230), but it can also be used for making graphical comparison of actual sales and forecasts.

Figure 12.3 shows a format that enables data to be collected relating to the original forecast, the budget which is the forecast figure after it has been adjusted following management's examination of the financial implications of such a forecast, and the actual sales which are entered as they occur. These three measures are entered as actual sales values, cumulative values (the new values are added to the previous totals as they occur, see page 222) and as Moving Annual Totals, (see page 224).

Figure 12.3 could provide three Z charges, budget, forecast and actual sales; the former two acting as predictive devices (as on page 230) and the latter, actual sales, acting as a control device as in the following example.

The Z emerges as sales figures become available. In Table 12.1 a hypothetical sales situation is developed and the data shown can be expressed as a Z chart, see Figure 12.4

In Figure 12.4 the Moving Annual Total and the cumulative total are calculated as shown earlier when the Z chart was used as a forecasting tool (Tables 7.25 and 7.26). The forecast is shown as a straight dotted line.

The forecast for 19X2 was £330,000. The total sales figure for the previous year, 19X1, was £345,000.

The forecast for 19X3 is £380,000.

The situation shown in Figure 12.4 poses a number of questions when considering forecast and sales performance. For example, why was the forecast for 19X2 set at £330,000 when the total sales figure for 19X1 was £345,000; were there indications that the market

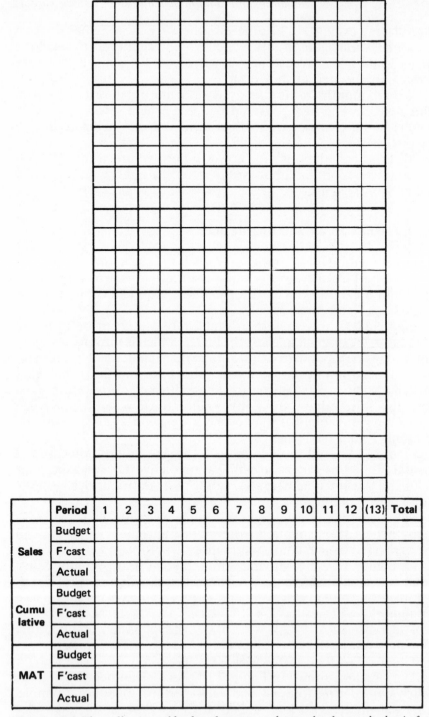

	Period	1	2	3	4	5	6	7	8	9	10	11	12	(13)	Total
	Budget														
Sales	F'cast														
	Actual														
	Budget														
Cumu lative	F'cast														
	Actual														
	Budget														
MAT	F'cast														
	Actual														

Figure 12.3 *The collection of budget forecast and actual sales as the basis for forming a Z chart to use as a control device*

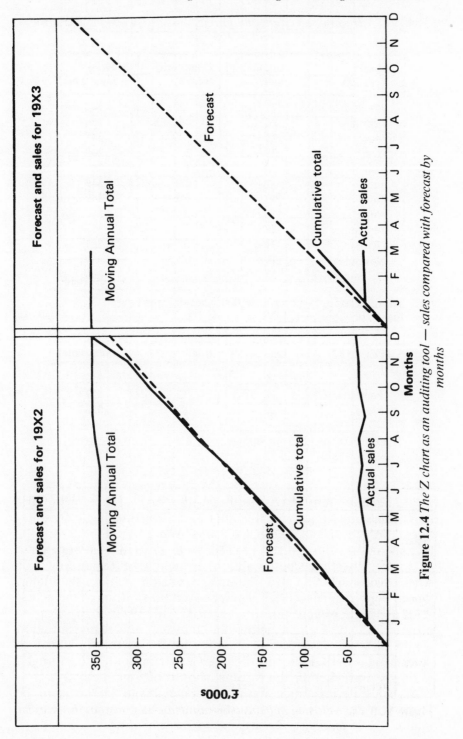

Figure 12.4 *The Z chart as an auditing tool — sales compared with forecast by months*

Table 12.1 *Historic sales data and forecasts used to develop a Z chart for auditing purposes*

Month Year 19X2	Actual sales	Cumulative total	Moving Annual Total
January	25	25	346
February	26	51	346
March	28	79	347
April	25	104	348
May	30	134	349
June	32	166	349
July	30	196	349
August	32	228	350
September	28	256	352
October	31	287	353
November	33	320	354
December	35	355	355

The forecast for 19X2 was £330,000. The total sales figure
for the previous year, 19X1, was £345,000.

Year 19X3	Actual sales	Cumulative total	Moving Annual Total
January	26	26	356
February	27	53	357
March	29	82	358

The forecast for 19X3 is £380,000.

would decline? Why were sales below the forecast line for the first half of 19X2 and above for the latter half? Was this due to seasonal fluctuations or are there other reasons? What were the reasons for increasing the sales forecast to £380,000 in 19X3 in what appears to be a relatively static sales situation? Is the market expanding or is some extra marketing effort being expended to achieve the higher figure? With regard to 19X3, it can be seen that, although the actual sales are higher each month compared with 19X2, total sales are proportionately further below the forecast line. This situation would indicate a need to re-examine all the factors involved, to determine whether the market and environment had changed radically and whether the forecast should be amended.

As sales performance figures become available they can be plotted on the second graph and a continuous comparison can be made.

Table 12.2 *The sales budget and forecast of XYZ Ltd for the month of April.*
19X5

Sales unit forecast	Product X 4,000		Product Y 7,000		Product Z 10,000		Total
	Each		Each		Each		
Sales at standard selling prices	£2.00	£8,000	£1.00	£7,000	£0.50	£5,000	£20,000
Standard cost of sales	£1.20	£4,800	£0.70	£4,900	£0.40	£4,000	£13,700
Standard profit on forecasted sales	£0.80	£3,200	£0.30	£2,100	£0.10	£1,000	£6,300

Table 12.3 *Profit/loss of XYZ Ltd if sales had been made on budgeted pattern giving a profit/loss variance*

Product	Budget pattern	Total actual sales at budget prices	Actual sales on budget pattern	Actual sales @ SP	Variance	Profit margin	Profit or loss
X	40% of	£18,200	£7,280	£6,000	− £1,280 ×	40%	− £512
Y	35% of	£18,200	£6,370	£7,500	+ £1,130 ×	30%	+ £339
Z	25% of	£18,200	£4,550	£4,700	+ £150 ×	20%	+ £30
						Total variance	− £143

The management accounting approach to auditing the forecast

An adaptation of accounting methods is useful where the sales forecast assessment is complicated during the forecasting period by changes in sales by units, price changes, sterling value changes, and perhaps by changes in the product mix. Further, in the previous chapter when the forecast was applied to product types, areas, and channels of distribution, profits influenced decisions. Therefore, a comparison of the effects of profit, sales and price performance against forecast is an important part of the total forecasting process. These relationships can be illustrated by the company situation depicted in Table 12.2.

Actual sales made during April 19X5 were:

> Product X 3,000 units sold for £6,500
> Product Y 7,500 units sold for £7,200
> Product Z 9,400 units sold for £4,200

It will be seen that a true assessment must take into account three possible variances, price, volume and product mix.

1. *Sales price variance* — comparing budget price and actual price obtained. This indicates the effect of changes in price made during the period, perhaps the result of special deals, increased discounts, etc.

Product	Budget price	Actual unit sales	Actual sales at standard price	Revenue obtained	Variance
X	£2.00	3,000	£6,000	£6,500	+ £500
Y	£1.00	7,500	£7,500	£7,200	− £300
Z	£0.50	9,400	£4,700	£4,200	− £500
				Overall sales price variance	− £300

2. *Sales volume variance* — relating the volume of sales to profit or loss.

Product	Budgeted sales volume	Actual sales at standard prices	Variance	Profit margin	Profit margin × variance
X	£8,000	£6,000	− £2,000	40%	− £800
Y	£7,000	£7,500	+ £500	30%	+ £150
Z	£5,000	£4,700	− £300	20%	− £60
				Overall volume variance	− £710

3. *Product mix variance* — comparing the budgeted pattern or mix of products within the total budgeted sales with the actual pattern during the period.

Product	Units sold	Budgeted price	Actual sales at standard prices
X	3,000 @	£2.00	£6,000
Y	7,500 @	£1.00	£7,500
Z	9,400 @	£0.50	£4,700
	Total actual sales @ standard price		£18,200

In Table 12.2 the mix or pattern of sales in the budgets is £8,000 of X, to 7,000 of Y, to £5,000 of Z; ie, 40 per cent, 35 per cent and 25 per cent respectively of total budgeted sales at standard prices (£20,000). If actual sales had been made on this pattern the sales mix variance related to profit or loss would be as shown in Table 12.3.

Table 12.3 shows how sales of individual products deviated from the pattern or mix laid down in the budget and the consequent effect on profits. However, within the pattern laid down in the budget it is possible for variances to occur within the sales mix. This can be seen by comparing budgeted sales with actual sales on the budget pattern as in Table 12.4.

The type of analysis shown in Tables 12.2, 12.3 and 12.4, clearly indicates where sales, revenue and profit are not according to forecast, and, therefore, where action should be taken.

Table 12.4 *A comparison of budgeted sales with actual sales on budget pattern*

1	2	3	4	5	6
Product	Budgeted sales volume	Actual sales on budget pattern	Variance (3 − 2)	Profit margin	Profit variance (4 × 5)
X	£8,000	£7,280	− £720	40%	− £288
Y	£7,000	£6,370	− £630	30%	− £189
Z	£5,000	£4,550	− £450	20%	− £90
				Quantity	− £567
		Total sales mix variance from Table 12.3			− £143
				Overall volume variance	− £710

Using probability in control of the forecast

Probability was used on a number of occasions in Chapter 7. Of particular application in auditing forecasts is the use of the probability control lines set two standard errors either side of a projected value. The graph from the earlier example is used to illustrate the usefulness of this device in Figure 12.5.

In Figure 12.5 a least squares trend line and control lines (two standard errors either side of it) were calculated on the original sales data available to the end of July, see Table 7.12 (page 177). The control lines have been projected to the end of the year, and the later sales values have been marked with an X.

The main use of this device is to indicate acceptable deviations away from the trend line. Thus the August, September, October and December values are within the acceptable limits. The November value, being just outside the lower limit line, would warrant investigation but not necessarily action. As two standard errors have been used there is a possibility that in five cases out of 100 the sales volume achieved will fall outside the limits. However, if the December value had also fallen below, this would increase the probability that there had been a fundamental change in the variables affecting the market place, although it could still be a matter of sheer chance. Investigation and action would need to follow; the result could be the amendment of the forecast.

Another use of this control method is that it affords comparisons to be made between different forecasts. Where the control lines are

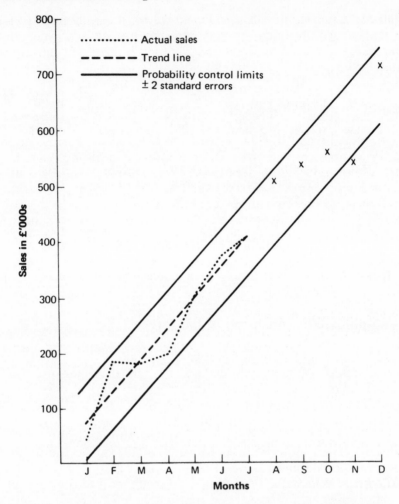

Figure 12.5 *A graph of monthly sales, a least squares trend line and confidence limits set two standard errors either side of the trend and projected into the future. The actual sales figures for later months are marked as X*

more narrowly placed in one case compared with another, it indicates that a greater degree of accuracy, and conversely a lower magnitude of variation in forecasting, could be expected. Where this is not the case, investigation as to the cause should be made and in many cases new factors, or the increased magnitude of some influencing factors, will be found.

By using probability (as shown in the section dealing with correlation (page 160)) it would be possible to calculate the chance of obtaining a particular sales performance by sheer chance. If in a particular case the odds are very high against an achieved sales value being obtained by sheer chance, then it must be determined which new variables are present.

Quantitative assessments and measurement values

In Chapter 5 (page 107) it was shown that there were various quantitative assessment values to which a forecast could be related.

In addition to these quantitative assessments there are also measurement values that imply relationships between the various quantities and these are necessary yardsticks by which to measure the effectiveness of the forecast or the company's performance in a market. Three that are widely used are:

1. Market segmentation

This indicates the number of special segments the market has been divided into. When a new generic product concept is introduced there is no market segmentation intitially, but, as the market develops and special consumer needs are identified and satisfied, the market becomes increasingly fragmented. Degrees of segmentation are possible either by using a scale of subjective values, ie a market can be seen to be 'highly segmented' or by quantifying. Quantification is possible by considering the number of special uses and/or applications, or by considering the use by socio-economic groupings, user industries, sex, age, location, etc.

2. Market saturation

This measurement term is usually expressed as a percentage, indicating the relationship of actual market volume to market potential. A market segment is saturated when actual market volume equals market potential (100 per cent) and degrees of saturation are expressed as percentages. The degree of saturation is useful to the forecaster as an unsaturated market indicates marketing opportunity.

3. Market penetration

This measuring device relates company actual market share and sales to actual market volume. Degrees of market penetration can be expressed as a percentage and can be used to assess the effectiveness of past marketing strategies and tactics, and also to set targets for the future, eg to increase market penetration from 10 per cent to 15 per cent in the next year.

The relationship between the various assessment terms, and between them and the measurement devices, can be seen in Figure 12.6.

Forecasts are made on assumed levels of segmentation, saturation and penetration. In the auditing process of forecasting, an assessment of actual sales compared with forecast in the light of these three factors may reveal that they have not progressed according to the anticipated pattern. Therefore, it may not be the machinery of a company forecast that is at fault but rather the assumptions and information on which the forecast was based.

Auditing the 'machinery' of forecasting

Earlier, it was stated that there should be a multi-technique approach to forecasting. From this a general pattern of forecasts will emerge and should there be any great difference between forecasts it will be a valuable exercise to discover why. Within the limitations of time, cost, availability of information, need, etc, as many techniques as possible should be used to build a composite forecast. The component forecasts can be used in total as a control device. They should be listed, compared with actual sales achieved, and the variances expressed as a percentage. The degree of accuracy between techniques is revealed, and over a number of periods a pattern of degrees of accuracy for each component forecast can be established. These degrees of accuracy will indicate the degree of reliability that can be placed on some methods of forecasting in the individual company situation, compared with others. Its reliable performance in the past must not cause unqualified acceptance of a forecast from a particular technique. All forecasts should be exposed to critical human judgement and intelligence, and assessed for credibility.

Further, an examination of the make-up of the various component forecasts in relation to their degrees of accuracy will often indicate the most important variables that are common to several forecasts. It might then be possible to improve the forecasting system by concentrating on methods that are dominated by these high priority variables.

Accuracy of forecasting methods

Listing the accuracy of the various forecasts also serves another purpose: it can be used as the basis for an audit of the techniques

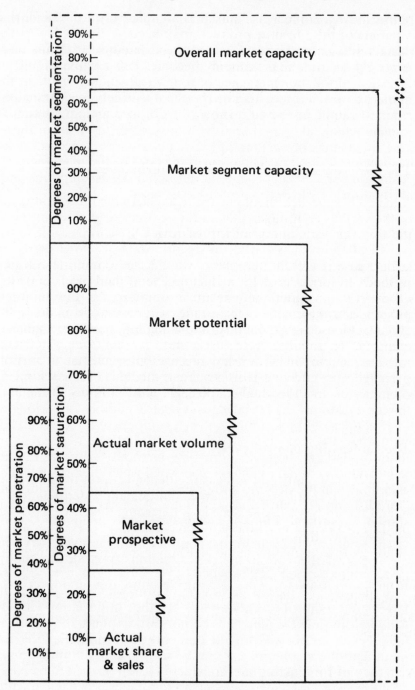

Figure 12.6 *Relationships between quantitative assessment and measurement values*

of forecasting. Some techniques that are relatively accurate during one part of the life of a product, may become ineffective as the market situation changes. A forecasting method that has been relatively accurate and suddenly becomes less reliable should be investigated for the emergence of a new influencing factor in the market. Unless a forecasting method that is widely inaccurate over a period can be improved it should be dropped and an alternative found.

The life-cycle approach to choice of techniques

A life-cycle approach should be made to determine the combination of the various techniques that could be used. At the beginning of the life-cycle for a new generic product it will be impossible to use statistical techniques based on historic data, as none exists. In such a case it will be necessary to use basic marketing research methods, historical analogy, and subjective methods such as panels of experts or panels of executive opinion. As the life-cycle progresses, adjustments to techniques will have to be made, eg the alpha factor used in exponential smoothing may have to be radically changed. As the life-cycle levels out, the constant percentage increase method will become less effective, but segmentation analysis becomes more effective. However, basic methods of forecasting the economy or an individual market will tend to apply throughout the life-cycle.

The forecasting control cycle

Any system of control of forecasting depends upon the quality of feedback information, the effective analysis and interpretation of it, and the ability to make decisions regarding the need to change the forecast or the machinery of forecasting.

The stages of the cycle for the control of forecasts will vary with the needs of the various market situations, but ideally should include the stages shown in Figure 12.7.

In Figure 12.7 a logical starting point from which to consider the forecasting control cycle would be the information inputs. Although in practice there will be no starting point, the results of the previous output will provide part of the information of the new input, and the whole process can be seen to be continuous.

If the information input is considered it will be seen to be based on the reaction (a) by management through changes in the marketing plan, (b) by the market, and (c) by competitors, all within the context of environmental change. Together with data from monitoring

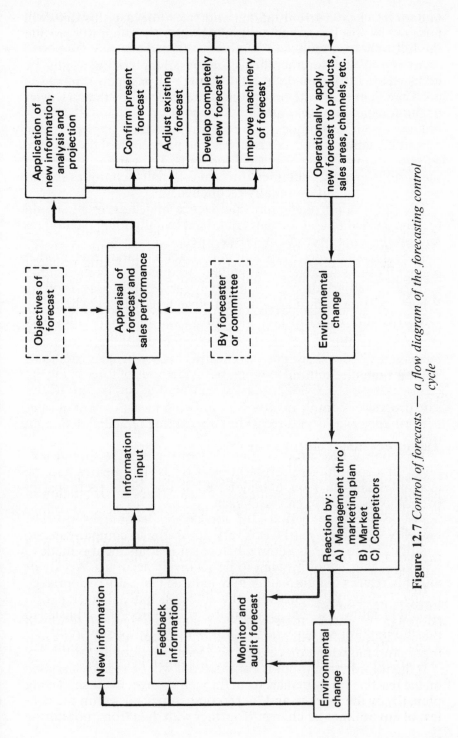

Figure 12.7 *Control of forecasts — a flow diagram of the forecasting control cycle*

and auditing the current market and sales forecast, this data will form the feedback information. Linked with new data it will provide the information input.

An appraisal of whether the techniques of forecasting need to be adjusted should be made in relation to their past performance as good predictors and the objectives of the forecast, by the forecaster or the forecasting committee.

The various techniques of forecasting are then applied to the new information input, and analysis and projection of the data are carried out to produce a series of forecasts. The variances between the various forecasts obtained through different techniques should be investigated and eventually reconciled.

The application of human intelligence and judgement should then be carried out on forecasts obtained by individual techniques and on the final overall composite forecast.

The integrated forecast (which may be for a total market, market segment, product range, or individual product type) is then either confirmed, adjusted, or a completely new forecast is evolved. Where existing techniques do not give forecasts in which the forecaster has a high degree of confidence, new techniques may have to be introduced or existing techniques modified.

Taking remedial action

The process of control involves not only the measurement of sales performance against a forecast but also taking remedial action on time.

The control flow process suggested in Figure 12.7 should take place on a continuous short-term basis (ie as sales figures become available) and also on a long-term ad hoc basis (perhaps an overall assessment once each year).

Just as the time periods for forecasting techniques (weekly, monthly, quarterly, yearly, etc) vary according to company needs, so will the time periods allowed before some adjustment is made to a forecast that is not proving to be relatively accurate. Weekly or monthly returns of information may indicate that sales performance is significantly different from the forecast, but a longer period should be allowed to elapse before the actual forecast is adjusted to the 'new pattern' of sales. But even when forecasts are adequate on a quarterly basis, the monitoring of weekly or monthly results will give an early indication of the need for possible change.

Re-forecasting

The time to re-forecast will be indicated when the acknowledged forecasting objectives are not being met and performance data are falling outside acceptable error limits or probability limits for that particular market. As a general rule this would not be done on a sample of one sales period unless it was obvious that the forecast was fundamentally poor. Usually, re-forecasting action will be taken after investigation and perhaps confirmation of a new emergent pattern through the results of further periods. The exception would be where factors change that are fundamental to the whole forecast, eg where a credit squeeze is imposed, thereby affecting the sales of products that have to be financed, or where a new competitor enters a market having achieved a technological breakthrough in a particular product area, etc.

The facts that emerge from auditing forecasts (already mentioned in this chapter) may also indicate the basis for a revised forecast. For example, an in-depth investigation and analysis of the variance between sales and forecast may indicate the need to change the forecasting objectives or to amend the policies and/or programmes by which the objectives are achieved. It may also indicate the need to develop new techniques that are more appropriate to the proposed revised forecast and show the need to re-train personnel involved in any change. It may even indicate the need to completely reorganize the forecasting function of a company.

By taking corrective action and revising the forecast, the forecaster is in effect setting new objectives, thereby starting the whole cycle (see Figure 12.7) again.

Setting forecasting objectives, standards and goals not only enables the development of policies and programmes to achieve them, but also permits the measurement of every piece of relevant environmental and sales performance data. Effective forecasting control is not imposed simply to discover how good or bad forecasts have been in the past, but also to determine what action to take today to improve forecasting results *tomorrow*.

'This is not the end. It is not even the beginning of the end. But it is perhaps the end of the beginning . . .'

Winston Churchill

Index